Speaking of Crime

The Chicago Series in Law and Society

Edited by William M. O'Barr and John M. Conley

Speaking of Crime

The Language of Criminal Justice

Lawrence M. Solan and
Peter M. Tiersma

The University of Chicago Press
Chicago & London

Lawrence M. Solan is professor and director of the Center for the Study of Law, Language, and Cognition at Brooklyn Law School and author of *The Language of Judges* (1993). Peter M. Tiersma is professor and Joseph Scott Fellow at Loyola Law School, Los Angeles, and author of *Legal Language* (1999).

The University of Chicago Press, Chicago 60637
The University of Chicago Press, Ltd., London
© 2005 by The University of Chicago
All rights reserved. Published 2005
Printed in the United States of America

14 13 12 11 10 09 08 07 06 05   1 2 3 4 5

ISBN: 0-226-76792-2 (cloth)
ISBN: 0-226-76793-0 (paper)

Library of Congress Cataloging-in-Publication Data

Solan, Lawrence, 1952–
    Speaking of crime : the language of criminal justice / Lawrence M. Solan and Peter M. Tiersma.
        p. cm.—(Chicago series in law and society)
    Includes bibliographical references and index.
    ISBN 0-226-76792-2 (cloth : alk. paper)—ISBN 0-226-76793-0 (pbk : alk. paper)
    1. Criminal justice, Administration of—United States—Language. 2. Criminal law—United States. I. Conley, John M. II. Title. III. Series.
    KF9223.S668 2005
    345.73'05'014—dc22

                                                                2004010382

♾ The paper used in this publication meets the minimum requirements of the American National Standard for Information Sciences—Permanence of Paper for Printed Library Materials, ANSI Z39.48-1992.

Contents

Acknowledgments

This book has been a long time in the making, and many people have been of great help to us. We would like to give special thanks to individuals who generously read earlier drafts
and provided us with comments: Kenworthey Bilz, Margaret
Berger, Bob Freidin, Susan Herman, Laurie Levenson, and
Michael Risinger. We are also very grateful to our respective
institutions, Brooklyn Law School and Loyola Law School, for
their generous support for this project through providing us
with summer research grants, research assistants, and overall encouragement. Solan conducted some of the work that
appears in this book while a visiting fellow in the Department of Psychology at Princeton. We also wish to thank that
institution, and especially John Darley. Loyola Law School
gave special assistance to Tiersma in the form of the Joseph
Scott Fellowship.

Numerous research assistants helped in the preparation
of the book, including Loyola Law School students and graduates Scott Bishop, Ana de Santiago, Irene Farinas, and Heidi
Brooks, and Brooklyn Law students and graduates Tara Lom-
bardi, Marji Molavi, Jerry Steigman, and Stacey Winograd.

Portions of chapters 3 and 4 appeared in our article *Cops
and Robbers: Selective Literalism in American Criminal Law,*

which appeared at 38 Law and Society Review 229 (2004). Chapter 7 is condensed from our article *Hearing Voices: Speaker Identification in Court,* which appeared at 54 Hastings Law Journal 373 (2003).

Part 1

A Good Time to Study the Language of Criminal Justice

This book is about the criminal justice system's adherence to deeply entrenched notions about language, many of which we now know are wrong. People do *not* always understand their rights, even if they have received the *Miranda* warnings and say that they do. When a suspect wishes to speak to a lawyer during a police interrogation, the request is *not* always honored, especially if the suspect's language is not precise and direct. Witnesses do *not* generally remember voices that they heard once in stressful situations, even if they are sure that they do. Nor are they likely to remember the exact words they heard, although they may testify as if they did. Jurors and even expert witnesses are *not* always able to identify correctly the author of an anonymous document, such as a ransom note, based on a comparison of the document with writings known to have been produced by the defendant. The language of statutes is *not* always as plain as some judges seem to think, as the debate about whether President Clinton committed perjury illustrated all too well. There are many more such examples.

Often enough, misconceptions about language can affect the outcome of a case. A key event in the Lindbergh baby kidnapping and murder trial, which led to Bruno Hauptmann's execution in 1936, was Charles Lindbergh's recollection of a voice that he had heard only briefly years earlier. We take no position as to whether Hauptmann was guilty or not. But whether Lindbergh could really have identified that voice certainly should have mattered. It also matters whether experts with phonetic training can identify voices, as is illustrated by recent debates over whether audiotapes unequivocally contain the voice of Osama Bin Laden. Likewise, whether the system should accept linguistic expertise on authorship is an important question. Identifying the author of the ransom note in the currently unsolved murder of JonBenét Ramsey, determining who wrote the letters accompanying the distribution of anthrax in 2001, and many other legal mysteries raise this issue.

The issues we discuss in this book are by no means mere technicalities. For example, a disturbing number of prisoners, some of whom have spent many years on death row, have had their convictions overturned in recent years, in many cases as the result of post-conviction DNA analysis. In a significant percentage of these cases, the original conviction was the result of a false confession to police, or sometimes a fabricated report of a confession by a jailhouse informant. A startling example is the Central Park jogger case, in which five individuals were exonerated in 2002 after having served prison sentences in New York for raping a woman in 1989. Their convictions were based in large part on confessions they made to the police. DNA testing showed the confessions to be false and the young men not to have committed the rape. Thus, whether a suspect understands that he has the right to stop an interrogation until he has consulted with counsel may have serious consequences, both for the defendant and more generally for the system of justice.

Two major themes emerge from this overview. One, as already mentioned, is that many participants in the legal system make assumptions or have preconceptions about language that are wrong or not supported by the evidence. This is a shortcoming that can be addressed by making the relevant research more accessible to those in the legal community. More difficult to remedy is the second major theme that winds its way through this book: that the legal system is often inconsistent in how it deals with linguistic issues. As we will see, most judges rule that "Maybe I should talk to a lawyer," uttered by a suspect during interrogation, is too tentative and thus does not function as a request for a lawyer. On the other hand, virtually any judge would hold that "Maybe I should blow your brains out," uttered to someone in a dark alley, can be a threat, even though it is expressed in equally tentative terms. Such double standards are particularly troubling if, as is often the case, they favor the prosecution.

As academics trained in both linguistics and law, our main goal in writing this book is to show how recent advances in the study of the human language faculty can help bring these and similar issues to light. In addition, we offer some suggestions for solving the problems that we discuss, and present ideas for how future work in linguistics and psychology might help the legal system better to realize its stated goals and ideals. In some instances, these suggestions concern standards for police conduct. In others, they concern evidentiary rules, including rules governing the use of experts. In still others, they concern problems that confront judges faced with the job of interpreting statutes such as the perjury statute, which defines a language crime. We also present suggestions for other players in the system, including lawyers and language experts themselves. We hope that readers with very different agendas, whether enhancing law enforcement techniques or protecting the rights of defendants at trial, will find the book interesting and useful.

We begin in chapter 1 by exploring some of the linguistic issues that commonly arise in the criminal law. Chapter 2 then explains some basic linguistic concepts, especially recent work in fields like speech acts and pragmatics, that are particularly relevant to any study of the language of crime.

Language and the Criminal Law

Language and the criminal law interact in a wide variety of ways. In this book our focus is on some of the more common and obvious illustrations of this interaction. Here we present some introductory examples of the main subject areas of the book: the language of police and suspects in pretrial proceedings, the admissibility of linguistic evidence during trial, and crimes that are committed by language.

The Language of Police and Suspects

Various linguistic issues arise in communication between law enforcement officers and persons suspected of committing a crime. For instance, the language of both police and suspects is relevant in deciding whether someone detained by the police has voluntarily consented to a search:

> A police officer believes that a car contains illegal drugs, but does not have probable cause to believe that a crime is being committed. He therefore has no right to initiate a search. He seeks permission to search the car by asking the driver, "Does the trunk open?" The driver opens the trunk, and the officer discovers a large stash of heroin under the back seat. Later, the driver, now the defendant, claims that he could not possibly

have knowingly waived his rights because he didn't have any idea that he had the right to say "no" to the police officer. Did the driver voluntarily consent to the search?[1]

It seems incredible that someone who knows that he has contraband in his car would "consent" to allow police officers to search it. Yet that is exactly what happens every day in countless encounters between police and citizens throughout the United States. In chapter 3 we analyze this riddle from a linguistic perspective. We show, using the tools of linguistic pragmatics, that courts are willing to take into account context and other pragmatic information in deciding that the police have indirectly *requested* that the driver open the trunk and that the owner has indirectly *consented* to the search, but stop short of using pragmatic information to conclude that the officer indirectly *ordered* the driver to open the trunk. We explore the implications of this practice on the controversy surrounding racial profiling.

Language is also an issue during interrogation. According to the U.S. Constitution, a suspect who invokes his right to counsel may not be further interrogated without his lawyer's presence and agreement:

> Police officers are questioning a suspect about a number of burglaries when suddenly they change the subject to a recent stabbing death. The suspect responds: "Wait a minute. Maybe I ought to have an attorney. You guys are trying to pin a murder rap on me, give me 20 to 40 years." Can the police continue questioning him about the murder? In other words, is the suspect merely thinking out loud, or is he invoking his constitutional right to consult a lawyer during interrogation?[2]

Courts frequently hold that such indirect or possibly ambiguous statements do not count as "requests" to have a lawyer present, allowing police to continue their interrogation. Again invoking the tools of linguistic pragmatics, we show in chapter 4 that people very often speak indirectly or somewhat ambiguously in such situations, and explain why they do so. We contrast the courts' attitude toward the language of suspects with their attitude toward the language of the police, where judges are much more accommodating in finding that an officer has made an indirect "request" to conduct a search.

Linguistic issues also arise when police read people their *Miranda* rights, which advise a suspect of her right to remain silent and to the assistance of counsel. Only if a suspect knowingly and intelligently waives those rights can an interrogation begin:

An individual is arrested and read her *Miranda* rights. She decides to talk with the police and confesses to the crime. When the government seeks to use the confession against her at trial, her lawyer claims that she did not understand her rights because she is mentally retarded—or a young child—or deaf—or not a native speaker of English. Should the confession stand? How can we tell if the defendant understood the *Miranda* warnings? What should the standard be for allowing these confessions to be used in court?[3]

We discuss this and similar cases in chapter 5, where we analyze the *Miranda* warnings and the ability of suspects to understand them. We will see that the average native speaker of English probably grasps the meaning of the warnings well enough. But not everyone is average. Whether juveniles or people who do not speak English well or who have mental problems comprehend the warnings and their implications is a serious concern that relates to the problem of false confessions.

Linguistic Evidence

Another major area of intersection between language and the criminal law is linguistic evidence. In a broad sense, just about any speech or writing could be considered linguistic evidence. We focus here somewhat more narrowly on linguistic issues that have an impact on what evidence should be admitted at trial. We discuss topics such as the ability of witnesses to remember exact words, how well people can identify a person by his or her voice, and whether people can be identified by their writing style.

Once a suspect is charged, he becomes "the defendant." As we have noted, an issue in many cases is the language used either by the police or the defendant in connection with a search or a confession that the defendant later challenges at trial. Sometimes these encounters have been taped, but often they have not. This is unfortunate, because so much rides on the exact words used.

When there is no recording, those involved must testify about their memories of what was said. Consider the following scenario:

A man is accused of bank robbery and is held in jail pending his trial. At the trial, his cellmate testifies, in exchange for a reduced sentence, that the man confessed to him and said that he used the money he stole from the bank to buy new clothes. He cannot remember the defendant's exact words, but is allowed to testify anyway about the gist of the confession. The defense lawyer is unable to cross-examine the cellmate effectively on the language that the defendant used in the alleged confession, because the cellmate never testified to the defendant's actual words. Should the legal system be concerned that there is no record of the defendant's exact words?[4]

We ask that question in chapter 6, where we discuss studies showing that our ability to remember exact words is typically not very good. An exception to the hearsay rule permits witnesses to testify about a party's admission to wrongdoing. The legal system allows such evidence to be admitted on the theory that the adversarial system should be able to root out inaccurate reports of confessions, largely through cross-examination. However, the research on verbal memory suggests that evidence of this sort may actually be less reliable than the system recognizes. We also look at other situations in which lack of access to the words that were actually used may have a significant impact on the administration of justice.

Another problem concerning recollection of linguistic information concerns our ability to identify people by their voices:

A police officer, pursuant to a valid warrant, tapes a brief telephone conversation about a proposed drug deal. Ultimately, the defendant is arrested for having participated in that transaction. The police officer appears in court to authenticate the recording. He testifies that he knows that the voice on the tape was the defendant's because he had interviewed the defendant some three years earlier. How likely is it that he is correct?[5]

Chapter 7 addresses how well we can remember and identify voices. Perhaps not surprisingly, people are not able to remember relatively unfamiliar voices over substantial periods of time. Research has also shown that the reliability of voice recognition is influenced by a variety of factors that courts often fail to recognize.

Chapter 7 also asks whether the legal system should allow the defendant to call an expert to testify about the results of experimental studies into our ability to recognize voices. If lay persons are not particularly good at identifying voices, are there experts in voice identification who are sufficiently skilled to compare the defendant's voice to that on the tape and to issue a reliable opinion as to whether the voices are the same or different? For a number of years, many courts allowed "voiceprint" experts to testify. Currently that practice is less prevalent, but still occurs periodically. We discuss the history of that technology, which we believe is properly excluded by most courts, and bring to light some new approaches that are likely to lead to more reliable results in the future.

Closely related to identifying a speaker is identifying the author of a writing:

> A woman is found dead at her home, along with a suicide note. The police suspect foul play. They think her husband killed her and wrote a bogus note. A careful reading of the note shows that it contains certain spelling errors that the husband sometimes makes in writings known to be his, and that the wife did not make those errors in her known writings. How much should we make of this evidence? And should we leave this task to the jury, or should we allow experts to offer opinions on authorship?[6]

Author identification has long been a tool for biblical and literary scholarship. It has recently been used in efforts to solve crimes, such as the Unabomber and JonBenét Ramsey cases. Yet the technique raises serious issues of reliability. For instance, we may not know how frequently spelling errors like those in the above scenario occur in the general population, or whether they occur more frequently among people with a particular educational background. Such questions are the subject of chapter 8.

All of these cases involve evidentiary issues. Some deal with the reliability of lay testimony, some with expert testimony, while others concern both. The law governing the admissibility of lay identification testimony has not changed much over the past half century. We will see that it is, at least to some extent, out of tune with what we now know about people's ability to remember exactly what was said or to identify speakers and authors.

As for expert testimony, there has been a great deal of change over the past few decades, starting with the adoption of the Federal Rules of Evidence in 1975 and followed by a trilogy of Supreme Court decisions in the 1990s regarding the standards for the admissibility of expert testimony in federal courts. We discuss these cases in chapter 2, and later scrutinize several areas of linguistic expertise in light of these important legal developments, pointing out how linguistics and psychology might develop to meet evidentiary standards, and pointing out ways in which the current perspective on evidence may be off the mark.

Crimes of Language

Sometimes crimes are committed through language. There are many such crimes, including solicitation, conspiracy, bribery, fraud, perjury, and making false statements to government officials. In part 4 of this book we will see that just as the police and suspects, in encounters with each other, perform constitutionally relevant acts of speech indirectly, acts of speech intended for bad purposes also tend to be committed indirectly, often to reduce the chance of being caught. Nonetheless, the law generally considers indirect acts good enough to meet the statutory definitions of a crime. Consider this case:

> A man whose wife has lupus tells a friend that his wife would be "better off dead," that he needs someone else to "pull the trigger," and that "she needs to die." Did the husband solicit his friend to commit murder, or did he just express some grizzly ideas or vague plans?[7]

Both a jury and appellate court found that the defendant had solicited his friend to murder the wife. In chapter 9, we explore similar examples and discuss the language that people use to solicit crimes.

Another language crime is threatening people:

> A man makes clear his desire to have sex with a woman and tells her, "I don't want to hurt you." She engages in sex with him, but later claims that she did so only out of fears for her safety if she did not. Did she freely consent, or did the defendant threaten her?[8]

A court held the statement not to be a threat, and therefore ruled the sexual encounter consensual. This scenario shows how important inferences drawn from context are in deciding whether an utterance is a threat, as we discuss in chapter 10.

Deciding, as a factual matter, whether an utterance is a threat or solicitation may be difficult under the best of circumstances. People engaging in language crimes typically take care to express themselves in ways that allow them later to deny that they were acting illegally (sometimes called "plausible deniability" when done by politicians). Yet we will see that it can be even harder to decide these issues when people make threats or solicit crimes for political reasons. Is a preacher who proclaims during a sermon that "we will kill" the president really issuing a threat, or is this just political hyperbole?

Perjury is another language crime. Lying is not usually criminal. When it occurs under oath, however, making a false statement may be punishable as perjury:

A general in the National Guard held a party in 1990 to raise funds from other National Guard officers for a political candidate he supported. It is illegal to solicit campaign contributions in this way. An officer who attended the party is later placed under oath and asked if such fundraising occurred at the 1991 party. No such party took place in 1991. The questioner, who misspoke, actually intended to refer to 1990, and there is evidence that the witness understood the question as referring to 1990. The officer says "no." Has he committed perjury?[9]

We argue in chapter 11 that essential to determining the truthfulness of an answer is the context of the question. The courts in this case held that the officer must have understood the question to refer to 1990, and that therefore he made a false statement, even though his words were literally true. We examine the so-called literal truth defense to perjury and explore its limits, focusing largely on the Clinton scandal. As we will see, President Clinton seems to have been well aware of the literal truth defense and tried his best to answer questions about his relationship with Monica Lewinsky in a way that was literally true, but misleading. How well did he succeed? We show that the answer to that question is far more complicated than commentators on both sides wanted us to believe.

Unlike the other crimes of language, where indirectness is the norm, perjury law looks closely at the "literal" meaning of a defendant's words. The principal reason is that perjury occurs in a courtroom in which the roles of the participants are strictly orchestrated. In that setting it is reasonable to require the lawyers who control the questioning to create a clear record of falsity before perjury liability can attach. Perhaps equally important, holding a person liable for making true, but misleading, answers in a setting where lawyers frequently ask misleading questions tilts the playing field unfairly in favor of the lawyers.

Some Goals and Limitations

Traditionally, the legal system hasn't spent much time asking or trying to answer the questions raised by these scenarios. Part of the reason is simply that lawyers and judges, many of whom are excellent users of language, may not have any particular expertise in the mechanisms that underlie our linguistic abilities. We will see in the next chapter that the field of linguistics has made great progress, especially in the past half century or so, yet many people remain woefully uninformed about the nature of human language. One of our goals, therefore, is to explain some of the basics of language and linguistics to people concerned with the legal system, especially those aspects of language that interact with criminal justice. We devote the first section of chapter 2 to this task.

But lack of knowledge is not the only reason that the linguistic questions raised by the scenarios above are seldom asked. Sometimes the goals of the legal system—whether putting a halt to drug trafficking, or solving a high-profile crime or fighting crime in general— induce the system to avoid asking these questions, or to minimize their importance even if they are asked. Our first scenario, for example, raises the perplexing question of why someone with contraband or evidence of an illegal activity would ever voluntarily consent to have police search his car. As we show in chapter 3, the answer lies largely in the relationship between police and suspects in this situation and the fact that what might ostensibly seem like a police "request" to search is usually interpreted as a command. The Supreme Court has failed to acknowledge this issue, in all likelihood because the Court considers consent searches to be an effective law enforcement technique. The linguistic analysis we present in this book cannot create the will to stop pretending that we are adhering to constitutional values when we are not. That is a political decision. But it can at least lead us to admit that we are pretending, and offer suggestions on how to ensure that people really do understand their rights.

Finally, we emphasize that this book is not intended merely as a critique of what is wrong with the criminal justice system, although we obviously do not shy away from pointing out its failings. Rather, we hope to show more broadly how a better understanding of the nature of language and cognition can improve its functioning. Our overriding goal is to explore how linguistic knowledge and expertise can help ensure that the guilty get their just deserts and, even more critically, prevent the innocent from going to prison.

In approaching these tasks, we do not intend this book to be encyclopedic. For example, each of us has written elsewhere about linguistic issues in the interpretation of statutes[10] and in the ways that courts instruct juries.[11] Space limitations prevent us from addressing those issues at length here, although both arise in various contexts in the book from time to time. Moreover, we have concentrated mainly on those cases that got it wrong, and consequently pay somewhat less attention to those that reached the right result. In other words, we have focused our attention on those areas where a better understanding of linguistics and related fields can improve the quality of justice.

With these goals in mind, we turn in chapter 2 to a brief discussion of how language works, and how receptive the legal system has been to linguistic research to date. The aspects of linguistic science discussed in the next chapter will serve as useful tools in getting to the bottom of the linguistic events that we analyze throughout the rest of the book.

Linguistics in the Law

The criminal process is full of language events from beginning to end. Among them are the initial encounters between the police and a suspect; the presentation of testimony at trial, including testimony about what was said in earlier language events; the identification of people by their voices or by how they write; the interpretation of statutes, including statutes that make various speech acts illegal; and the presentation of instructions to a jury. Rules of evidence, constitutional doctrine, and principles of statutory interpretation all contain tacit assumptions about how accurately we recall language events and how we interpret language. For example, the Federal Rules of Evidence make identification of a voice on a tape a relatively trivial matter of authenticating the tape.[1] An exception to the rule against hearsay allows the admission of testimony reporting a defendant's alleged confession even if the witness cannot recall the defendant's exact words.[2]

Enormous advances in linguistics and cognitive psychology during the past several decades now make it possible to evaluate these assumptions systematically. Beginning in the 1950s and 1960s, Noam Chomsky and others effected a shift in the field of linguistics from an inquiry into language as an external object to an inquiry into the language faculty as part of the human mind.[3] Chomsky's work focused on what he saw to be the creativity of the human language faculty: we are all endowed with the power to articulate and understand infinitely many new linguistic expressions as a routine matter. We do so with almost no training as children, and we do so automatically and unselfconsciously. For example, the sentences on the previous page may never have been uttered or written before, yet they are easily enough understood.

Many of the regularities that enable us to speak and understand language so quickly and easily, according to Chomsky and others engaged in similar research, can be found in the relationship between syntax and meaning, which is at the heart of Chomsky's work. There is broad debate about how these systems are structured, and Chomsky's theory of syntax continues to be controversial as the field matures. Nonetheless, the mentalistic approach to the study of language is widely accepted and forms a significant part of the background of our work. Most linguists now agree that their work involves important questions about how the mind works. Of course, in the decades preceding Chomsky's entry into the field, linguists had been conducting significant research, often with important insights.[4] Paradigm shifts do not typically occur in a vacuum. But the fact that the paradigm shift has indeed occurred is difficult to deny.

For that matter, there is a long history of linguistic investigation in the Western intellectual tradition, a tradition that has included other noteworthy shifts in paradigm. One of the most influential early linguists was Sir William Jones, to whom both of us have an affinity because he—like us—was both a linguist and a lawyer. "Oriental Jones," as he is often called, was born in England in 1746 and as a young man was renowned as a scholar of Asiatic languages. He later became a barrister and wrote a highly regarded treatise on the law of bailments. Eventually he was appointed to a judgeship in British India, where he studied the local Hindu and Muslim law and sought to improve the British colonial legal system. But language was his passion. Jones is famous in linguistic circles for a speech that he made to the Asiatic Society of Bengal in 1786, in which he pointed out the similarities that Sanskrit bore to Greek and Latin, languages that we now know to be part of the Indo-European language family.[5] His discovery led to great advances in our understanding of the historical relationships of languages to each other.

Some two hundred years later, Chomsky's early publications again energized the field of linguistics, this time by focusing on the study of language as a part of human psychology, and ultimately, human biology.[6]

In the ensuing decades, linguistics has made great strides in developing this paradigm. While the field is a vibrant one, full of lively debate and some sharp disagreements, there is at least rough consensus on some very important issues. We now know a great deal about what makes language plain when it is plain, and what makes language vague or ambiguous when it is unclear. We know something about what makes one sentence harder to understand than another, even when they are both grammatical. We know much more about how adept people are at identifying individuals from their voices, and about the circumstances in which identification becomes harder. We know a great deal about the sound patterns of languages, and which sounds are most likely to be confused with one another. We also know how the structure of a discourse affects the inferences that people are likely to draw from the language that they hear. This chapter discusses a number of these legally relevant advances, which are woven throughout the book.

At the same time that linguistics has been making progress, the legal system has taken advantage of advances in other areas of psychological study. To take one prominent example, psychologists have demonstrated beyond any question that people are not always very good at identifying faces. Simply put, we make a lot of mistakes in eyewitness identification, and these mistakes can lead to people being convicted of crimes that they did not commit. Leading work in this area has been conducted by psychologists such as Elizabeth Loftus[7] and Gary Wells,[8] with many others making important contributions. Both the scholarly literature and the popular press frequently report cases in which witnesses, although acting in good faith, just got it wrong. Our visual memory is fallible and, perhaps most frightening, is susceptible to suggestion. We may actually remember seeing things that never happened if those events are suggested to us.

In their dramatic book describing the work of the "Innocence Project," Barry Scheck, Peter Neufeld, and Jim Dwyer point to mistaken identification as the leading factor in the conviction of people later found to be innocent.[9] The legal system has given these advances in understanding the limitations of eyewitness testimony a mixed reception. Some courts allow experts to testify about its questionable reliability; others do not, a fact to which we return later. But there can be no doubt that basic research into the limits of human memory has begun to infiltrate the criminal justice system. While research into the structure of our language faculty has played less of a role in the judicial decisionmaking process, it too is clearly relevant to many important legal issues. Let us look briefly at how our linguistic capacity is structured.

The Subsystems of Language

It is useful to imagine our linguistic abilities as containing various modules that interface with one another.[10] For example, languages all have sound systems. The study of the sounds of language is called *phonetics,* and the study of how sounds interact and how sound systems are structured is called *phonology.*[11] The sounds of language, of course, feed into other linguistic systems. We put together sounds to form words, words to form sentences, sentences to form discourse, and so on. In fact, language is typically thought of as a system that relates sound and meaning.

Sounds can be strung together into meaning-bearing elements called *morphemes.* Some words, like *cat,* consist of a single morpheme. *Cats* consists of two morphemes: *cat* and the plural marker *s.* Other words have a more complex structure, as examples like *disembodiment* (DIS-EM-BODI-MENT) illustrate. The linguistic subfield that studies these structures is called *morphology.*

Syntax is primarily the study of sentence structure, an area on which modern linguistics has focused a great deal of attention for the past half century.[12] Semantics, the study of meaning, acquires its substance from words, syntax, and discourse, all of which contribute to meaning. It is self-evident that words contribute to meaning. The investigation into how they do so is sometimes called *lexical semantics.* In addition, we glean a lot of meaning from context; linguists study regularities in the ways that context is used in fields such as pragmatics and discourse analysis.

Let us examine some of these subsystems of language, focusing our attention on aspects of the language faculty that will provide a window into legal issues raised later in this book.

A Look at Sound Systems

Sounds are the basic building block of language. The sound systems of languages are full of generalizations that we use routinely without noticing them. Consider the following example, which is well known in the linguistic literature and legally relevant in a surprising way. The two initial consonants in *bat* and *pat* are closely related. They are both made by closing the lips and then allowing a burst of air to escape from the mouth after the lips are released. Linguists call these sounds *bilabial stops.* The difference between *b* and *p* is that the *b* is *voiced,* while the *p* is *voiceless.* Readers can experiment (privately, we recommend) by beginning to pronounce *bat* and *pat,* but stopping before the first sound is actually produced. You will hear a noise in the first instance, but not in the second. It is easier to hear the difference between voiced and voiceless consonants by comparing the sound of *zzzz* (a voiced fricative) with *ssss* (the corresponding voiceless fricative). The vibration of the vocal cords with the *z*, which produces the voicing, is even more noticeable if you plug your ears while saying first *ssss* and then *zzzz*. Other pairs of stops, *d/t* and *g/k*, are made by cutting off the air at different parts of the vocal tract. The members of these other pairs differ from each other in just the way that *b* and *p* do: the first is voiced, the second, voiceless.

In English, we pronounce voiced and unvoiced stops differently when they come at the beginning of a word. If you put your hand in front of your mouth, you will feel a puff of air after the *p* in *pat* but not after the *b* in *bat*. The same holds true for words beginning with *t* and *k*, in contrast to words beginning with *d* and *g*.[13] Linguists call this *aspiration,* and say that initial unvoiced stops in English *(p, t, k)* are aspirated. Note that in other languages, such as French and Spanish, these consonants are not aspirated when they occur at the beginning of a word. Part of what it means to have an American accent is to succumb to the temptation of aspirating these sounds in a language where aspiration is inappropriate.

German also has both voiced and unvoiced stops, but has a different set of phonological rules that make use of the distinction. English distinguishes between voiceless and voiced stops throughout a word, including at the end. Aspiration doesn't occur there, but the sounds clearly differ, as in *slap/slab* or *bat/bad*. This is not true in German, however. Although German speakers normally distinguish between voiced and voiceless stops, they do not make this distinction phonetically at the end of words. Only voiceless stops can occur in that position. Thus, even when a letter like *d* is written at the end of a word, German speakers will pronounce it as a *t* (*Bad* ["bath"] is thus articulated as *bat*). Most linguists believe that German speakers store this word in their mental lexicons with a *d* (compare the plural *Bäder* ["baths"] and the verb *baden* ["bathe"]). When this *d* or any other voiced stop occurs at the end of a word, a phonological rule called *final devoicing* converts the underlying *d* into a *t*. German speakers apply the rule of devoicing without thinking, just as English speakers employ aspiration without being consciously aware of it.

The result of final devoicing in German is that the sound *t* (or *p* or *k*) is possible at the end of a German word, but the sound *d* (or *b* or *g*) is not, however a word is spelled. This often has consequences for Germans speaking English. Unless a German speaker is very fluent in English, she is likely to pronounce the *d* in the English word "good" as a *t;* in fact, this is part of what it means to have a German accent. Likewise, when writing English, a German immigrant with little education might write the *d* at the end of a word as a *t,* or overcorrect and write a final *t* as a *d.*

The fact that German speakers sometimes confuse voiced and voiceless stops at the end of words when writing English was one of the pieces of evidence used to convict Bruno Hauptmann, a German immigrant, of kidnapping the Lindbergh baby, as we discuss in chapter 8. Another application of phonetics to a legal issue arises in chapter 7, where we discuss people's ability to identify speakers by their voices.[14]

Syntax: The Algebra of Language

Peculiarly little of this book is about syntax,[15] although much research in linguistics over the past half century has focused on syntactic regularities in languages throughout the world.[16] Apart from discussions of the best way to draft, say, a jury instruction or a statute, the legal system does not engage in much debate over syntax. But it does engage in a great deal of debate over meaning, and meaning is in part a by-product of syntax.

We use syntax to derive meaning so routinely and efficiently that it often goes completely unnoticed. Consider the following:

Who did you think Bill saw in the park?

We know without reflection that *who* is related to a place in the sentence in which a gap has been left, namely the direct object position of *saw:*

Who did you think Bill saw _____ in the park?

That means that we must somehow "know" that *see* takes a direct object, that the object is missing, and that the question is about the identity of the direct object. We can also ask about the subject:

Who did you think saw Bill in the park?

While we have done nothing more than reverse the order of *saw* and *Bill* in this sentence, it has an entirely different meaning. In this case, what is missing is the subject of *saw:*

Who did you think _____ saw Bill in the park?[17]

Again, we must take note of what is missing in order to understand the question, which means that we somehow must "know" that *saw* ordinarily requires a subject, which is missing in this sentence. Consequently, we are able to figure out that *who* represents a missing object in the first example, and a missing subject in the second.

What is so interesting about seemingly mundane linguistic facts like these is that they are most readily explained by reference to some rather abstract elements of a language, like subject and direct object.[18] Since we all seem to agree on the interpretations of these sentences, it would appear that whatever explains the differences must be part of our internalized knowledge of English. Otherwise, we would not have and share these judgments in the first place.

Many syntactic principles, like the example presented above, work smoothly and quite predictably. Yet syntax is also riddled with systematic ambiguities and variables. When these correspond to issues of syntactically driven meaning, we might expect to see them raised in legal disputes. A classic illustration of linguistic ambiguity from the linguistic literature comes from Noam Chomsky's early work. Sentences like "Flying planes can be dangerous" are subject to two distinct interpretations. One is about the danger of engaging in aviation, the other about the danger of planes that are aloft.[19] Language is full of such ambiguities, which we typically resolve from context without even noticing them. Consider one more:

A picture of a man I admire is on the wall.[20]

The sentence can refer to a picture of "a man I admire" or to "a picture of a man" I admire. It is ambiguous as to whether I admire the man or the art. But consider:

A picture I admire of a man is on the wall.

Now the ambiguity disappears, although the sentence is a bit more awkward. The trade-off between syntactic clarity and stylistic elegance produces an ongoing tension in legal language.[21]

To illustrate from an actual case, the federal child pornography statute (shortened and paraphrased) says that "any person who knowingly distributes a depiction—if the depiction contains child pornography—shall be punished."[22] In *United States v. X-Citement Video, Inc.,*[23] the defendant was convicted of violating this statute. He attempted to argue that he knew he was distributing pornography, but he didn't know that it was *child* pornography. The trial court did not permit him to assert this defense, since it appears that the statute requires knowledge only that one is sending a depiction—not that the depiction involves children in sexual situations.

On appeal, the defendant argued that the statute was unconstitutional if one could violate it unknowingly. He won the appeal on those grounds. But the Supreme Court reversed. The Court acknowledged that the statute is best read as not requiring knowledge on the part of the defendant that he was distributing child pornography, which would make it unconstitutional for criminalizing innocent conduct. But instead of throwing out the statute, the Court added such a requirement, and ordered a new trial. Interestingly, it is very difficult to write this statute so that the scope of "knowingly" unambiguously encompasses the entire act. Our best stab is: "Any person who knowingly distributes a depiction, and who knows that the depiction contains child pornography, shall be punished." As this case shows, the trade-off between precision and simplicity is not always an easy one to evaluate.

Word Meaning: Two Ways of Thinking

A great many legal disputes concern the meanings of words. For example, most disagreements about statutory interpretation involve debates over whether a word in the statute should apply to the situation in a particular case. We use words to express concepts, so unless language and thought are the same (and we do not believe that all thought requires language), then there must be some interface between language and conceptualization that allows us to access words and use them to express the concepts we want to convey. This interface has some legally relevant consequences. For one, our recollection of the things we talked about on a given past occasion may be sketchy, but it is much more accurate than our recollection of the actual language used in the conversation. This means that when the exact words of unrecorded speech matter in a legal dispute, perhaps in determining the propriety of a police officer's request to search a car, or in deciding whether a cellmate's report of the defendant's jailhouse confession is true, we must decide the issue without having available to us the actual words used in the interaction.

Even when we know the exact words that were used, we need to understand what was meant by them. One way to understand the meanings of words is to provide definitions for them. A definition should accurately describe the circumstances in which it is proper to use the word for the concept. For example, *Webster's Third New International Dictionary*, a leading dictionary of American English, defines the word "circle" as "a closed curve every point of which is equidistant from a fixed point within the curve." It is a good definition in that it describes all and only circles. If it is not a closed curve, or if it is a closed curve but not all points on the curve are the same distance from a point inside the closed curve, then it is not a circle. Each of the two conditions is necessary, and together they are sufficient to describe a circle.

This approach to word meaning, sometimes called the "classical" or the "definitional" approach to word meaning, looks very law-like. Just as a dictionary defines words, judges and legislatures define legal obligations and remedies in terms of necessary and sufficient conditions. Consider New Jersey's statutory definition of robbery:

A person is guilty of **robbery** if, in the course of committing a theft, he:

(1) Inflicts bodily injury or uses force upon another; or
(2) Threatens another with or purposely puts him in fear of immediate bodily injury; or
(3) Commits or threatens immediately to commit any crime of the first or second degree.

An act shall be deemed to be included in the phrase "in the course of committing a theft" if it occurs in an attempt to commit theft or in immediate flight after the attempt or commission.[24]

Like the dictionary definition, the statute describes a set of conditions. The first is that the person must commit a theft. The second condition is satisfied by any one of a set of three alternatives. To prove that a person has committed a robbery, therefore, it is necessary to show both that the first condition is met, and that one of the alternatives in subsections 1, 2, or 3 is met. Together, they are sufficient.

But sometimes we expect too much of definitions. The common law definition of burglary, as students learn in their first year of law school, is "a breaking and entering into an occupied dwelling in the nighttime with the intent to commit a felony."[25] Each element of the crime is necessary, and together the elements are sufficient to determine whether someone has committed a burglary. The common law definition, however, is both broader and narrower than our everyday understanding of that crime. It is broader in that we usually think of burglary as involving theft, while the law includes any felony. In fact, a mere intent to commit a felony inside will suffice at common law. The definition is narrower than the ordinary meaning in that burglary at common law had to occur at night, while today we would consider a break-in and theft at any time of day to be a burglary. Modern statutes no longer limit burglary to nighttime crimes, but they still include felonies other than theft.

Thus, some burglaries appear to be more "burglary-like" than others. This fact illustrates a problem with the definitional approach to word meaning that has been a source of debate among philosophers, psychologists, and linguists for the past quarter century: people are strongly influenced by prototypes.[26] Consider the chair—a common illustration. At least for us, the prototypical chair has several features, including four legs, a seat large enough for one person, two armrests, and a backrest. These features are not necessary and sufficient conditions, however. An object that otherwise qualifies but has no armrests would probably still fit within the category of chair (in fact, it might be the prototype for some people). Take away the four legs and replace them with a single stand that rests on three to five wheels (a common piece of office furniture), and you would still have a chair, although this one would deviate somewhat more from the prototype.[27]

Prototype analysis even shows up in the dictionary. Consider the definition of the word "chair" in *Webster's Third:* "a usu[ally] movable seat that is designed to accommodate one person and typically has four legs and a back and often has arms." Little is rule-like in this definition. It seems that a chair must be a seat that is designed to accommodate one person. But that's about it. Everything else in the definition describes the typical chair: portability, a back, arms. Moreover, while being a place to sit appears to be a necessary condition of chairhood, it is not sufficient, since ottomans and other pieces of furniture also fit that description, but are not chairs.

Thus, some concepts, including something as basic as a chair, seem to be characterized not by a definition, but by a complicated array of information that includes some definitional features, along with some typical features. Approaches to word meaning that focus on similarity to either prototypical examples or the most salient features of a concept are often called *prototype* approaches, named after the pioneering work of Eleanor Rosch in the 1970s.[28] Current work in linguistics and psychology supports the position that our understanding of words is rooted in theories we develop that contain both types of information: definitional features, and features based on prototypical mental models we form from experience.[29]

This tension is obviously relevant in the area of statutory interpretation, including how we understand the concept of lying in the context of perjury, which is the subject of chapter 11. Yet it also arises in a legal context that we discuss later in this chapter: not only do we think in both ways when deciding the meaning of a word, but we think both in terms of rules and experience in our reasoning generally. The law governing evidence, expert testimony in particular, has recently been construed to favor strongly those experts who are able to testify in terms of identifiable procedures. Easier to exclude are those who are able to say that they have formed opinions based on experience, but cannot articulate the specific mechanisms or principles from which their opinion derives. This issue is critically important for understanding when courts are willing to permit the testimony of experts in linguistics.

Discourse and Inferences from Context

If linguistic systems such as phonology and syntax are bodies of knowledge that we share, more or less, as native speakers of our language, the question that immediately arises is how we put these systems of knowledge to use. After all, we use language to communicate. Words contain a great deal of the communicative content of language, and we have just seen that the syntactic relationships among words and phrases in a sentence contribute a great deal to meaning as well. How these systems interact with one another is an interesting problem for linguists, but is beyond the scope of this book.[30]

Here, we will focus on the aspects of meaning that must be determined from context. Even after all of the technical linguistic material has contributed what it can to the process of communicating, there may still be a great deal of residual ambiguity and uncertainty about what the speaker or writer meant. Courts are well aware that context is a necessary element in determining meaning. Statements like the following, from a 1993 Supreme Court opinion, are commonplace: "[L]anguage, of course, cannot be interpreted apart from context. The meaning of a word that appears ambiguous if viewed in isolation may become clear when the word is analyzed in light of the terms that surround it."[31] Fortunately, people are excellent contextualizers. Given a word with multiple meanings, both experimentation and everyday experience show that people do a good job inferring from context which of the possible meanings is intended.[32]

But we use context far more broadly in communicating with one another. Consider the simple sentence, "It's two o'clock." Literally, it is nothing more than a statement about the time of day. But when uttered by one concerned parent to another, it may be a way of saying, "I'm worried about our teenager not being home yet," even though worry is never mentioned. When uttered by a teacher at the end of a test, it may mean, "Time is up." When uttered by a sports fan, it may mean, "The game is about to start." This broader use of context, which includes not just the verbal context, but also the surrounding circumstances and shared background information and assumptions, is the domain of what linguists call *pragmatics*.

In making legal judgments, we use context all the time, not just to glean which of several senses of a word was intended, but also to determine why the speaker uttered the statement at all. The use of context to infer communicative intent is a recurring theme of this book. When a policeman stops a car in the middle of the night and the officer asks, "Does the trunk open?" we understand it as an indirect request or a command—not an inquiry into the design of the automobile or the condition of the trunk. Similarly, people engaged in illegal activity often speak indirectly about their plans. How do we know what they are really intending to communicate?

To address these questions, we rely on two lines of research in the area of linguistic pragmatics. The first is Paul Grice's theory of conversational implicature. At the heart of Grice's theory is the Cooperative Principle: "Make your conversational contribution such as is required, at the stage at which it occurs, by the accepted purpose or direction of the talk exchange in which you are engaged."[33] Cooperation is essential to communication. People employ several strategies to accomplish this goal, strategies that Grice calls "maxims of conversation." Among them are the maxim of quantity ("make your contribution as informative as is required for the current purposes of the exchange") and the maxim of relevance ("be relevant").[34]

Like the syntactic principles discussed earlier in this chapter, the Cooperative Principle explains not just how we produce utterances, but also how we understand them. In other words, not only do we generally follow the maxims of conversation when we speak, but we assume that our conversational partner is also cooperating, and we thus use the maxims to infer what she means.[35] Returning to the case of the police officer asking whether the trunk opens, the Cooperative Principle tells us that the officer said what he did in order to advance the conversation with respect to a purpose that he had in mind. This flows from the maxim of relevance. To interpret the officer's words as nothing more than an idle query about the design or condition of the trunk would make the statement irrelevant to the purpose of the traffic stop. We thus infer that the officer was asking the car's occupants to open the trunk. Why else would he ask whether it opens?

The second line of pragmatic research that we use throughout this book is the theory of speech acts, first conceived by the philosopher J. L. Austin,[36] and later developed by John Searle,[37] among others. Utterances not only convey meaning, but can also function as acts that have an impact on the surrounding world beyond mere communication of information. An important category of speech acts includes what are called *performatives*. When one says, in response to a reminder that guests are coming, "I promise not to be home late for dinner tonight," one has performed the act of promising just by using that word. The word "promise" is a performative verb because using it performs the act that the verb identifies when the conditions are right. I can promise by saying "I promise."

One indicator that a sentence is being used as a performative is that it allows for the insertion of "hereby" before the verb. Thus, it is possible to say, "I hereby promise to buy you dinner." In contrast, the word "cook," which is not a performative, can only describe actions, it cannot perform them. Unless I am a magician, I cannot cook vegetables by saying "I cook the vegetables." Inserting "hereby" does no good either; in fact, it makes the sentence sound rather odd. The relevance of the theory of performatives to legal domains such as contracts has been studied in detail.[38]

What complicates matters is that even when a performative verb is available, it is not usually essential to use it to perform a speech act. In other words, we can promise without saying "I promise." We can say: "I'll be home for dinner on time. You can count on me." Moreover, we can and often do perform speech acts indirectly.[39] Depending on the nature of the relationship, it might be enough simply to respond to a question about whether we'll be home on time by saying, "Don't worry."

Judges often have to decide, based on a person's words, whether he or she performed a specified speech act. We consider in chapter 4, for instance, whether a suspect has made a "request" for a lawyer if he tells interrogating officers, "Maybe I should talk to a lawyer," instead of using a direct performative ("I request a lawyer"). And as we will see throughout this book, people use words to solicit, threaten, lie, command, and request; all of these are speech acts with significant legal consequences. These speech acts are usually best characterized by the speaker's intent in making the utterance, which is referred to as its *illocutionary force*. The statement "I'll be there at nine o'clock" can have the illocutionary force of a promise. "I have a gun" may well have the illocutionary force of a threat.

On other occasions we may be less concerned with the speaker's intent and more with the effect that a speech act is likely to have on others, which is called the utterance's *perlocutionary effect*. Deceiving, coercing, and persuading are illustrations. There is no performative verb "entice." I cannot entice you to go home by saying, "I entice you to go home." I may, however, be able to achieve the perlocutionary effect of enticing you to go home by using the performative verb "promise" (for instance, I could promise you an ice cream cone in order to persuade you to go home.) In that case, my illocutionary intent is to make a promise, which is intended to accomplish the perlocutionary effect of inducing you to go home. Similarly, the illocutionary act of threatening is often used to accomplish the perlocutionary effect of intimidating or coercing.

Deception requires that the speaker effectuate a perlocutionary effect: inducing someone to believe as true something that we believe not to be true. Lying is one way to accomplish the goal of deceiving, but not the only way. For instance, we can also deceive by giving less information than is appropriate in a certain context. This explains why people were so offended by President Clinton's defense to charges that he committed perjury. His claim to have deceived without lying distinguished between acts with different illocutionary forces, but with the same perlocutionary effect. The distinction was real, but not morally relevant to many. We return to the Clinton scandal in chapter 11.

Of course, it is not always easy to pigeonhole language into predefined speech acts. Sometimes we don't know our own state of mind well enough to specify which speech act we are performing. Moreover, we can often characterize our speech in terms of a number of overlapping and sometimes even contradictory goals and effects, all of which may be operating at the same time. Our motivations are complicated, and our acts of speech are no less so. Philosophers have pointed out these and other problems with speech act theory.[40] We also recognize the indeterminacy of speech act categories. In fact, actors in the legal system often argue over the characterization of an act of speech, with both sides making reasonable points. Nonetheless, we hope to show that it is a useful heuristic for describing a wide range of legal problems involving inferences drawn from utterances.

Linguistics in the Courts

There is no doubt that the sorts of linguistic knowledge that we discuss in this book can be very useful in understanding aspects of the legal system. Yet if the research that we describe remains buried in academic journals, it will have precious little practical importance. To make a difference, the research will have to find its way into the legal institutions that can make use of it.

There is now enough experience with linguistics in the courts to draw some preliminary conclusions. Lawyers offer expert testimony by linguists with some regularity. This phenomenon is recorded in two very different ways. First, there now exist many opinions from trial courts and appellate courts concerning offers of testimony by linguists. Often—but by no means always—these opinions affirm a trial court's decision not to allow the linguist to testify.[41] This should not be surprising. Appellate courts are extremely deferential to the evidentiary decisions by the trial courts, and the issue of linguistic testimony is most likely to arise in a published appellate opinion when a defendant appeals a conviction and wishes to raise the exclusion of an expert witness as one of the grounds for appeal.

But a more careful look at the case law shows that linguists are routinely permitted to testify in some kinds of cases, are sometimes permitted to testify in other kinds of cases, and rarely if at all in still others. For example, linguists are almost always accepted as experts in trademark cases, where the issue is usually the likelihood of confusion.[42] They are also generally allowed on issues such as proficiency of non-native speakers in the English language. They are sometimes accepted as experts on the meaning of statutes or contracts and on the identification of speakers by their voices. However, they are generally excluded when asked to use discourse analysis to draw inferences about a speaker's intent, or to identify the author of a document from its style.

Most interesting are issues such as the comprehensibility of legal documents. Linguists are generally accepted as experts when the document in question is a public notice or other document that is supposed to be understandable to a broad audience. Yet courts balk at allowing linguists to testify about the comprehensibility of jury instructions. Apparently, the system is willing to ask serious questions about how understandable language is so long as the answers do not threaten important legal institutions.

The second record of participation by linguists in the judicial system consists of reports by linguists on their own experiences as experts. These are captured in a number of recent anthologies,[43] three books by the linguist Roger Shuy, discussing some of his many experiences as an expert witness in criminal and civil cases,[44] and numerous articles published in the journal *The International Journal of Speech, Language and The Law* (formerly *Forensic Linguistics*).[45] We periodically refer to this literature.

Our point here is that the legal system is not in principle hostile to expert testimony by linguists.[46]

We thus approach our task with the assumption that the legal system will take this kind of learning seriously when it meets ordinary standards of admissibility. During the 1990s, the law governing expert evidence became increasingly focused on issues of scientific validity and reliability. In the next section we summarize standards governing the admissibility of expert evidence, and how linguistic expertise may or may not meet those standards.

Linguistics and the Admissibility of Expert Evidence in American Courts

The American legal system's perspective on scientific evidence has undergone significant change in the past quarter century.[47] First, Congress in 1975 adopted the Federal Rules of Evidence, which apply to all federal cases. Some states have also adopted the federal rules, although many continue to adhere to their own evidence codes. Second, the Supreme Court decided a trilogy of cases in the 1990s that has had a significant impact on how scientific evidence is regarded. Finally, the introduction of DNA evidence has had a dramatic impact on the legal culture. Although it was controversial at first, and continues to encounter problems at the margins, DNA has become the paradigm for what science in the courts should look like.

Not only is DNA analysis based on well-established scientific principles, but samples of DNA can be compared to a reference set to yield a statistical analysis of how likely it is that the DNA in question comes from a known individual. Moreover, as Jennifer Mnookin highlights in an interesting article that compares the history of forensic identification by fingerprints with DNA identification, DNA won its status by responding to vigorous challenges as it developed into a law enforcement tool.[48] In contrast, fingerprint comparison, handwriting analysis, microscopic hair analysis, ballistic comparison, and certain other forensic "sciences" routinely accepted by the courts for decades without evidence of validity are now being questioned, as DNA analysis has set the standard for what it means to draw inferences based on science.[49]

For much of the twentieth century, the admissibility of expert testimony was governed by the *Frye* test, named for a 1923 U.S. Court of Appeals decision, *Frye v. United States*.[50] *Frye* involved a trial court's refusal to admit the results of a lie detector test (called a "systolic blood pressure deception test") offered through an expert to prove the defendant's veracity in a murder case. The court of appeals affirmed the trial court's decision, articulating a standard for admissibility that was followed routinely for some fifty years, not only by other federal courts, but by many state courts as well:

> Just when a scientific principle or discovery crosses the line between the experimental and demonstrable stages is difficult to define. Somewhere in this twilight zone the evidential force of the principle must be recognized, and while courts will go a long way in admitting expert testimony deduced from a well-recognized scientific principle or discovery, the thing from which the deduction is made *must be sufficiently established to have gained general acceptance in the particular field in which it belongs.*[51]

Many observers soon began to argue that the *Frye* standard is inconsistent with the way scientific inquiry is conducted. Science often involves controversy, and many significant scientific theories never gain general acceptance. The critics argued that when controversial, but arguably helpful, expertise is offered, it would make more sense for courts to permit arguments on both sides and to weigh the evidence, rather than to preclude the jury from hearing the evidence at all. On the other hand, defenders of a more restrictive test worried about admitting "junk science."[52]

Rule 702 of the Federal Rules of Evidence was written to replace the *Frye* test. As originally adopted, it read:

> If scientific, technical, or other specified knowledge will assist a trier of fact to understand the evidence or to determine a fact in issue, a witness qualified as an expert by knowledge, skill, experience, training, or education, may testify thereto in the form of an opinion or otherwise.

On its face, the rule's standard that expert knowledge must "assist the trier of fact" is more relaxed than *Frye*'s requirement of "general acceptance in the particular field in which it belongs." Rather than clarifying the issue, however, the adoption of Rule 702 led to a period of confusion as to just what the standard really was. Some federal courts understood Rule 702 as replacing *Frye*, while others continued to follow *Frye*, which had become deeply entrenched over the decades.

This lack of consensus continued until 1993, when the Supreme Court decided *Daubert v. Merrell Dow Pharmaceuticals, Inc.,*[53] the first of three rulings on expert evidence decided by the Court in the 1990s.[54] The issue in *Daubert* was whether Bendectin, an anti-nausea drug taken during pregnancy, had caused birth defects in the plaintiffs' children. The established epidemiological literature said that it did not. The plaintiffs in *Daubert* wanted to call experts to undermine this literature and discuss the results of animal studies. The trial court, however, refused to let the plaintiffs' experts testify because their work had not been published, and therefore failed to meet the standards of scientific reliability that the courts had developed under *Frye*.[55] The court of appeals affirmed the trial court's decision.[56]

The Supreme Court reversed. It held that the Federal Rules of Evidence had replaced the *Frye* standard. In its view, Rule 702 requires courts to engage in a "preliminary assessment of whether the reasoning or methodology underlying the testimony is scientifically valid and of whether that reasoning or methodology properly can be applied to the facts in issue."[57] To be "scientifically valid," the proffered evidence need not be generally accepted by the scientific community. Rather, "[t]he adjective 'scientific' implies a grounding in the methods and procedures of science."[58]

Daubert set forth four nonexclusive criteria for deciding whether evidence is scientifically valid:

1. whether the theory offered has been tested;
2. whether it has been subjected to peer review and publication;
3. the known rate of error; and
4. whether the theory is generally accepted in the scientific community.[59]

Although a number of states have retained the *Frye* test or tests similar to it, there is no doubt that *Daubert* has become the leading opinion in this area.

Four years later the Supreme Court decided the second case in the trilogy, *General Electric Company v. Joiner*.[60] The question in that case was the standard that appellate courts should apply in reviewing the *Daubert* decisions of trial courts. The Court adopted the very lax "abuse of discretion" standard, which means that very few evidentiary rulings concerning the admissibility of expert testimony will be reviewed seriously. It also means that the appellate courts will usually not play the role of correcting unintended effects of the *Daubert* regime. One unfortunate consequence is that jurors may be presented with evidence that requires explanation, but the relevant expertise is excluded as not sufficiently scientific, leaving unsophisticated jurors to their own devices. Whatever the best solution to this puzzle might be, a matter we pursue in chapter 8 in connection with authorship identification, appellate courts are not addressing it adequately in the wake of *Joiner*.

The *Daubert* opinion did not say whether the standards it established should be applied to testimony that is not strictly scientific. One could argue, for example, that testimony that describes the possible interpretations of a legal text is more descriptive than theoretical. Therefore, the *Daubert* approach should not apply. In an opinion published in 1999, *Kumho Tire Co. v. Carmichael,*[61] the Supreme Court rejected this line of argument.

Kumho Tire was a products liability case concerning automobile tires. The issue was whether a tire expert should be allowed to testify based on his experience in the industry. The Court held that *Daubert*'s principles apply not only to scientific evidence, but also to experts basing their testimony on experience.[62] While the Court admitted that the *Daubert* factors may not all be applicable in such cases, it stressed that the overall approach should be followed. The key to deciding the admissibility of expert evidence, according to the Court, is whether the expert "employs in the courtroom the same level of intellectual rigor that characterizes the practice of an expert in the relevant field."[63]

We cannot, therefore, avoid asking how linguistic testimony stands up to the *Daubert/Kumho Tire* factors. In fact, Rule 702 has been amended to incorporate some of them. It now reads:

> If scientific, technical, or other specialized knowledge will assist the trier of fact to understand the evidence or to determine a fact in issue, a witness qualified as an expert by knowledge, skill, experience, training, or education, may testify thereto in the form of an opinion or otherwise, if (1) the testimony is based upon sufficient facts or data, (2) the testimony is the product of reliable principles and methods, and (3) the witness has applied the principles and methods reliably to the facts of the case.[64]

As we will see, linguistic analysis generally meets any evidentiary standard, whether governed by *Frye* or *Daubert*. Linguistics is a field whose work is published largely in peer-reviewed journals. It is intellectually active, with disagreements among scholars aired publicly, and consensus typically acknowledged only when perspectives merge.

But we will also see instances in which the admissibility of linguistic expertise is questionable. For example, there exists substantial controversy in the courts over whether "voiceprint" experts should be permitted to testify about whether two taped speech samples were uttered by the same person. There is also some controversy over the acceptability of expert witnesses in forensic stylistics: individuals who analyze the writing styles in two sets of documents to opine about common authorship. We believe that the courts should move slowly with respect to these areas, and offer suggestions about how the fields might respond to the issues that the evidentiary standards raise.

At the heart of these debates is a policy decision related to observations we made earlier in this chapter discussing the meaning of words. Psychologists have observed that we think in two different ways: from the top down, based on rules and principles, and from the bottom up, based on experience. As Joseph Sanders points out, *Daubert* clearly privileges rule-like thinking in determining whether expert evidence should be permitted.[65] To take one of Sanders's examples, the beekeeper who knows in which direction bees will fly as they leave the hive, but who cannot explain why, has knowledge as valuable—perhaps more valuable—than the engineer who can explain the physics behind the bees' behavior. The *Daubert/Kumho* regime favors the latter over the former.

Perhaps, as Sanders argues, this is the right approach. While the legal system will lose out on some relevant knowledge, the stricter approach helps keep the adversarial system honest and promotes more exacting work among experts who might wish to appear in court. In the linguistic context, it means that people who are adept at author identification may not, at present, be welcome in the courtroom. This provides all the more incentive for linguists to develop methodologies that are proven valid and can withstand scrutiny, a positive goal in its own right.

In contrast to such controversial areas of linguistics, there is no reason for courts to reject linguistic expertise on comprehensibility, on linguistic competence in English or other languages, or on the range of meanings that ordinary people are likely to give such legal texts as a statute. The issue should always be whether the expert is in a position to assist the trier of fact and to do so in a reliable way, which is just what Rule 702 demands.

We return to the question of linguistic evidence in part 3. Before doing so, however, we proceed in part 2 to delve into some of the applications of pragmatics and discourse analysis to the criminal law, especially with respect to pretrial procedures such as searches, interrogation, and confession.

Part 2

Gathering the Evidence

Before a trial can begin, it is necessary to gather the evidence that is to be presented to the judge or jury. There are two major categories of evidence used in criminal and other cases: testimonial and demonstrative evidence. Testimony consists of statements made under oath by witnesses. Demonstrative evidence is virtually any other type of proof, including blood or hair samples, documents, and photographs, to name just a few.

The distinction between the two categories of evidence can be critical. The Fifth Amendment of the Constitution protects a person from being compelled to be "a witness against himself." As a consequence, a criminal defendant cannot be forced, for example, to state whether he had been drinking alcohol at the time of an automobile accident. But he might be compelled to give demonstrative evidence, such as a blood or breath sample. Even though it may be used as evidence against him, giving a blood sample to authorities is not equivalent to stating "I am drunk." This was essentially the holding of the U.S. Supreme Court in *Schmerber v. California*,[1] in which the Court noted that the privilege against compelled self-incrimination extended only to being forced to provide the state with "evidence of a testimonial or communicative nature."[2] Likewise, speaking aloud certain words to allow for voice identification or providing a handwriting sample is not usually considered testimonial.[3] Even though these acts clearly involve language in some sense, they are not intended to communicate a message when the only purpose is to identify a person's voice or handwriting.

In the following chapters, we discuss efforts by law enforcement authorities to gather both types of evidence. Chapter 3 is primarily concerned with demonstrative evidence, which police officers sometimes try to obtain by means of consensual searches. Testimonial evidence is the topic of chapters 4 and 5. Our focus is not trial testimony per se, but rather efforts by law enforcement officers to obtain confessions or other information from suspects by means of searches and interrogation before trial. As we will see, linguistic issues are raised in the process of gathering both types of evidence.

Chapter 3

"Consensual" Searches

You don't mind if we look
in your trunk, do you?

In 2002, the U.S. Supreme Court decided *United States v. Drayton*.[1] The case involved two defendants who had been sitting in a bus when three police officers entered. One of the officers sat in the driver's seat at the front, another positioned himself at the back, and the third then approached various passengers in an effort to find drugs. The officer asked one of the defendants if he had any luggage, and then asked, "Do you mind if I check it?" After the officer found nothing, he continued, "Do you mind if I check your person?" The defendant agreed; the officer found drugs strapped to his body and he was arrested. This scenario was reenacted with Drayton, the second defendant. The Court determined that the defendants consented to let the officer search their bodies, even though they must have known that they were carrying drugs and would almost certainly be arrested and convicted. Surely they would not have consented if they believed that they had a choice in the matter. Nonetheless, the Supreme Court held the consent to be voluntary and expressly rejected any requirement that police advise people in this situation that they are free to decline. The holding follows a line of cases dating back thirty years to the seminal case of *Schneckloth v. Bustamonte,*[2] to which we now turn.

The *Bustamonte* Case

Joe Gonzales, accompanied by Robert Bustamonte, Joe Alcala, and a couple of other young men, was driving an automobile in northern California during the wee hours of the morning. A police officer stopped the car, having observed that a headlamp and the license plate light were not operating properly. Gonzales could not produce a driver's license; in fact, only Joe Alcala, one of the passengers, had a license with him. The automobile, it turned out, belonged to Alcala's brother.

By then, the occupants of the car had stepped outside and two additional officers had arrived on the scene. For reasons that are not entirely clear, the police were interested in searching the trunk of the car. Perhaps they had a hunch that the occupants of the car had been up to no good. They may have had previous encounters with the car's occupants. Or maybe they routinely attempted to search automobiles of people who fit a particular profile—in this instance, young Latino men driving an older car in the middle of the night.

Unfortunately for the police, they had no warrant, nor were there any grounds for a warrantless search. The Fourth Amendment's prohibition against "unreasonable searches and seizures" generally requires the police to obtain a warrant issued on a showing of probable cause unless there are extraordinary circumstances, such as evidence that a crime is in progress. Although the Supreme Court has recognized an "automobile exception" to the warrant requirement,[3] probable cause that a crime has been committed is also required to trigger the exception. Neither the lack of a driver's license nor a hunch or vague suspicion is enough to overcome the probable cause requirement. The police therefore did what they often do in these situations: they asked the occupants of the car if they might have a look in the trunk. Joe Alcala said "yes" and opened it. The officers found three stolen checks. Largely on the basis of this evidence, Robert Bustamonte was later convicted of possessing a check with intent to defraud.[4]

Bustamonte appealed, arguing that the search of the trunk violated the Fourth Amendment. The case eventually made its way to the U.S. Supreme Court, which upheld the constitutionality of the search. The Court emphasized that even when there is no other legal basis for conducting a search, law enforcement officers are free to seek consent. If the person who controls the property (Alcala in this case) "freely and voluntarily"[5] consents to a search, it is valid.

Addressing the requirement that the consent must be "voluntary," the Court deemed it self-evident that "neither linguistics nor epistemology will provide a ready definition" of its meaning.[6] Instead, it drew inspiration from the law of confessions, which must also be voluntary, and adopted the test set forth in *Culombe v. Connecticut:* "Is the confession the product of an essentially free and unconstrained choice by its maker? If it is, if he has willed to confess, it may be used against him. If it is not, if his will has been overborne and his capacity for self-determination critically impaired, the use of his confession offends due process."[7]

To decide whether a suspect's will had been overborne, the Court held in *Bustamonte* that judges should examine the totality of the surrounding circumstances, such as the suspect's age, education, intelligence, and whether he had been advised of his rights. Knowledge of the right to refuse consent is one of the factors that should be considered, according to the opinion, but it was not a dispositive issue.[8] The Court therefore affirmed the decision of the trial court that consent to search had indeed been freely and voluntarily given. Both a police officer and the car's driver testified that Alcala's consent to the search seemed voluntary, perhaps even casual. The officer described the atmosphere as "congenital" (no doubt meaning "congenial"), and Alcala even aided the officers in the search. At no point, however, were the car's occupants informed that they could refuse to allow the officers to conduct their search, and there was apparently no evidence in the record that they realized they had this right.[9]

Assuming that the occupants of the car genuinely and voluntarily consented to the officers' rummaging through the trunk, the abiding mystery of this case—and many others like it—is why they would do so. Why, indeed, would *any* rational person *ever* agree to let the police search his possessions? At best, you will be forced to stand by and wait while suffering the indignity of having a stranger ransack your personal belongings. At worst, the police will find incriminating evidence and use it to send you to prison. Of course, many of us would like to think of ourselves as being cooperative with law enforcement, and therefore willing to endure some inconvenience.[10] Nonetheless, the innocent have little to gain by allowing a search, while the guilty have much to lose.

So, why do people consent so frequently? Despite the Supreme Court's comment that linguistics has little to do with the matter, we believe that the answer to this riddle is very much a linguistic one. The problem, as we will see, is that people who are stopped by the police tend to interpret ostensible requests as commands or orders.

Requests versus Commands

As we saw in chapter 2, speech act theory attempts to explain how people use language in order to accomplish certain goals. Requests and commands are both speech acts. In particular, they are both performatives—you can actually request or command someone just by saying "I request that you do x" or "I command that you do y." Lawyers use many performative verbs in legal documents. In contracts, wills, and other legal instruments, it is usually wise to make yourself as clear as possible, so legal texts are full of explicit performative phrases like "I hereby promise" or "we hereby warrant." In ordinary speech, however, we usually express ourselves more indirectly. We can promise without using the word: "I will take you fishing tomorrow—you can count on it." In other words, we can promise directly (by saying "I promise") or indirectly (by intentionally communicating to the hearer in some other way that we are committing ourselves to do something in the future).[11]

It is common to make requests and to issue orders or commands indirectly, and that seems to be just what happened in the *Bustamonte* case. According to the testimony, one of the officers, after searching the inside of the car, asked the occupants, "Does the trunk open?" Joe Alcala replied "Yes," got the key, and opened the trunk.[12] Literally, the officer merely inquired whether the trunk was capable of being opened. He never directly requested permission to search the trunk. Yet Alcala's response—taking the key and opening the trunk—indicates that he understood this ostensible question as a request or command to open the trunk. So did the Supreme Court, whose opinion fails to recognize that, understood literally, all the officer did was ask whether the trunk was capable of being opened.

The use of indirect directives in *Bustamonte* corresponds with our everyday experiences. Consider a person who asks a fellow diner, "Can you pass the salt?" This is usually not taken as a question about the addressee's ability to pass the salt, but as a request or command to do so.[13] If the addressee answers "Yes" but does nothing, she has acted inappropriately, or perhaps made a rather juvenile joke by playing on the literal meaning of the words. One of us, as a child, was often asked by his mother whether he "would like" to wash the dishes. This was never intended to be taken literally as a question about his desires, but was obviously intended as a command. An historical example is the offhanded remark attributed to King Henry II regarding his enemy, Thomas Becket: "Will no one rid me of this turbulent priest?" On the surface, this was merely a question. But not long afterward, four of Henry's knights took it upon themselves to assassinate Becket.[14]

The reason we tend to issue requests, commands, and orders indirectly is that it is usually considered bad form to make a blunt order, even if we have the authority to do so. Consequently, a boss may ask his secretary, "Could you type this memo?" A father may ask his son, "Would you clean up your room?" or tell him, "I'd like you to clean up your room." None of these are literally commands, but they all function as such.[15] Requests and commands are thus closely related speech acts. Both of them are attempts to induce the addressee to do or not to do some act. And both speech acts are typically made indirectly. As linguist Robin Lakoff has pointed out, we do so because a direct request or command could cause its recipient to lose face by being viewed as someone who is subject to being ordered about.[16]

The problem for the legal system is that indirect requests and indirect commands are practically indistinguishable on the basis of the language alone. Suppose that Bob says to Alice, "Would you like to wash the dishes?" after eating dinner with some friends. This is a question or request that can be refused, especially if Bob and Alice have already agreed to wash the dishes but have not agreed who is going to wash and who is going to dry. When Mom says it to Junior, however, it is an indirect command. Or suppose that one friend says to another: "Your shoes are dirty." This is taken merely as an observation, or perhaps as a well-meaning suggestion. But if a corporal says it to a private in the army, it is tantamount to an order or command to polish the shoes.

Despite the great similarity between requests and commands, the distinction between them is critical to the voluntariness of consent to a search, and thus to its constitutionality. When a uniformed police officer commands a car's driver to open a car trunk, any subsequent "consent" can hardly be termed voluntary, because the driver will assume that the officer has the authority to ensure compliance and that she therefore has no choice in the matter.[17] Obeying the commands of a uniformed and armed officer ("Pull over" or "Place your hands on the car") is never voluntary in any real sense.

Thus, an ostensible question like "Does the trunk open?" might be either a request that can be refused or a command that must be obeyed. Only if it is a request can we deem the response to be free and voluntary. If it is a command or order, the voluntariness of any acquiescence is highly questionable. The Supreme Court in *Bustamonte* implicitly recognized that

"Does the trunk open?" might be an indirect request to open the trunk. But it failed to consider the other logical possibility: that it might also be a command.

If requests and orders are so similar, how do speakers know the difference? The most important factor in deciding whether an ostensible question is a request that can be refused, or a command that cannot be, is the power relationship between the speaker and addressee. As the philosopher John Searle has pointed out, "If the general asks the private to clean up the room, that is in all likelihood a command or an order. If the private asks the general to clean up the room, that is likely to be a suggestion or proposal or request, but not an order or command."[18]

It is therefore highly relevant that the "request" to search is usually made by a police officer who has already exercised his authority in stopping the automobile and ordering the occupants to get out. Whether or not he has the legal power to search the car without permission, the officer certainly projects that power when he purports to ask the occupants to allow a search. Any ostensible request under these circumstances is likely to be interpreted as an indirect command.

Suppose that a police officer pulls over a car and asks the driver, "May I see your license?" "No" is just not an appropriate response. Moreover, while flashing the license to give the officer a quick glimpse and then putting it back into one's wallet would literally comply with the officer's request to "see" the license, most of us understand that we must hand it over so the officer can inspect it more closely. We assume that police officers have the right to examine our licenses, that they can enforce this right, and that playing linguistic games or refusing to comply will only get us into trouble. The officer's polite request, asking whether he "may see" the license, is nothing short of a soft-spoken command: "Give me your license!"

Now consider how the driver is likely to react when that same officer uses very similar language to "request" permission to search the car. Is there any real likelihood that the driver will know that the coercive part of the traffic stop has ended and the voluntary part begun? We doubt it. It is worth mentioning that the opinion of the Ninth Circuit Court of Appeals in *Bustamonte* revealed greater linguistic sophistication than the Supreme Court on this score. The Ninth Circuit noted that "under many circumstances a reasonable person might read an officer's 'May I' as the courteous expression of a demand backed by force of law."[19]

Power relationships are not the only relevant factor. If they were, a policeman would never be able to make a true request; every effort to do so would be interpreted as a command. An ostensible request is most likely to be interpreted as a command when the person in power appears to the subordinate to have the right, in this specific situation, to order the subordinate to perform the requested act. This will generally be the case when a police officer is acting in his official capacity. If an officer asks a driver whether he "may see" her license, his utterance will be interpreted as a command because he has not just the power to force compliance, but appears to have the right to request her driver's license in this situation. The same police officer who enters a restaurant just after midnight and asks if he "may have" a grilled cheese sandwich is making a request. The waiter can, without fear of legal repercussions, tell the officer that the kitchen closed five minutes earlier. Likewise, if a police officer asks a motorist, "May I see your credit card?" or "Do you mind having sex with me in the back seat?" most people would realize that these requests are not within the officer's authority and refuse.

Let us now return to the plight of Robert Bustamonte and his friends, whom we left standing outside the car. Most probably the occupants of the vehicle, young men driving a borrowed car with some nonfunctioning lights at 2:40 in the morning, were not educated in the law. They would not have been aware of their constitutional right to refuse to allow a search of their private possessions. In any event, with three armed police officers now on the scene, the lights on their squad cars flashing, Bustamonte and his friends might quite reasonably have concluded that the wisest course of action was to cooperate. Like the speeder who says nothing, but simply hands the officer her driver's license when the officer asks if he "may see" it, Bustamonte and his friends opened the trunk when the officer "asked" to look inside.[20]

People who are stopped by the police alongside the road in the middle of the night quite logically assume that if the police "ask" them to do something, the police have both the power and the right to force them to comply. Consider an actual case in which an officer was questioning several persons about what was in their luggage, and then said to one of them: "Why don't you put your hands behind your back, all right?" Most of us would assume that this is not a question that can be answered by stating a reason ("Because I don't want to" or "It wouldn't be comfortable"), but an order to which the appropriate response is to put our hands behind our back.[21] Similarly, if the police ask to look into the trunk of someone's automobile, many people will assume the police can legitimately force them to comply. Only those who are aware that the police do not have the legal right to search without a warrant will construe the words as a request that they can refuse without adverse consequences.

Now consider the situation of Mr. Gomez, who had been stopped beside the highway and was asked by an officer, "May I search the vehicle? May I look?"[22] Or in another case, "May I look into your car?"[23] Or, "May I search your bag, your jacket, and your person?"[24] The natural assumption is that if police officers ask this question, they have the right to search your possessions, making this a polite command that it would be foolish to refuse. As the New Jersey Supreme Court has observed, "[m]any persons, perhaps most, would view the request of a police officer to make a search as having the force of law."[25]

"Requests" to search are even more coercive when they begin with the phrase "do you mind . . ." Some actual examples include:

> *Would you mind* if I took a look around there?[26]
> . . . *do you mind* if we search your vehicle?[27]
> Well then *do you mind* if we search the truck?[28]
> *Do you mind* if I take a look?[29]
> *Do you mind* if I search?[30]
> *Do you mind* if I pat you down?[31]

This formulation places the burden on the suspect to object to the search. It suggests that the police officer intends to perform the search unless the suspect has a valid objection. This is hardly a neutral way to request permission, even if the inherent coerciveness of having the question posed by a law enforcement officer could be overcome. Nonetheless, in each of the above cases the courts held the subsequent consent to have been voluntary.

The coerciveness of the question is even more apparent when it is phrased as a statement with question intonation ("you don't mind . . .") or as what linguists call a *tag question* ("you don't mind . . . , do you?"). Some actual examples include:

> *You don't mind* if I search the truck?[32]
> *You don't mind* if I search your car?[33]
> Well, then, *you don't mind* if I look around in the car then, *do you*, or would you?[34]

These so-called requests or questions are really just statements with question intonation, an utterance form that tends to be considered relatively coercive and is typically allowed at trial only during cross-examination.

Also problematic about the "do you mind" or "you don't mind" phrasing is that people are sometimes uncertain whether "yes" or "no" is the appropriate way to signal consent. The problem is that we normally consent to something by saying "Yes." In contrast, saying "No" is typically the way to *refuse* consent. The "do you mind" formulation forces us to refuse consent by saying "Yes," which can be confusing:

Officer: Ok. Do you have any guns or drugs in that car?
Suspect: No (shaking his head).
Officer: *Do you mind* if I take a look?
Suspect: *Sure* (no head movement).[35]

Despite the suspect's refusal to later sign a consent form, the court held that he freely and voluntarily consented to a search.

Equally confusing is the following exchange:

Officer: Would you have any problems with me searching the van and the contents of the van?
Suspect: (nods head).
Officer: Would you mind if I search it?
Suspect: Yes.
Officer: It's ok?
Suspect: It's ok. Everything is ok.
Officer: You don't—do you mind if I search the van?
Suspect: (no response).
Officer: Is it all right for me to search the van?
Suspect: Yes.[36]

Again, this was held to be a valid consensual search, even though all the suspect did was to repeatedly say "Yes" or signal the affirmative, whether or not it was contextually appropriate. It is only on the last turn that the officer finally seems to hit on the idea of phrasing the request in a way that would make "Yes" the response that he was seeking.

Even more egregious is the "rolling no's" technique. As one court described it, a police officer posed a series of questions to the suspect, each intended to elicit a negative response. The final question in the series was, "You don't mind if we search your car, do you?" The suspect, once again, responded by saying "No." He voluntarily consented to a search, the court concluded.[37]

Consider finally cases where the officer uses the phrasing "can I":

Can I have a look in your truck?[38]

Well, if there is nothing important [in the bag], *can I* look in it?[39]
Can I have permission to search your vehicle?[40]

In each of these cases, the suspect nodded or responded by saying "Yes," which was deemed to be voluntary consent to the search.

Ironically, the same courts that interpret "may I" as a literal request for permission (which it is) are now interpreting "can I" in a relatively nonliteral sense. Although "can I" is used to express a number of related concepts, we tend to regard its literal meaning as asking whether the speaker has the *ability* to do something.[41] An affirmative response simply confirms that, according to the respondent, the speaker is able to do the act; it does not confer permission to do it. This is why some parents reprimand their children for asking "Can I have a snow cone?" According to traditional rules of grammar, one ought to say "may I" when making a request.

The reality, of course, is that "can I" is routinely used in ordinary language to request permission, even though some language purists continue to insist that "may I" is the only correct choice.[42] It is interesting that judges seem to have no trouble understanding that a question using "can I" is really a request for permission ("may I"). But they have a much harder time going the final step: grasping that often police requests for permission are really commands.

As we explained in chapter 2, whenever we interpret language, especially spoken utterances and conversation, we make use of pragmatic information.[43] Roughly speaking, pragmatic information can include just about anything beyond the actual language of an utterance. In addition, the search for meaning is, as philosopher Paul Grice suggested, a cooperative venture. Thus, the meaning of a question beginning with a "can you" phrase (*"Can you* pass the salt?") depends on a critical piece of pragmatic information: whether the addressee is evidently able to perform the act. If so, the question is probably a polite request to perform the act. But when the addressee's ability is uncertain (*"Can you* lift one hundred pounds with one arm?"), a question with "can you" will probably be understood as relating to ability. The reason for the difference is explained by Grice's maxim of relation, part of the Cooperative Principle, which states that a speaker's contribution to a conversational exchange should be relevant (and will be interpreted as such). If it is obvious that the hearer is able to pass the salt, asking whether the hearer can literally pass the salt is not relevant to the conversation. In an attempt to cooperate by making the question relevant, the hearer infers that the speaker is really requesting the hearer to pass the salt.

Courts in the cases discussed above properly took pragmatic information into account in deciding whether officers were making a request for consent to search. A "literal" interpretation of a question such as "Can I look in your trunk?" makes little sense when it is obvious that the officer has this ability. Consequently, the addressee takes it as a request for consent to actually inspect the trunk. Similarly, recall this interaction:

Officer: *Do you mind* if I take a look?
Suspect: *Sure* (no head movement).[44]

The court held that "Sure" constituted consent, even though this interpretation is nonsensical under a literal reading of the question. The court obviously took the question to mean something like "Do you give your consent to my looking in the trunk?" The *Bustamonte* case provides another illustration. "Does the trunk open" is not a literal request for consent to search the trunk, but merely seeks information. Yet the Supreme Court did not hesitate in assuming that the officers had requested consent to search.

Despite their willingness to take pragmatic information into account in deciding that an officer made a request for a suspect's consent, many courts refuse to take seriously the same kind of information when deciding whether the officer might, in fact, have given a command. As we observed earlier, in the context of consent searches the pragmatic information needed to determine whether a question is a request or a command is the power relationship between the parties and whether the suspect believes that the police officer has the right to conduct the search. In the *Busta-monte* case, only if the occupants of the car were aware that the police had no authority to order them to open the trunk could the "request" to search the trunk be interpreted as a genuine request that could be refused without negative consequences. If, on the other hand, the car's occupants believed that they could be forced to submit to a search, they would naturally interpret the so-called request as actually being a command. That, of course, is exactly what seems to have happened.

Bustamonte is hardly an isolated case. It is highly likely that many people do not realize that they have a right to refuse in this situation. *Drayton* is a more recent example. Consider also another recent Supreme Court case, *Bond v. United States*.[45] A Border Patrol agent boarded a bus in Texas. Walking down the aisle, he squeezed the soft luggage that passengers had placed in the overhead storage space. When he squeezed a canvas bag belonging to a certain Mr. Bond, he noticed that it contained a "brick-like" object. He asked Bond if he could search the bag, and Bond consented. The agent discovered a "brick" of methamphetamine inside, leading to Bond's conviction on federal drug charges and a prison sentence of fifty-seven months. The Supreme Court held that initially squeezing the bags of the passengers constituted a "search," and that this warrantless search was unconstitutional. Consequently, Bond's later consent was irrelevant. This seems to us to be the right decision. Yet notice that Bond "voluntarily" consented to let the agent open the bag, even though he must have known that it contained a large quantity of drugs and would almost certainly lead to his arrest and conviction. Surely he would not have consented unless he believed that he had no choice but to do so.

In another of many similar cases, a deputy sheriff stopped a Mr. Harris, who was weaving through traffic while driving a rental car. The deputy asked if he could search the car and Harris consented, leading to the discovery of nineteen kilos of cocaine. Again, no rational person with this amount of illegal drugs in a car would consent to its search if he realized that he could decline and be on his way. Yet people do routinely consent, and the only explanation that makes any sense at all is that they believe that they must comply. In other words, they interpret these ostensible requests to be, in effect, commands.

Consenting

If courts sometimes hesitate to take pragmatic information into account when deciding whether police officers have made a command (as opposed to a request), they are far more willing to use such information in deciding that a suspect has consented. In one instance, a man placed his briefcase on a conveyer belt that led to an x-ray machine at an airport. Operators of the machine spotted an object in the briefcase that turned out to be cocaine; the man was arrested. At trial he challenged the constitutionality of the search, arguing that he had never expressly consented to it. The lower court agreed and suppressed the evidence. The court of appeals reversed, however, holding that the act of placing luggage on an x-ray conveyer belt at a security station in an airport constitutes implied consent to a search of the luggage by the machine, as well as a limited hand search if the x-ray scan is inconclusive.[46] Several other cases involving airport security have reached similar conclusions.[47]

In another case, United States v. Griffin, the police came to the defendant's apartment and asked to be allowed inside. The defendant slammed the door in their faces. When they requested entry a second time, the defendant opened the door, turned around, and walked inside; the officers followed him in. By these actions, the court held, he had consented to a search of the apartment.[48] This case is especially troublesome because the defendant had clearly denied permission at first, relenting only when the police persisted. One can imagine many situations in which the police can obtain consent by outlasting an intimidated suspect who quite clearly refused to give it at first.

Likewise, in *United States v. Benitez,* a man in a car appeared somewhat suspicious to officials at a border crossing. An officer asked if he "minded if we looked in the trunk," in response to which the man said nothing but opened the trunk. Eventually, the officer found marijuana. On appeal, Mr. Benitez argued that he interpreted the officer's utterance as an order.[49] Recall that this phrasing ("do you mind") is relatively coercive, even apart from the stark differences in power between officer and detainee. Nonetheless, the court held that the officer's utterance was a request, and that Benitez's actions signaled voluntary consent.

In *United States v. Wilson* an officer asked the defendant if he "minded" if the officer search his person. In response, the defendant shrugged his shoulders and raised his arms.[50] Though shrugging one's shoulders often indicates an equivocal or uncertain attitude, or perhaps resignation, the court held that the defendant's actions constituted consent. Fortunately, at least two other courts have recognized that merely shrugging the shoulders, without more, does not indicate an affirmative response, especially when the suspect speaks little English.[51] Perhaps the critical factor in *Wilson* was that the suspect also raised his arms to facilitate being patted down.

The area of consensual searches reveals that courts are not, as is sometimes supposed, invariably literal-minded. Judges are obviously capable of understanding that people often speak or communicate indirectly. Passengers are deemed to be aware of security procedures at airports and the action of placing luggage on the conveyer belt is held to be consent to an x-ray scan. Whether they realize it or not, courts use inferences drawn from pragmatic information to reach this result. On the other hand, we would not suppose that driving our automobile into an ordinary parking lot would constitute consent to having our cars surreptitiously x-rayed as we drive in, or that placing a suitcase in an airport locker constitutes implicit consent to having the locker opened at night and the contents searched by hand. Pragmatic information regarding the circumstances of an act or utterance is essential to understanding its meaning.

Yet after reading the cases, it is hard to avoid the impression that courts have somewhat of a double standard when it comes to considering pragmatic information. They are significantly more likely to take it into account when it benefits the government, and less so when it helps the accused. Pragmatic information that suggests a defendant consented to a search is generally credited, while pragmatic information that suggests refusal is less likely to be.

Most importantly, courts are reluctant to take seriously the notion that police–citizen encounters are almost always, to a greater or lesser degree, coercive. This inherent coerciveness invariably colors how people interpret what, to a dispassionate judge removed from the scene, is nothing more than a polite request by a police officer to a person who is technically free to leave at any time. The inherent coerciveness of the situation is the only explanation for why so many people allow perfect strangers to rummage through their private belongings.

Racial Profiling

Does any of this really matter? It is critical to remember that the Fourth Amendment guarantees the "right of the people to be secure in their persons, houses, papers and effects, against unreasonable searches and seizures" and further provides that warrants shall issue only upon probable cause, supported by an oath or affirmation. Evidently, the framers of the Constitution contemplated that the warrant requirement would form a bulwark against unreasonable searches and seizures.[52] Nonetheless, the Supreme Court has carved out exceptions to the warrant requirement, one of which is consent searches. While statistics are scarce, a study by the National Center for State Courts found that most searches were conducted without a warrant, usually by obtaining consent.[53] A major reason that people consent, as we have seen, is that the nature of the power relationship between the police and those they detain, combined with how police request consent, creates the perception that "requests" to search are really commands.

The distinction between a request and a command is sometimes a subtle one, so it may not be surprising that judges can have trouble telling the difference. Encounters between the police and suspected offenders are always going to be somewhat tense; there will inevitably be an inequality in power and, as a consequence, anything the police do is likely to be perceived as coercive. And—at least in the case of consent searches—the defendants must have been doing something illegal, or they would not be trying to suppress the fruits of the search.

Yet these subtle distinctions are far from purely academic, as is shown by the widespread public discussion about what is sometimes called "racial profiling." According to research in the United States, a relatively high proportion of drivers stopped by police for routine traffic violations are African American and Latino, especially along major interstate highways that are thought to be drug corridors. One study by journalists in Florida was based on videotaped traffic stops along a freeway through Volusia County. Their analysis of over one thousand police videotapes revealed that even though only around 5 percent of all drivers on that freeway were African American or Hispanic, over 70 percent of traffic stops involved drivers of those two ethnic groups. Blacks and Hispanics were detained, on average, twice as long as white drivers. Most significantly for our purposes, approximately half of all stops were followed by a search, and 80 percent of all searched automobiles belonged to black and Hispanic drivers.[54] All of the stops were purportedly the result of traffic violations, such as swerving, exceeding the speed limit, burned-out license tag lights, improper license tags, and failing to signal before a lane change. Yet surprisingly, police issued tickets to only nine drivers—less than 1 percent![55]

Similar disparities, sometimes also characterized as "Driving While Black," have been documented elsewhere. In a New Jersey study, 77 percent of the motorists whom state troopers stopped and subjected to consensual searches were members of a racial or ethnic minority. And on an interstate freeway in Maryland, on which 17.5 percent of the drivers and speeders are black, 70 percent of those stopped for traffic violations and searched were African American.[56]

A routine traffic stop does not normally provide a legal basis for inspecting the interior of the car (beyond what is in "plain view"). It is therefore noteworthy that so many traffic stops in these studies were accompanied by a search. The most likely explanation is that drivers are "consenting" to searches in large numbers.[57] The ease of obtaining consent encourages police to stop cars that look like they might be involved in drug running or other illegal activity. What is disturbing about this practice is that minority drivers are apparently being stopped and searched in rates substantially greater than their proportion of the driving population, presumably because some police officers believe they are more likely to be transporting drugs. Recall that in the Florida study 80 percent of all searched automobiles belonged to minority drivers.

The ability to obtain consent so easily under current law is almost certainly a factor that encourages the practice of racial profiling. Thus, one reaction to the controversy surrounding racial profiling has been to ban consent searches entirely. In California, for instance, a lawsuit has alleged that the California Highway Patrol (CHP) stops vehicles driven by black or Latino motorists significantly more often than those driven by whites, and that occupants are two to three times more likely to be searched by drug interdiction officers. Although the CHP denied that its officers are instructed to stop suspects based on racial criteria, it was concerned enough about the problem to impose a six-month moratorium on consensual searches.[58] Moreover, New Jersey has interpreted its state constitution to require that police may conduct a consent search only if the officer has a "reasonable and articulable" suspicion that an offense has been committed.[59]

One of us (Tiersma), while a student at Stanford University, participated on a ride-along program with a San Jose, California police officer as part of a course on criminal law. San Jose happens to be close to where the *Bustamonte* case transpired, and the ride-along occurred at around the same time (the 1970s). Very early in the morning, the officer stopped an older car occupied by four young Latino men for a minor traffic violation: an inoperative light above the license plate. He visually inspected the inside of the car and collected all their drivers' licenses, returning to the patrol car to note their names and other information. The officer explained that he did so in order to be able to find the four and question them if later something suspicious happened in the area. The officer also explained that he would not ticket the driver for the inoperative light. If he did, they would probably repair it. As it was, he could stop them again for the same violation whenever he deemed it necessary to question them. Although the officer did not ask to search the car, it is easy to imagine that in a place with a great deal of drug trafficking, such as Florida, the object of such a strategy would be to search for drugs or other contraband.

Pretextual traffic stops that are really aimed at finding drugs would not cease if, as we recommend, police routinely advise people that they do not have to consent to a search and are free to leave.[60] But police would have less of an incentive to carry out such stops if they were required to apprise motorists of their right to refuse and if people exercised that right in greater numbers. Consent searches are what make racial profiling appear to pay off, because if the police stop and search enough vehicles driven by people who fit their profile of drug runners (a profile in which race and ethnicity play a major role), they will at some point find contraband, reinforcing their belief that the strategy works and leading them to continue pursuing it. Whether and how well it works is impossible for us to determine, but the damage that profiling inflicts on notions of racial equality and fairness almost certainly cancels out any possible benefit in the war against drugs.

Conclusion

Interactions between police and citizens will always be inherently coercive to some degree. Yet this coerciveness can be mitigated in a number of ways. For example, if police officers want to make a noncoercive request instead of a command, they should make it evident that they are doing so. A general who tells a private that she "might want to clean her boots" will normally be interpreted as making a command. If it is actually no more than a suggestion or request, the general would have to add "This isn't an order, private" or "That's just an informal suggestion." Even then, of course, the general's "suggestion" would be hard to ignore.

In the context of searches, the inherent coerciveness of the situation mandates that if consent be freely and voluntarily given, the police must explicitly acknowledge that they are making a request rather than a command. In practice, this will require them to inform suspects that they have a right to refuse.[61] Such a solution goes beyond what the Constitution requires of the police. The Supreme Court explicitly rejected requiring such warnings in *Bustamonte*[62] because "it would be thoroughly impractical to impose on the normal consent search the detailed requirements of an effective warning."[63] Recently, the Court reaffirmed *Bustamonte* in the *Drayton* case, rejecting emphatically the notion that any type of warning or legal advice was required.[64]

Of course, simply appending "You have the right to say no" to any search request, which is probably all that police would have to say, is not really very burdensome. In fact, some law enforcement officers already give such a warning: "Do you mind if I search—are you sure you don't mind that I search your person? You don't have to let me if you don't want to."[65] Just adding a few words—"You can say no and are free to leave"—would make the request less coercive and the ensuing consent more legitimate. A few states now require under their own constitutions that people asked to undergo a consent search understand their right to refuse and that they are free to go at any time.[66]

It is possible, of course, that even after suspects are told that they have a right to refuse and are free to go, the inherent coerciveness of the situation will nonetheless induce them to consent.[67] If that turns out to be the case, the only logical conclusion we can reach is that the pragmatic context of a traffic stop is so coercive that a police officer simply cannot make a genuine request in this situation, but will always be understood as issuing an order or command. Any subsequent consent can therefore never be voluntary. The result would be that consent searches in the context of a traffic stop would inevitably be unconstitutional. No doubt the likelihood of this conclusion is a major reason that courts are so reluctant to seriously consider the pragmatic context.

As a linguistic matter, therefore, the notion that most of the suspects discussed in this chapter freely consented to various searches is dubious. The real animus behind the *Bustamonte* decision becomes apparent in the Court's observation that "[c]onsent searches are part of the standard investigatory techniques of law enforcement agencies"[68] and its insistence on the "legitimate need" for such searches.[69]

The Court's concern seems to be that advising suspects of their constitutional right to refuse will encourage them to exercise that right, thus leading to less incriminating evidence being found and fewer criminals being apprehended.[70] While punishing wrongdoers is an important social goal, one hopes that it can be attained without manipulating the meaning of consent. Because more experienced criminals have probably learned that they have nothing to gain by cooperating in a search, it is the inexperienced and less dangerous criminals who are most likely to be caught in this snare. Moreover, allowing police to subtly pressure suspects into consenting undermines public confidence in the rule of law and the basic fairness of the criminal justice system.[71] This is even more problematic when those who are stopped and whose consent is sought for a search are predominantly members of racial and ethnic minorities.

Chapter 4

Interrogation, Confession, and the Right to Counsel

Maybe I should talk to a
lawyer.

Obtaining confessions from suspects has long been a favorite technique for solving and proving crimes. Morally, there is a lot to be said for confessing. People ought to accept responsibility for wrongful acts that they commit. Practically, confessions save the legal system a great deal of time and money.

Unfortunately, the obvious benefits of confessions have sometimes made law enforcement officers a bit too eager to obtain them. A long-practiced method involved the use of threats and torture. Although we tend to associate such investigative techniques with the Middle Ages or the Spanish Inquisition, beating confessions out of suspects is hardly unknown in the history of the United States. It wasn't until 1936 that the U.S. Supreme Court invalidated a confession obtained by whipping and threatening to hang three black men thought to have murdered a white farmer.[1] But even as physical torture became less acceptable, psychological torment took its place. About a decade later, in 1944, the Supreme Court again held invalid a confession that was made after police conducted a "relay interrogation" of a suspect for thirty-six hours, without allowing the suspect to rest or sleep.[2] Even today, physically coercive interrogation remains a problem in many parts of the world.[3] The abuse of Iraqi prisoners by American and British military personnel in 2003 and 2004 serves as a reminder that interrogation by torture is more than an abstraction.

The Supreme Court has long adhered to a rule that any valid confession must be "voluntary" and thus cannot be the result of coercion.[4] In 1957, the Court developed a "totality of the circumstances" test to decide whether a confession is voluntary.[5] This test considers factors such as the length and location of the interrogation, the nature of the police tactics, and the suspect's mental condition and education.[6] Using such factors, courts decide whether a confession was voluntary or whether the suspect's "will was overborne at the time he confessed."[7]

The "totality of the circumstances" test proved not always easy to apply. Confessions were often made to police behind closed doors, generally with no reliable record made of the event and without the presence of a disinterested witness who could later describe exactly what took place. Add the fact that the suspect was usually not free to leave, and it's clear how such a situation could be inherently intimidating and coercive. Deciding whether, under these circumstances, a confession was voluntary is almost always a speculative venture.

In 1964, to address such concerns, the Supreme Court held in *Escobedo v. Illinois* that a suspect being interrogated by the police has a right to have a lawyer present to assist him.[8] The right was reaffirmed and strengthened in *Miranda v. Arizona,* which we discuss in chapter 5. In a later opinion, *Edwards v. Arizona,* the Supreme Court elaborated that once a suspect invokes the right to counsel, the police may not resume questioning until a lawyer has been provided or until the suspect voluntarily resumes the discussion.[9]

An important linguistic issue raised by these cases is whether a suspect has invoked his right to counsel by "requesting" the assistance of a lawyer. As we saw in chapter 3, courts typically take pragmatic information into account in deciding, for example, that during a routine traffic stop a police officer's question about whether the car's trunk opens is in fact a request to search inside the trunk. As we will see, courts are much more reluctant to consider such pragmatic information when suspects indirectly request to speak to an attorney.

Invoking the Right to Counsel

There are doubtless a few people who during interrogation will expressly invoke their right to counsel by saying something like "I hereby invoke my right to counsel," or "I request to have an attorney present before questioning continues." In written legal documents, using direct speech acts like these is the norm. Yet as we saw in chapter 3, most people speak less directly in ordinary conversation, especially when they impose on someone else by making a request or command.

Consider how we request or order something in a restaurant. We seldom say, "I request your salmon special" or "Bring me the salmon special." Instead, we might simply express a *desire:*

> I'd like the salmon special.
> I'm in the mood for the salmon.

Even though we have—strictly speaking—not ordered anything, our utterance will be viewed as a request or command if we say it to the waitress. The pragmatic context, as always, is critical. Were we to make this utterance to the friend who is dining with us, before the waitress arrives, it would be interpreted "literally" as a statement about what we desire to eat, rather than being taken as an indirect request for the friend to go to the kitchen and fetch us some fish.

Another way to request or order something in a restaurant is by expressing a *need:*

> These potatoes need to be cooked a little longer.
> I need some milk for my coffee.

We might also speak the language of *obligation:*

> I have to take the rest of this food home.
> I must try a piece of your delicious chocolate cake.

Or we could make a statement about the *future:*

> I'll have some coffee with my dessert.

A request or command can also be made to seem less of an imposition, and thus more polite, by asking a *question:*

> Could you bring me a glass of water?
> Why don't I try the Pad Thai?
> Might I have some butter?

A question ostensibly allows the addressee some choice in the matter, and is therefore a device to help the server save face.

An analogous result can be obtained by *hedging,* which refers to methods that "soften" a claim or statement, or make it weaker. People tend to hedge when they are uncertain about something, but they may also hedge out of politeness, often in combination with the other strategies listed above. One way to hedge is to add adverbs of uncertainty, like "maybe" or "perhaps":

> Maybe you could bring me the check.
> Could you perhaps get me a knife?

Another method of hedging is to use verbs that express the speaker's mental state, which make a weaker claim to the truth than an outright assertion:

> I guess I'll have the vegetarian tacos.
> I think I'd like the Chardonnay.
> I believe you brought me the wrong dish.

Finally, we can make a request or command more polite by making it *conditional* on the good will or convenience of the addressee:

> If you have a moment, could you bring me some salsa?
> Charge it to my credit card, if you don't mind.

Note that the condition is obviously one that the speaker presumes will be met, so that in this context these statements are actually unconditional requests, or perhaps even commands or orders.

Suppose now that instead of eating out, you have been picked up for questioning regarding the untimely death of your neighbor, with whom you had an ongoing feud. You are being interrogated by two detectives in a small, windowless room. You have been read your rights. After two hours of relentless questioning, you desperately need to visit the toilet. What do you say to the detectives? "Let me use the toilet" or "I request permission to use the restroom facilities" is possible, of course, but most of us would be inclined to speak more politely under these circumstances. What most of us would say is something like:

> Do you mind if I use the restroom?
> I need to use the toilet.

I'd like to go to the bathroom, if that's all right.

Maybe I could use the toilet.

Where is the men's room?

The detectives are obviously in control of this situation, so any request that we might make will naturally be phrased fairly indirectly and politely.

Requests for counsel are comparable. People in custody do not normally make a direct request or a demand for a lawyer. Instead, they are naturally inclined by the situation to be polite and indirect, perhaps by using expressions of need or desire, or by making the request in the form of a question. All too many judges, however, tend to read these requests for counsel the same way they would read a deed or promissory note. They expect that suspects during interrogation will speak the way that lawyers write, and thus interpret the statements literally. Consider the following interaction:

> Officer: [I]t's my understanding you don't want to sign the rights form now is that right?
> Defendant: Not 'til you know?
> Officer: Ok.
> Defendant: When I talk to my lawyer I'll.
> Officer: Ok. But you don't want a lawyer at this time, is that correct?
> Defendant: I will get a lawyer.
> Officer: Ok. But you don't want one now is what I'm saying. Ok.
> Defendant: I'd like to have one but you know I [sic] it would be hard to get hold of one right now.
> Officer: Well what I am asking you Clayton is do you wish to give me a statement at this time without having a lawyer present?
> Defendant: Well I can I can [sic] tell you what I did.
> Officer: Ok, that's what, that's what [sic] I'm asking.[10]

Despite the defendant's statement that he would "like to have" a lawyer, the court held that he did not invoke his right to counsel. If what matters is the suspect's communicative intent, then the court got it wrong. This is obviously a statement of desire that functions as a request. The dialogue is all the more troubling because it appears that the defendant really did try to invoke his constitutional rights, but was ultimately too intimidated to force the issue when the officer did not abide by his wishes. Moreover, this case is not an isolated one. Another person being questioned by law enforcement officers commented that he "felt like he might want" to talk to a lawyer; he was likewise held not to have invoked his right to counsel.[11]

The same result obtained for a suspect who told his interrogator: "I think I would like to talk to a lawyer."[12]

Expressions of need may be equally ineffective. In *People v. Krueger,* police were questioning a suspect about a number of burglaries and then suddenly asked about a stabbing death. The suspect responded: "Wait a minute. Maybe I ought to have an attorney. You guys are trying to pin a murder rap on me, give me 20 to 40 years." Another policeman recalled that he said, "Maybe I need a lawyer." In any event, the Illinois Supreme Court held that he had not clearly enough invoked his right to counsel.[13] Likewise, a defendant who told police: "I think I might need a lawyer," was also held in *People v. Kendricks* not to have effectively invoked the right to counsel.[14]

In both *Krueger* and *Kendricks,* the suspects' statements were hedged ("maybe" and "I think"). Hedging is common in this situation.[15] Similar are conditional requests, which in the following example is combined with hedging: "If I'm going to be charged with murder maybe I should talk to an attorney." The Minnesota Supreme Court held that the woman who made this utterance did not clearly request that a lawyer be present.[16]

Not only do judges tend to take hedged statements literally, without considering the pragmatic context, but they often do the same with questions. According to the Virginia Supreme Court, for instance, a suspect's comment, "Didn't you say I have the right to an attorney?" was not a valid assertion of the right to counsel.[17] In fact, this question is really a statement that seeks confirmation that the speaker does have this right, equivalent to: "You said I had a right to an attorney, didn't you?" Like so many of these ineffective invocations, it is an indirect—and thus more polite—way of asserting that the speaker wishes to assert this right. Consider again the restaurant analogy. Suppose that a customer is told that she gets a free glass of wine with her meal, but sees that she was charged for the wine when she receives the check. Unless the patron is a lawyer, a direct demand would seem out of place: "I assert my right to a free glass of wine and hereby demand that you adjust the check accordingly." Somewhat more polite, but still rather direct, is to assert "The wine is supposed to be free." More polite is to phrase it as a confirmation-seeking question, "Didn't you say that the wine was included?" or as an observation, "I think you accidentally charged me for the wine." These are exactly the strategies that many suspects employ during interrogation, much to their disadvantage.[18]

Not all courts have taken such a hyperliteral view of the matter.[19] According to Janet Ainsworth, who has written a thoughtful analysis of the problem, courts in the past employed three main approaches in deciding whether an individual invoked the right to counsel. One approach used the *threshold of clarity* standard, which applied the very literal interpretations illustrated above. Unless the suspect clearly invokes his constitutional rights, questioning can continue. At the opposite end of the spectrum, the *per se* approach recognized indirect requests as being valid invocations and requires that interrogation cease immediately. That is, a suspect's mentioning legal counsel counts as a *per se* invocation of Fifth Amendment rights. The third line of cases identified by Ainsworth—the *clarification* standard— represented a compromise of sorts between the other two approaches by allowing police to clarify a request for counsel that is considered ambiguous.[20]

While the clarification approach may initially seem to be the most reasonable, we must not forget that those seeking clarification—interrogating officers—have a strong interest in proceeding without a lawyer present. Most lawyers advise their clients to invoke their right to remain silent. Assuming that the police have indeed detained someone involved in the crime, the presence of a lawyer may frustrate their ability to obtain evidence from one of the people who knows the most about it, perhaps the perpetrator himself. Under these circumstances, it would not be surprising if the questions purportedly seeking clarification doubled as indirect warnings advising the suspect that it might not be in his best interest to have a lawyer present.

Suppose once again that we are in a restaurant. The waitress asks what you would like to order, and you reply "I believe I'll have the steak." The waitress attempts to clarify your ambiguous statement: "Are you ordering the steak?" "Yes," you answer, but by now you are beginning to waver. "Well," replies the waitress, "I just wanted to be absolutely sure that you really wanted the steak. Some people order the steak but when it arrives they are sorry they did. So I just want to confirm that you really and truly want the steak, because once you order it, your choice is final." Many people, we imagine, would decide at this point to order something else. The unstated message of the waitress's confirmatory questioning is that our decision was not a wise one.

This is exactly what some interrogators do to clarify what they regard as an ambiguous invocation of counsel. As Ainsworth points out, they suggest, directly or indirectly, that having an attorney present may not be in the suspect's best interest, or that finding a lawyer will be a slow and cumbersome process, or that the suspect does not yet need a lawyer.[21] Coming on the heels of an indirect invocation of the right to counsel, such "clarification" can only discourage suspects from persisting.

Aggravating the situation is that those who make indirect requests for counsel are likely to be less empowered members of society who are particularly susceptible to such pressure tactics. Research by linguists over the past several decades has shown that an indirect speech style and greater use of hedging is associated with people of lower socioeconomic status. Initial studies focused on the differences between men's and women's speech. Robin Lakoff, who conducted pioneering studies on women's language, reported that women tend to speak in a less direct and more polite way than men. Whereas men are more likely to make direct orders or requests, such as "Close the door" or "Please close the door," women tend to use what are considered more polite formulations: "Will you close the door?" or "Won't you close the door?"[22] According to Lakoff, women also avoid stating strong opinions, preferring to use constructions that indicate some uncertainty or seek confirmation.[23] This is consistent with the more frequent use of hedged or conditional expressions, as well as the use of questions to make requests, as in the examples above.

Subsequent research has confirmed what many readers are doubtless thinking: this speech style may be characteristic of Aunt Mable, but does not necessarily reflect how younger and more educated women talk. One study confirming this impression was based on an analysis of the language of witnesses conducted by a team of researchers including John Conley and William O'Barr. They found that some women did indeed resort to the female style described by Lakoff, but that others did not. And although more women used this style than did men, there was nonetheless a significant number of men who employed it as well. Examining the data more closely, they discovered that women who used a "women's" speech style tended to be housewives or have lower social status. In contrast, the speech of well-educated professional women did not reflect these features nearly as much. The researchers noted the same distinction among men: those who spoke in the style that Lakoff described usually held lower status jobs or were unemployed. The study concluded that what Lakoff described as women's speech was in fact better characterized as a "powerless" speech style that was typical of both men and women who were less well educated or of lower socioeconomic status.[24]

It is evident that indirect invocations of counsel reflect this "powerless" style of speaking. In contrast, better-educated and more affluent people, who probably have a clearer understanding of their rights, will be inclined to assert them more directly. And their right to counsel is more likely to be respected by interrogators. Thus, a rule requiring detainees to invoke their right to counsel with clarity may result in a disproportionate number of people with less education and socioeconomic clout having to navigate through police interrogations without a lawyer. No doubt this has some effect on the demographics of the prison population.

These findings suggest that the legal system should begin to recognize indirect requests for counsel, just as they recognize indirect requests by the police to search a car, and just as they recognize indirect acts of consent by suspects. At the very least, law enforcement officers should be required to explain, once a suspect raises the right to counsel, that his request will be respected and that if he wants to have a lawyer present, all he has to do is say "I want a lawyer."

The law is now settled and contains no such requirement. In 1994—the year after Ainsworth's article was published in the *Yale Law Journal*—the Supreme Court held in *Davis v. United States* that a suspect's statement that "Maybe I should talk to a lawyer" was not an invocation of the right to counsel, adopting the literalistic threshold of clarity approach. The Court also held that interrogating officers were under no duty to ask clarifying questions, emphasizing that unless and until a suspect makes an *unambiguous* or *unequivocal* request for counsel, the police can continue questioning.[25] The ruling was especially aggressive in rejecting the clarification standard, which the government itself had agreed may be the best path to take when a suspect makes an equivocal invocation.[26]

The Supreme Court's ruling in *Davis* sets a minimal standard and thus precludes courts from imposing a stricter requirement as a matter of federal constitutional rights. But state courts may do so under their own constitutions, and law enforcement agencies may do so as a matter of adopting professional and fair police practices. Whether imposed by statute, local ordinance, judicial decisions, or departmental policy, we believe that police officers at the very least should clarify ambiguous requests.

Another approach would be to have interrogators inform the suspect that specific "magic words" will stop an interrogation. For example, they might explain: "At any time, if you say the words, 'I want a lawyer,' we will stop questioning you and give you the chance to consult with an attorney."[27] In fact, this approach could also solve potential problems with the clarification approach. If a suspect makes an ambiguous request, officers could just repeat this warning: "Are you saying you want a lawyer? Remember, if you say the words, 'I want a lawyer,' we will stop questioning you and give you the chance to consult with an attorney." While formalism is sometimes the enemy of successful communication, a clear procedure that is easy to understand may be appropriate in this instance. Although we doubt that courts will insist on this procedure as a constitutional imperative, legislatures and police departments might work together to produce a more professional approach to the problem.

We also vigorously recommend that encounters between suspects and the police be recorded, to eliminate disputes about what actually happened and to give judges first-hand evidence of what happened during the interrogation. Because the exact words that the suspect used in potentially invoking his right to counsel are so critical under the Supreme Court's ruling in *Davis*, it is particularly important to record this aspect of the proceedings. Recall that in *Davis* it was the addition of the single word "maybe" that doomed the defendant's claim that he had asserted his right to a lawyer.

It is enlightening to now return to the Supreme Court's decision in *Schneckloth v. Bustamonte,* discussed in chapter 3, and to compare it with *Davis*. In *Bustamonte* the Court held that the police officers, by asking "Does the trunk open?" had requested consent to search the trunk. Literally, of course, the officer's utterance was nothing more than a question about the condition of the trunk. Yet the indirect or nonliteral meaning is so natural under these pragmatic circumstances that the Court automatically interpreted this utterance as a request to open the trunk, or—depending on who is asking—a demand to do so. Likewise, Joe Alcala never literally consented to the search. He simply confirmed that the trunk was capable of being opened and proceeded to open it. The Court, once again, interpreted his actions as constituting consent. In contrast, when the defendant in the *Davis* case told police that "Maybe I should talk to a lawyer," the Court suddenly assumed a very literal bent, insisting that requests for counsel be unequivocal and unambiguous.

It appears, therefore, that people subject to interrogation are held to a higher linguistic standard than the police: they must be direct in invoking their right to counsel. If anything, it seems to us, the situation should be reversed. A police request to search should be direct and clearly indicate that it is truly nothing but a request. People suspected of having committed crimes, who are typically under great stress while being interrogated and who may not have the benefit of much formal education, should be allowed to invoke their rights by using the types of indirect requests that are so common in everyday speech.

The Meaning of "Interrogation"

We have seen that once a suspect invokes his right to counsel, interrogation must cease. Clearly, this means that police can no longer ask questions about the case ("Where did you hide the gun?"), nor can they demand information ("Tell us where you hid the gun").

Now consider the facts of *Rhode Island v. Innis*. A man suspected of having killed a taxicab driver with a sawed-off shotgun was arrested on the street. He received the customary *Miranda* warnings (see chapter 5) and asked to speak to a lawyer. The suspect was then placed in a vehicle bound for the police station. Having invoked his right to counsel, the officers in the car could not question him further during the drive to the station. But they were eager to find the murder weapon. En route to the station, one of the officers happened to mention to another policeman that there was a school for disabled children near the scene of the crime. "God forbid one of them might find a weapon with shells and they might hurt themselves." The other officer concurred, adding that they should redouble their efforts to find the weapon. At this point the defendant, who overheard the conversation, spoke up and volunteered to show the officers where the gun was located.[28]

Did the police pose a question about the case to the defendant, and thus "interrogate" him? If so, they did not honor his invocation of the right to counsel, which would require the court to suppress both his response and the weapons found as a result of the response. An easy solution would be to observe that the policeman did not literally ask a question and to hold that this was the end of the matter. After all, on one level the officer only expressed legitimate concern about the school children.

The Court in *Innis*, however, was linguistically sophisticated enough to understand that people often speak indirectly. It held that the prohibition against further interrogation in this situation extends not just to express questions, but also to the "functional equivalent" of a question. The Court defined the functional equivalent of questioning as any words or actions on the part of the police (other than those normally attendant to arrest and custody) that the police should know are reasonably likely to elicit an incriminating response from the suspect. Ultimately, however, the Court decided that the officers did not, under this definition, engage in interrogation.[29]

The Court's definition of "interrogation" seems sensible. Just as there is more than one way to make a request or command, there is more than one way to elicit information from someone. When a parent says to a child, "I just heard from your teacher, and she isn't happy about what happened today," any reasonable youngster will understand this statement as an invitation to tell her side of the story.

Whether the Court was correct in concluding that the officers in *Innis* did not, under this definition, interrogate the defendant about the location

of the weapon is more debatable. The policeman directed his utterance to
the other officer. As the Court noted, there is no reason to expect that a
suspect's eavesdropping on a private conversation will arouse pangs of guilt,
leading to a confession. But it is also possible that, somewhat deviously,
the policeman overtly directed his utterance to his fellow officer while in
fact intending or hoping that the defendant would respond. In that event,
the defendant would have been what linguists sometimes call an "intended
overhearer." If that is actually what happened, we would have to conclude
that the officer was indirectly interrogating the defendant. On the other
hand, if the utterance was truly nothing more than a comment to the other
officer, which the defendant unintentionally overheard, it would not be the
functional equivalent of a question.

Under the circumstances of *Innis*, we think it likely that the police
officer was indeed attempting to provoke a response from the defendant.
Perhaps part of the reason for the Court's decision is that it is hard to be
sympathetic to the defendant. He knew where the murder weapon was hidden, which is strong evidence that he killed the taxi driver. Other possible
scenarios are more troubling, however. Suppose that officers, as in *Innis*,
are transporting to a local jail a defendant who has invoked his rights. One
officer says to the other, "Man, I feel sorry for this guy. He's facing a murder
rap and refuses to cooperate. The prosecutor is going to go for the death
penalty and I bet he fries. If he would just tell us where the body is, I bet
he could cut himself a pretty good deal." Or consider this possible comment
by one officer to another, in the presence of a suspect: "This poor guy is
going to get beaten pretty badly when the other prisoners find out he's
a child abuser. If only he would cooperate, we should be able to get him
into a mental hospital, where he'd be a lot safer. And that lawyer he wants
to talk to is a useless windbag." Courts would likely hold these comments
to constitute interrogation, and would almost certainly do so if they were
directed at the suspect himself.[30]

In the famous "Christian burial speech" case, the Supreme Court found—
under circumstances very similar to *Innis*—that an officer's "comments" to
a suspect were in fact questions that constituted interrogation. In *Brewer
v. Williams*, a man suspected of killing a young girl invoked his right to
counsel before being transported by police to Des Moines for further proceedings. The officers agreed with the man's lawyer not to interrogate him
until he arrived in Des Moines and had a chance to speak to another lawyer.
As they were driving, one of the officers turned to the suspect, who was
known to be quite religious, addressed him as "Reverend," and said:

I want to give you something to think about while we're traveling down the road. . . . Number one, I want you to observe the weather conditions, it's raining, it's sleeting, it's freezing, driving is very treacherous, visibility is poor, it's going to be dark early this evening. They are predicting several inches of snow for tonight, and I feel that you yourself are the only person that knows where this little girl's body is, that you yourself have only been there once, and if you get a snow on top of it you yourself may be unable to find it. And, since we will be going right past the area on the way into Des Moines, I feel that we could stop and locate the body, that the parents of this little girl should be entitled to a Christian burial for the little girl who was snatched away from them on Christmas Eve and murdered.[31]

Soon afterward, the man led police officers to the body.

Unlike *Innis*, the Supreme Court held in *Brewer* that there was "no serious doubt" that the detective "deliberately and designedly set out to elicit information" and that these efforts were tantamount to interrogation, even though the "speech" contained nothing remotely similar to a question. Why the difference? In both cases the Court acknowledged that people can elicit information indirectly. The distinction may lie in the fact that in *Innis* the officer spoke to another policeman, while in *Brewer* the officer's comments were directed at the suspect.[32] Thus, while the Court correctly realized that people can ask questions by making what seem to be statements, it appears to be less willing to acknowledge the "intended overhearer" scenario: that person *A* can speak to person *B*, even while ostensibly addressing person *C*.

A different way to "question" someone is to confront a suspect with evidence, either the actual evidence itself or a description of evidence that police claim to have found. In *People v. Ferro*, a man was being investigated for having stolen furs; he invoked his rights. Officers then placed some of the stolen furs next to his cell. A New York court acknowledged that the police placed the furs there with the intent of trying to obtain a statement, but held that the action did not constitute interrogation.[33] The case was later reversed, largely for other reasons, but it does illustrate the tactics to which police sometimes resort.[34] The officers clearly intended to communicate a message to the defendant, roughly speaking as follows: "We have the evidence; you might as well confess!" Why else would they place the stolen furs outside his cell?

Deciding whether an utterance or action is the functional equivalent of a question depends on a relatively subtle analysis of the language used

and the surrounding circumstances. This creates somewhat of an evidentiary problem: people generally recall how they interpreted an utterance
at the time, but remember less well the exact words that were spoken, the
intonation, accompanying gestures, and so on (see chapter 6). These cues
can be critical in determining whether an officer's words were reasonably
likely to elicit an incriminating response from the suspect, the standard in
Innis. For this reason, we recommend that courts adopt a bright-line rule
that should be easier for both police and reviewing courts. Once a suspect
invokes his right to silence or the presence of an attorney, police should
no longer discuss the case in his presence, nor should they drive him to
the scene of the crime or present him with evidence pertaining to the case.
Without such a rule, the temptation for police to reinitiate interrogation
under the ruse of making ostensibly harmless comments is simply too great.

Interrogation and the Problem of False Confessions

As mentioned at the beginning of this chapter, courts assessing the admissibility of a confession have traditionally concentrated on whether it was
voluntary—the product of the free will of the speaker. If a confession is
found to be involuntary, or coerced, it will not be admitted into evidence.

Voluntariness is surely a critical element of any valid confession, but
it does not go far enough. Voluntariness does not inevitably guarantee
reliability or trustworthiness, which is the ultimate issue. It is true that the
average person would not voluntarily confess to a crime that she did not
commit. Not everyone is average, however. Children, people with mental or
learning disabilities, and those who do not speak English well or have little
familiarity with the American legal system are particularly susceptible to
making false confessions.[35]

It is impossible to determine the exact extent of the problem of false
confessions.[36] The vast majority of confessions are almost certainly true.
Once police place them in custody, most suspects probably assume that
the gig is up and decide that they might as well cooperate with police in
the hope of obtaining a lighter sentence. Others may confess to relieve
themselves of the psychological burden of having to hide the truth, or
because they believe that it is the right thing to do.

Still, a not insignificant number of people have been convicted of crimes
they did not commit, often because of a false confession. Some dramatic
evidence comes from the Innocence Project, started in New York by Barry
Scheck and Peter Neufeld.[37] As of March 2004, 143 people convicted of and
imprisoned for crimes had been exonerated by DNA evidence. Roughly one-

fifth of the original convictions had resulted at least in part from false confessions. Stories of exonerations based on DNA analysis continue to be reported in the press, often involving inmates who falsely confessed to crimes and subsequently spent long periods of time in prison, some even on death row.[38]

Because interrogations are seldom taped, there is no definitive way to study systematically the linguistic devices that police officers use. Nonetheless, using materials from cases on which he has worked as a consultant or expert witness, linguist Roger Shuy has identified some of the linguistic features of the coercive questioning techniques that may lead people to confess to crimes they did not commit. Examples of these techniques include framing questions in such a way that the respondent is left with only two possible answers, as in a "yes/no" question: "Was he still alive at the time?" Even more coercive are questions that steer the respondent toward one specific answer. A common question type of this sort is what linguists call *tag questions:* "You hated Mr. Jones, didn't you?" These questions consist of a statement or accusation that the respondent is expected to confirm. Or a question might presuppose a fact that has not yet been established: "Why did you kill him?"

During a trial, such coercive questions are generally restricted to cross-examination, when it is permissible to "lead" a witness.[39] No such limitations apply during interrogation, however, despite the highly suggestive nature of such questioning. Most adults can probably resist suggestions implanted by questions of this kind, but it is less evident that some of the more vulnerable members of society can do so. Police often conduct an interrogation believing that the suspect committed the crime, or they suggest that this is so, resulting in "questioning" that consists largely of statements or accusations cloaked in interrogatory form.[40]

Sometimes, in fact, interrogators do not even bother to disguise their accusations as questions. Consider the following example, taken from the work of Richard Ofshe and Richard Leo. The suspect was being questioned about a mass murder case that took place at a Phoenix temple; the interrogator was obviously trying to undermine the suspect's alibi that he was in Tucson at the time:

Interrogator: Now Victor, ah Leo, you know that that's right. I mean you're
    shakin' your head trying to convince yourself, you know, but you cannot
    erase what happened. You cannot erase what happened. You were there.
Suspect: No I wasn't.
Interrogator: You went there (unintelligible).

Suspect: I was not there!
Interrogator: You know who you were with.
Suspect: No I don't.
Interrogator: You know who the people were that were there and you know
    what you know about what happened.
Suspect: I don't know anything.
Interrogator: Sooner or later, you know, you've got to say it.
Suspect: I, I wasn't there, I was not there.[41]

The suspect, who actually was innocent of the crime, eventually confessed
to having participated in the murder. But, of course, neither he nor two
others who also falsely confessed could provide police with any further
details about the crime, including what they might have done with the
loot. Eventually the real killers were found, along with the items that they
had stolen.[42]

According to Ofshe and Leo, who have studied the problem extensively,
the most common reason for false confessions is the use of threats of harm
if the suspect persists in denying involvement, or promises of leniency if
he makes admissions.[43] Of course, if interrogators were to tell a suspect
that they have evidence that will almost surely lead to her conviction and
execution, but that if she cooperates and confesses they will make sure she
gets no more than five years in prison, a judge would likely find the resulting confession to have been involuntary. The U.S. Supreme Court held over
a century ago that a confession induced by hope or fear is not voluntary.[44]
Nonetheless, interrogators sometimes continue to make promises (to induce
a confession by hope) or threats (using fear), but tend to do so indirectly,
so that a resulting confession will not be found to have been involuntary.
As Ofshe and Leo write, "[t]he modern equivalent to the rubber hose is the
indirect threat communicated through pragmatic implication."[45]

The following interchange illustrates how an interrogator might indirectly promise that the suspect, accused of sexually abusing a child, will
receive a lighter sentence or perhaps medical institutionalization in exchange for cooperation:

Interrogator: If you want that family, you're going to have to pull yourself
    together. You're going to have to be strong. Ok? You can start today or else
    you can go sit in jail and think about it. I don't care.
Suspect: Where . . . where do I go?
Interrogator: It doesn't matter to me because it's your—you go right here. You
    start talking right here. You start on your way to recovery. The District

Attorney knows that you're on your way to recovery. You're not putting these kids on (unclear). You're not just thinking about yourself. Ok? All right. That's how you start. And then no matter what comes of it. You know, the main thing is that you recovered. Ok? That you get that counseling. All right? All right? Ok? So you can become a productive person.[46]

The use of promises to induce a suspect to talk is problematic not only because it can be unduly coercive, but also because the police generally lack the authority to make such promises. Plea bargaining is the domain of prosecutors. And sentencing is the responsibility of the judge. Thus, interrogators cannot make promises regarding how a judge will sentence a suspect, nor can they promise that the defendant will be granted a particular type of plea bargain. Notice how the interrogator tries to sidestep this issue when the suspect begins to inquire:

Suspect: Still have to go to court, right?
Interrogator: That's up to you.
Suspect: (Unclear) If I don't go to court there's got to be a set time.
Interrogator: A set time for what?
Suspect: For jail time.
Interrogator: For jail time? Yeah.
Suspect: Prison or wherever the hell I go.
Interrogator: That doesn't mean that you have to go to court. Of course a judge would have to send you, yeah. Or . . . put you in a program for . . . you know . . . to make sure you get your treatment that you need. All these things will be taken into consideration.[47]

The interrogator here tries to avoid making any express promises that he cannot keep. But the subtext is clear: "We'll go easy on you if you confess." Suspects unfamiliar with the criminal justice system may be dismayed to find out later that the interrogator's indirect promises of leniency are unenforceable, and need not be honored by the prosecutor or the judge. Indirect threats played a role in the false confessions made by at least one of the suspects in the Phoenix temple murder case:

Interrogator 1: You've been sentenced before . . . you've been sentenced before for little things and you know that if that judge gets pissed off at you it's a lot different than if he's not. And you right now you can make a decision to make a difference about how the judge feels about you and you need to take it.

> Interrogator 2: What if he might send you to the gas chamber, and I don't say
> that to scare you, Dante, but in this situation that's a real possibility and I'm
> not gonna sit here, Wayne's not gonna sit here and lie to you about these
> things cause that's not gonna serve us any purpose.[48]

Obviously, police cannot tell a suspect that he will go to the gas chamber if
he does not confess; such a threat would clearly be coercive. Yet by "predicting" that this result is likely, they can in essence make a veiled threat
that has much the same effect. The legality of this tactic becomes even
more dubious when we see what happens to defendants who are accused of
making threats to others. In that case, the legal system has no problems
recognizing indirect utterances as actual threats, a topic that we explore
in chapter 10.

Making analysis more difficult is the quality of the accounts of the
interrogation that the police create.[49] Sometimes police produce what they
claim is a verbatim written record of what transpired; and if the suspect
signs the report, it may become a written confession. Such accounts are inherently limited because writing fails to include a great deal of information
conveyed by the speaker—information, for example, that can be gleaned
from intonation and gestures. Consequently, even if a report is truly a verbatim transcription, nonverbal indications that police are overbearing or
that the suspect is lying would be absent. This problem aside, the report
may not be accurate in the first place.[50]

Even worse is that often there is no record, either written or taped,
of the interrogation at all. Thus, what happened during questioning may
devolve into a swearing match between the police and the suspect. This is
especially problematic when the voluntariness of a confession is at issue.
As we have seen, threats and promises are often made indirectly, which
may leave the suspect with the impression that there was a threat, while
allowing interrogators to suggest that all they did was predict that, absent
cooperation, a death sentence was likely. This can be a problem even when
interrogators and suspects are both being entirely honest. As we will see in
detail in chapter 6, people seldom remember exact words, even though in
cases such as these, knowing the precise words that were spoken may be
critical.

In order to reduce the possibility of such problems, we endorse pro-
posals that all police interrogation intended for courtroom use should be
videotaped.[51] A videotape of a valid confession would be very convincing
to a jury. And when there is any question that a confession might not
be reliable, a videotape can reveal the conduct of the interrogation and

help determine whether the suspect spoke of his own accord or had words planted in his mouth. In the United Kingdom and Australia, police interviews have been recorded as a matter of law for years.[52] Illinois, motivated in part by the exoneration of several death row inmates who had been convicted based on questionable confessions, recently began requiring the taping of interrogations in homicide cases.[53] It is time for the rest of the states, as well as the federal government, to do the same.

We also believe that judges should evaluate the substantive reliability of confessions before admitting them into evidence, at least where the reliability or truthfulness of a confession is put at issue by one of the parties.[54] As we observed above, voluntariness is just one element in the equation. It is true that a rational actor would never voluntarily confess to a crime that she did not commit. Even the ploys often used during interrogation would probably not induce such a person to falsely confess. But a suspect who is a juvenile or mentally handicapped in some way, or someone who does not speak English and is unfamiliar with American culture, may not always act in ways that judges or lawyers would consider rational. Confessions of such vulnerable defendants should be closely scrutinized.

Some may object that the jury can decide for itself how truthful a confession is. This, of course, is the current state of affairs. But juries tend to give tremendous weight—perhaps too much weight—to a confession. Much of a judge's responsibility during trial is to function as a "gatekeeper," deciding which evidence should be admitted and which should not. Reliability is usually an important factor in those decisions. Where there is substantial doubt that a confession is truthful, especially if made by a vulnerable defendant, judges should not admit it into evidence.

Conclusion

The interrogation process is without question an important law enforcement tool. It can lead police to evidence that helps solve a crime and in some cases may prevent future crimes from happening. Moreover, when a suspect makes a reliable confession, the case is essentially closed, saving everyone involved the further expenditure of resources and providing comfort to victims and their families. As we noted throughout this chapter, however, the inherently coercive nature of the process means that the specter of false confessions always lurks in the background. While the exact number of people imprisoned because of a false confession will never be known with certainty, a civilized society should not tolerate any miscarriage of justice that could have been avoided.

One way to reduce the possibility of false confessions is to encourage police to use less coercive questioning strategies. The purpose of interrogation should be to obtain truthful information about a crime, which in many cases will include a confession; it should not be to bully suspects into incriminating themselves, sometimes falsely, through tactics such as indirect threats and promises. While the legal system is at least somewhat aware of the problems of physical and psychological coercion, it is time to acknowledge the linguistic devices that contribute to these practices.

Another safeguard is to ensure that suspects are provided with the assistance of an attorney if they request it. This, of course, is a constitutional right during interrogation. Yet the right to counsel loses much of its effectiveness if a suspect's request for a lawyer can be ignored when it is made indirectly. As we have sought to show, people in situations like interrogation do not normally make requests directly, because it is considered impolite. Chapter 3 illustrated that courts have no trouble recognizing that an indirect request to search an automobile is an actual request that can justify a consent search. Why are courts so reluctant to reach the same conclusion when it comes to a suspect's indirect request to have a lawyer present? Our view is that courts should take pragmatic information into account in both situations.

A final type of protection against the inherent pressures of interrogation is to advise suspects of their constitutional rights before questioning begins. While suspects have a right to counsel while being interrogated, many do not know it, or may forget about it under the stress of the situation. This, of course, brings us to the famous (or notorious) *Miranda* warnings, which is the subject of the next chapter.

Chapter 5

Understanding Miranda

```
You have the right to
remain silent...
```

Virtually anyone who has watched American television is familiar with the *Miranda* warnings. First articulated in the Supreme Court case of *Miranda v. Arizona* in 1966,[1] the rule has become one of the most familiar elements of American criminal law. Indeed, the opening words of the warning—"You have the right to remain silent"—have come to signal on television and in film that the crime has been solved and that the perpetrator is now under arrest. The credits roll on the screen and the show is over. In real life, the reading of *Miranda* rights to a suspect is in many ways just the critical first step in a long legal process that may involve interrogation, trial, sentencing, and prison.

The Rise of *Miranda*

Even with the vast array of crime-solving weapons available to the police these days, especially DNA evidence, the venerable process of interrogating suspects, confronting them with evidence, and encouraging them to confess remains an extremely important and common law enforcement technique.

At the same time, there have long been concerns about the coercion inherent in the process, particularly with vulnerable suspects who are minors, have low intelligence, are unfamiliar with American language and culture, or are mentally challenged. In the worst cases, this coercion can lead to false confessions.

We saw in chapter 4 that in the middle of the twentieth century, the U.S. Supreme Court began to address these issues. It applied the Sixth Amendment's right to counsel to the context of police interrogation, thus lessening the pressures of the process by affording suspects the assistance of a lawyer.[2] And it gave some teeth to the Fifth Amendment right against compelled self-incrimination by reversing convictions based on coerced confessions.[3] Taken together, these two fundamental constitutional rights went far in protecting the average citizen from the coercion that is inherent—and to some degree inevitable—in interrogation.

Yet practical problems continued. Not all suspects were aware of these rights or how they applied to their situation. It is not immediately obvious that the right to counsel extends to interrogation or that the right not to be a witness against yourself means you do not have to answer questions at the police station. Because the police had little incentive to inform the suspect of these rights, it was up to the suspect to invoke them on his own by requesting a lawyer or by expressly refusing to answer questions, something that might not have been easy to do under the circumstances. These considerations are important because, as we have seen, confessions were and are admissible only if they are voluntary. And it is virtually impossible to determine whether a confession was voluntary if the suspect did not realize that he could have ended questioning if he had invoked his right to counsel or to remain silent.

The Supreme Court therefore held, in *Miranda v. Arizona,* that suspects who were in custody should be advised of their rights before police begin interrogation. In particular, a suspect must be told that he has the right to remain silent, that anything he says can be used against him in a court of law, that he has the right to the presence of an attorney, and that if he cannot afford an attorney, one will be appointed for him prior to any questioning if he so desires.[4] Although the rule has been attacked over the years,[5] the Supreme Court recently reaffirmed its *Miranda* decision in *Dickerson v. United States.*[6]

Reading Rights

The *Miranda* warnings have never been standardized, but in virtually all cases, what police officers say or read to suspects closely tracks the language of the Supreme Court's opinion. Typically, officers read the warnings from a card:

1. You have the right to remain silent.
2. Anything you say can and will be used against you in a court of law.
3. You have the right to talk to a lawyer and have him present with you while you are being questioned.
4. If you cannot afford to hire a lawyer, one will be appointed to represent you before any questioning, if you wish one.[7]

The Supreme Court was obviously concerned that people be able to understand the warnings, and its proposed language in the *Miranda* opinion was relatively plain. The language on this card is even more straightforward, substituting "lawyer" for "attorney," for example, and using the more common "before" in place of the literary "prior to."

The average *Miranda* warning is written at about a sixth- to eighth-grade reading level, which means that most American adults should be able to understand it.[8] Studies confirm this general impression. Thomas Grisso tested 260 adults, including 203 parolees residing in half-way houses and 57 workers in custodial or maintenance crews at universities and hospitals. Using a variety of instruments, he tested both the subjects' understanding of the words and phrases in the warning, as well as their grasp of the function of the rights conveyed by it. Grisso found that when asked to paraphrase the four rights listed in the warning, around 69 percent of the participants received either seven or eight points out of a possible total of eight. A test of their knowledge of critical vocabulary items revealed that "entitled," "appoint," and "attorney" were comprehended by over 75 percent of the respondents. Fewer than half, however, properly understood "consult" and "right."[9]

A fair conclusion is that most English-speaking adults probably understand the warnings. But this is not good enough. The warnings must actually be understood by all interrogated suspects, including minors, people with mental problems, and those who do not speak English or do not speak it well. Actual understanding is critical because *Miranda* and related cases require not just a talismanic reading of a suspect's rights, but stipulate that a suspect may not be interrogated unless and until she has *waived* those rights. The Supreme Court summarized the waiver requirements in *Moran v. Burbine:*

> First, the relinquishment of the right must have been voluntary in the sense that it was the product of a free and deliberate choice rather than intimidation,

coercion, or deception. Second, the waiver must have been made with a full awareness of both the nature of the right being abandoned and the consequences of the decision to abandon it. Only if the "totality of the circumstances surrounding the interrogation" reveals both an uncoerced choice and the requisite level of comprehension may a court properly conclude that the *Miranda* rights have been waived.[10]

Thus, a waiver of a suspect's rights must not just be voluntary, but must be "knowing" and "intelligent," which requires a court to evaluate the suspect's "age, experience, education, background and intelligence and . . . whether he has the capacity to understand the warnings given to him, the nature of his Fifth Amendment rights, and the consequences of waiving those rights."[11]

To help ensure that a waiver will be upheld, police officers often follow the reading of the *Miranda* warnings with two questions:

1. Do you understand each of these rights I have explained to you?
2. Having these rights in mind, do you wish to talk to us now?[12]

Anyone who answers both of these questions affirmatively is usually deemed to have waived her right to silence, opening herself up to further interrogation and making her answers admissible at trial.

If someone listens to the *Miranda* warnings and then confirms that she has understood her rights and is willing to talk, can there be any doubt that she has made a knowing and intelligent waiver? Initially, it might seem highly implausible that a person would falsely claim to have understood something. There seems to be no logical reason for people to lie about something that is so significant.

Yet haven't most of us from time to time laughed at a joke without "getting" it? And haven't most of us, especially when speaking a foreign language, nodded or otherwise indicated we understood something when we did not, or did not understand it very well? Perhaps we exaggerate our understanding to avoid embarrassment, to save face, or simply to keep the conversation moving along. The fact is that people find silence awkward; most of us have a tendency to want to keep a discussion going.[13] That suspects might claim to understand something that, in reality, they do not comprehend very well is hence not all that surprising. What *is* surprising is how few courts are willing to dig a bit deeper to assure themselves that a suspect actually understood the warnings and that an apparent waiver was truly voluntary, knowing, and intelligent.

The question of comprehension is particularly relevant for some of the more vulnerable groups in our society: people with low levels of education or mental problems, recent immigrants, and children. In this context, we examine below evidence showing how poorly members of such groups understand their _Miranda_ rights, and the limited protection that the law affords them.

Suspects with Low Intelligence or Mental Problems

If an English-speaking person says that she understands her rights, or signs or initials a _Miranda_ card, courts tend to find that she has made a knowing and intelligent waiver of her rights even when the level of her knowledge and intelligence is quite low. Consider a case from Texas, where the defendant stated that he understood the rights that had been read to him from a card. The following interchange ensued:

> Officer: Ok, Mr. Faulkner, do you knowingly, intelligently and voluntarily waive these rights as I have read them out to you on this _Miranda_ warnings?
> Defendant: I don't understand that. Could you translate that down for me?
> Officer: Ok. Do you knowingly, intelligently and voluntarily, do you know what I read you? Do you understand it? Are you intelligent enough to understand what I've read you, and do you voluntarily waive these rights that I've read you? Are you willing to talk to me?
> Defendant: Yes, sir.[14]

Note that the defendant states that he does _not_ understand the request to waive his rights, and the officer never really explains what it means. Instead, the officer asks no less than five separate questions without waiting for an answer. It is impossible to determine which question or questions the "Yes, sir" refers to, and the officer makes no attempt to clarify it. Nonetheless, the court held the waiver valid.

Sometimes evidence of actual mental retardation leads to a finding that the person could not validly have waived her rights.[15] Yet too often courts find retarded people capable of doing so.[16] For example, _Taylor v. Rogers_ involved a confession made by a thirty-four-year-old man who was mildly to moderately retarded[17] and had a mental age of eight or nine. Based on testimony from the police officer who read Taylor his rights, and a government expert psychologist who testified that "there was no reason to suppose simply based on Taylor's intellectual level that Taylor could not understand his rights," the court held that this evidence was sufficient to uphold the man's waiver of his rights.[18]

A growing literature has made it clear that mentally retarded people are not likely to understand their rights.[19] Using Grisso's instruments to test the understanding of *Miranda* rights, Solomon Fulero and Catherine Everington compared the comprehension levels of two separate groups of mentally retarded individuals. The first group (MR1) had little contact with the criminal justice system, the second (MR2) had more. One of the tests required the subject to paraphrase each of the four *Miranda* warnings, for which the subject would receive a score of 2, 1, or 0. According to the researchers, a score of 2 was required to reach "adequate understanding." Table 5.1 shows the percentage of the two groups of retarded people that achieved this level of understanding, compared with Grisso's data from the general population of adults. In addition, the researchers compared the data on the different groups of subjects in terms of all four *Miranda* warnings taken together, with a total possible score of 8 (a maximum of 2 points on each of the four warnings). The two mentally retarded groups had average total scores of 2.24 and 4.60, respectively. In contrast, Grisso's earlier study found that 80.7 percent of his total adult sample scored 6 or higher.

It is clear that while experience in the criminal justice system improves comprehension, people with mental retardation do not typically understand their *Miranda* rights at anything approaching an acceptable level. In particular, people cannot understand the second or third parts of the warning without some knowledge of the workings of the criminal justice system.

Recent research by a team led by Morgan Cloud of Emory University confirms the conclusion that mentally retarded people simply do not understand their rights:

> [Our] empirical study . . . confirms what many have suspected: mental retardation makes some people incapable of understanding either the text of the *Miranda* rights or the consequences of forsaking them. For these people, the words of the warnings literally have no useful meaning. The harsh reality is that for mentally retarded suspects, the *Miranda* warnings cannot serve the instrumental functions for which they are intended—ensuring that confessions are the product of knowing, intelligent, and voluntary waivers of the right to remain silent, and not the result of the pressures inherent in custodial interrogation.[20]

Suspects who do not meet the threshold of mental retardation may also be sufficiently impaired that they have great difficulty understanding their rights. In one case, a defendant who claimed that he did not realize that he could stop the interrogation at any time was found to have validly waived his rights by initialing the warning form.[21] A murder defendant

Table 5.1. Percentages of Subjects Scoring 2 (adequate understanding) on *Miranda* Comprehension Test

Miranda Statement	General Population	MR Sample 1	MR Sample 2
1. Right to remain silent	88.5	17.2	56.0
2. Anything you say	68.1	3.4	28.0
3. Right to an attorney	66.5	24.1	32.0
4. Attorney provided	85.4	31.0	76.0

Source: Thomas Grisso, *Instruments for Assessing Understanding and Appreciation of Miranda Rights* 84 (1998); Solomon M. Fulero and Caroline Everington, *Assessing Competency to Waive Miranda Rights in Defendants with Mental Retardation*, 19 Law and Human Behavior 533, 538, table 1 (1995). Note that the two MR groups were not matched for IQ, so it is also possible that MR Sample 1 had a lower mean IQ, accounting in part for the disparity in results.

claimed at trial that he did not understand what the words "attorney," "appoint," "represent," or "right" meant within the context of the *Miranda* warnings. Psychological experts who tested him found his comprehension to be around the third or fifth grade level, with an IQ of 78. Nonetheless, the Illinois Supreme Court held that he knowingly and voluntarily waived his rights. The court noted that the warnings were repeated more than once, he signed a waiver form, and he never told questioning officers that he did not understand them.[22] Similarly, a functionally illiterate, borderline mentally retarded twenty-year-old defendant who suffered from organic brain damage was held to have validly waived his rights, despite testimony from two expert witnesses to the contrary.[23]

In summary, a person cannot intelligently waive rights that he does not understand, and people with diminished intellectual capacity do not seem to understand their rights very well. The consequence is a potentially serious one. As we noted in our discussion of the problem of false confessions in chapter 4, it is primarily the more vulnerable suspects who are likely to make false confessions. It is well established, for example, that the mentally retarded are especially likely to agree to suggestions by people in authority. In addition, research suggests they are particularly susceptible to the effects of coercive questions (e.g., leading questions) that contain false or misleading information,[24] an issue we raised in our discussion of interrogation techniques in chapter 4. It is unfortunate that the *Miranda* warnings seem to be least effective in protecting those who need them the most.

One solution is for interrogating officers to receive training in identifying and dealing with mentally vulnerable suspects and witnesses. No doubt this already occurs to some extent. Once officers identify someone with mental problems or particularly low intelligence, they should make careful

efforts to ensure that the person understands his rights and the consequences of waiving them. Perhaps a simple and reliable multiple-choice
test could help determine whether a suspect really understands these issues. Seeking the assistance of mental health professionals might also be
advisable in certain sorts of cases. And, of course, any reference by the
suspect to a lawyer should be dealt with in light of our discussion in the
previous chapter. Such steps will lead to more reliable evidence, which
ought to be the goal of everyone involved in the criminal justice system.

If a mentally vulnerable suspect has waived his rights and is prosecuted
for a crime, the court should consider appointing an expert to evaluate his
Miranda comprehension. Admittedly, appointing an expert in every case
of this type would involve certain costs. At the very least, when the defendant is prepared to offer an expert's testimony, it seems to us that the
offer should be accepted and the testimony taken seriously. And in those
cases in which the government presents expert evidence on this issue, the
defendant should be provided with funds to hire his own expert.

In any event, waivers of *Miranda* rights by people with diminished intellectual capacity, especially the mentally retarded, should be examined with
great care. The government has the burden to prove by a preponderance of
the evidence that a waiver was made voluntarily, intelligently, and knowingly.[25] When a defendant is found to be mentally retarded, that standard
should be taken very seriously. And the greater the degree of retardation,
the higher the burden ought to be.

Juveniles

Similar issues arise when the defendant is a juvenile. Even though children
might have difficulty understanding legal concepts, they are read their
rights just as adults are. They are then asked to waive those rights just like
adults. If they do so, they can be interrogated and pressed to confess in
much the same way that adults are. Often enough, courts find the waivers
of their rights to have been voluntary, knowing, and intelligent, and allow
the confessions into evidence.

These fact-specific determinations are difficult to make, and it is easy
to second-guess a court's decision. Still, to us it seems rather unlikely that
an illiterate thirteen-year-old defendant with an IQ around 47 and a mental age of six or seven could understand even a simplified version of the
Miranda warnings; nonetheless, an Illinois court decided that such a child
had validly waived his rights.[26] Or consider a fifteen-year-old murder suspect who had a mental age of just over six years and who suffered from

attention deficit disorder and a learning disability; he was held to have understood the warnings despite his youth and low level of mental ability.[27]

The cases just cited involved young defendants who also had mental
difficulties. Not surprisingly, studies show that IQ and age both contribute
in predicting ability to comprehend *Miranda* rights. In Grisso's study, mentally retarded sixteen-year-olds scored an average of 4.30 out of 8 on a paraphrase test, while children the same age with IQs of over 100 scored 7.45.[28]
At age thirteen, the respective mean scores were 3.40 and 6.15. Moreover,
Grisso found that only 30 percent of juveniles adequately understood the
right to counsel, and that 55 percent of them could not paraphrase that
part of the *Miranda* warnings.[29] Overall, Grisso's data show that even without intellectual deficits, children under fifteen years of age are relatively
unlikely to understand their legal rights adequately.

Young age appears to combine with poor comprehension of *Miranda*
rights to increase the risk of false confessions. In another study, Naomi
Goldstein and her co-authors asked juvenile offenders (ranging in age from
thirteen to eighteen) how likely they would be to confess falsely to a
crime under specified hypothetical circumstances. They found that the self-
reported probability of a juvenile's believing that he would make a false
confession increased as age decreased, and also depended on how well the
youth understood the *Miranda* warning concerning the right to counsel—
just the right that children least understand.[30]

The law is not entirely in tune with these findings. Shortly after deciding *Miranda,* the Supreme Court held that procedural safeguards to protect
Fifth Amendment rights were also necessary in juvenile proceedings.[31] However, twelve years later, in 1979, the Court decided in *Fare v. Michael C.* that
the same "totality of the circumstances" test used for adult suspects should
apply to evaluating waiver of Fifth Amendment rights by children. Among
the circumstances to be considered are "the juvenile's age, experience, education, background, and intelligence, and . . . whether he has the capacity
to understand the warnings given him, the nature of his Fifth Amendment
rights, and the consequences of waiving those rights."[32] The Court held
that the Fifth Amendment was not violated when police did not honor a
child's request to speak with his probation officer before questioning him.
The result has been a haphazard array of decisions of the sort illustrated at
the beginning of this section. Even retarded youths are sometimes deemed
to have intelligently waived rights that they cannot conceivably have comprehended.

The law refuses to let children of these ages get married, make wills,
or engage in most other legally significant acts. No matter how mature

they are, minors must obtain the approval of a parent or a guardian precisely because society considers them too young to make certain important
decisions for themselves. Why not apply the same rule to interrogation?
Given their linguistic limitations and suggestibility, children should at a
minimum be advised that they have a right to have a parent or other "interested adult" present during questioning. Some jurisdictions now require
that children be offered the assistance of an adult before they can waive
their rights.[33] For example, in a case where the accused was a ten-year-old
boy, a Kansas court held that no waiver by a juvenile under age fourteen
could be valid unless he had been given an opportunity to consult with a
parent, guardian, or attorney.[34] Another possibility is to require the participation of a state-appointed attorney.[35] Because the Supreme Court has in
recent years tended to limit procedural rights, advances in this area of the
law will probably have to be undertaken by state legislatures and courts,
and by law enforcement agencies.

Suspects Whose Native Language Is Not English

Courts have been somewhat more sympathetic toward people who do not
speak English very well but who received a *Miranda* warning only in that
language. For instance, a Spanish-speaking defendant who was read his
rights in English and was not shown a Spanish version of the *Miranda* card
was held not to have made a valid waiver.[36] Nor did a Kickapoo Indian, who
was read the warnings in Spanish in the absence of a Kickapoo interpreter,
knowingly waive his rights.[37] The same result obtained for a German defendant who spoke English poorly and could not understand court proceedings
without an interpreter.[38]

   On the other hand, when a non-native speaker of English claims to understand the language and answers questions in it, courts tend to have little
sympathy if he later claims he did not understand his rights.[39] Thus, one
court noted that a Hispanic defendant testified in English at trial and used
an interpreter only on a "standby" basis; it upheld his waiver, which was
made in English.[40] Likewise, an Apache in the eleventh grade, accused of
killing his father, was held to have understood his rights, based on evidence
that he read them back to investigators and was able to converse coherently
in English with an FBI agent.[41] A speaker of Black English was found to have
understood and validly waived rights that were read to him in standard
English, particularly since he was able to answer questions posed in standard English.[42] Many other cases have concluded that suspects must have
understood English-language warnings on the basis of similar evidence.[43]

Results are more mixed when a suspect's rights are read to him in one dialect of a language and he speaks another, although cases of this sort are rare. According to press reports in Los Angeles, a confession by a speaker of the Cantonese dialect of Chinese was ruled inadmissible after it appeared that he had been advised of his rights in another dialect.[44] On the other hand, a suspect advised of his rights in an Italian dialect different from his own was held to have made a valid waiver. One reason is that he told investigators at the time that he understood the warning read to him.[45] Perhaps more important is that dialect differences in Chinese are far greater than those in most European languages.

When the *Miranda* rights are translated or interpreted, the accuracy of the translation may be an issue. Many police officers carry with them cards that contain the warnings in other languages. Merely handing the card to a defendant and having her read it may be inadequate, as in the case of a Chinese woman suspected of credit card fraud.[46] Yet if the detained person responds affirmatively or nods when asked if he understands the rights as printed on a card, courts view it as very strong evidence that he must have actually understood.[47] Often enough this may be true, but it is also the case that suspects generally try to be cooperative. Nodding or saying "Yes" may simply be part of that strategy.

Courts also seem willing to tolerate some fairly loose interpretation practices. In one case, the police asked a passenger in a car, who had been drinking, to convey the warnings in Spanish to the driver; a court held later that the translation need not be perfect, as long as the defendant generally understands his rights.[48] Having a co-defendant, who had been in police custody before, administer rights to a suspected drug trafficker has also been held valid.[49] Another defendant complained that the Spanish version did not advise him of his right to stop the interrogation at any time. In rejecting this objection, the court noted that *Miranda* never required a "ritualistic recital of words" but merely "an intelligent conveyance of the rights to remain silent and of the general right of counsel."[50]

More serious translation errors, however, can invalidate a waiver. In *United States v. Higareda-Santa Cruz*, the court commented on the language of a Spanish *Miranda* card, which was translated back into English as follows: "In case that you do not have money, you have the right to petition an attorney from the court." The first part of the statement incorrectly suggested that a person must be completely indigent to have a state-provided attorney, and the second clause stated that the defendant must "petition" the court in order to obtain a lawyer.[51] In reality, a suspect need not be completely penniless and is entitled to have a lawyer present during interrogation simply by requesting one, without going through the formality of petitioning a court. More accurate is the following warning (as translated into English): "If you don't have the money to employ a lawyer one will be appointed to you before you answer any questions."[52]

An important limitation on *Miranda* rights is that suspects normally do not have to understand the broader implications of a warning, but merely—as one court put it—the "plain language." In particular, suspects do not have to appreciate the tactical advantage of remaining silent in the American legal system.[53] This right to silence might be far from obvious to people coming from countries where confessions are highly valued and lead to lighter punishment, but where refusing to cooperate with authorities may have dire consequences.

American courts historically have shown scant sympathy for arguments resting on such cultural differences. Thus, a Vietnamese suspect who stated that he understood the language of the warnings but because of his background believed that officers would "turn him upside down and put fish salt in his nose if he did not talk to them" was held to have adequately understood his rights.[54] The same result has obtained for people from China, Cuba, and Mexico who claimed to have waived their rights only because in their original cultures it was unthinkable to refuse to cooperate with police.[55]

While there is no single "officially approved" text of the *Miranda* warnings, variations throughout the country track the Supreme Court's language fairly closely. When the Court's words are translated into other languages, however, such variation becomes more of a concern, especially because legal terminology depends a great deal on background knowledge about the justice system. A relatively literal translation would not work well in most languages. Telling people in another language that they have the right to remain silent could well come across as suggesting that they do not need to volunteer information, for instance, but it might not advise them that they can refuse to answer questions, a practice that is regarded as rude in ordinary life.

What is essential is to convey the content in a way that is understandable to speakers of the language in question. This might require a bit more than the terse warnings dictated by *Miranda*. We believe it would be helpful if certified court interpreters, who now exist for most major languages, would work together to formulate a version of the warnings that will sensibly convey the meaning to speakers of their respective languages, and that could then be distributed as a public service to police departments around the country. When there are remaining questions about whether the suspect understood the warnings, a police officer who speaks the language should be called, or officers should request the assistance of a qualified interpreter.

Deaf Defendants

People with serious hearing impairments encounter problems similar to those who do not speak English. Indeed, for deaf people English is as much a foreign language as it is for someone from Guatemala or Thailand. English may, in fact, be more difficult for deaf Americans to learn than it is for foreigners. Speakers of other languages will at least be familiar with many of the sounds of English, most of which will be similar to those in their own language. Those who are prelingually deaf,[56] on the other hand, are expected to learn to read—and sometimes to speak—a language that they have never heard and without ever having learned the structure of another spoken language.

Perhaps the least effective way of communicating with deaf people is by expecting them to lip-read. This requires, first of all, that the lip-reader have an excellent command of English, which many deaf people lack. A further difficulty is that different sounds (or phonemes) may be articulated with the same lip position. As noted in chapter 2, the sounds *p* and *b* are both *bilabial,* which means they are created by putting the lips together and then opening them. They are distinguished by what phoneticians call *voicing:* the *b* is voiced and the *p* is not. Voicing is created by the vibration of the vocal cords, which are invisible to a lip-reader. As a consequence, a lip-reader would normally not be able to distinguish between these sounds, along with many other pairs of consonants that differ only in voicing. Not surprisingly, average lip-readers are estimated to understand around 5 percent of what is said, and the best ones decipher approximately 25 percent of spoken language.[57]

Finger-spelling is another means of communication employed by those who have hearing problems. Fingers are used to represent the letters of the alphabet. Because this process also relies on knowledge of English (or some other spoken language), it is once again not an ideal way to communicate with people who are deaf from birth. Of course, for deaf people with a good command of written language, finger-spelling may work well enough.

Another method of communicating with the deaf, Signed English, involves using signs that represent English words and morphemes. It requires people to first formulate their message in English, and then to convert the English words into gestures that represent those words. For those who learned English as children and later became hearing-impaired, Signed English may also work well, but like all English-based systems it is bound to be less successful for people who never acquired English naturally.

Most deaf Americans communicate using American Sign Language (ASL).[58] ASL derives from French sign language, although at present only about 60 percent of its vocabulary is still of French origin. The signs of ASL can be described along three parameters: hand configuration, motion of the hand(s) toward or from the body, and the locus of the sign's movement. Thus, the sign for "arm" involves a flat hand that moves to touch the upper arm. It is important not to confuse ASL with what are sometimes informally referred to as "sign languages," but which are really limited gestural systems. ASL is a full-blown language capable of expressing anything that hearing people can say.[59]

Despite the fact that deaf suspects are more likely to understand their rights when communicated in ASL, some courts have held that deaf suspects do not need an interpreter and allow the *Miranda* warnings to be administered in writing.[60] One court, however, concluded that a deaf defendant with limited ability to write English had not waived his rights; efforts to give the *Miranda* warnings to him using finger-spelling and ASL were not effective.[61] Similarly, courts in California and Wisconsin have recognized the inadequacy of using Signed English to explain rights to defendants who use ASL and have a low English reading level.[62]

As usual, these cases depend very much on the facts. Linguistic abilities differ among the various suspects depending on their educational level and whether they learned English as children or were deaf from birth or early childhood. Some deaf individuals are highly educated and can communicate using written English quite well. This may explain why a federal court was unsympathetic with a deaf drunk driving suspect who tried to avoid the consequences of a consent form that he signed, based on his having been denied an ASL interpreter. It turns out that the man was a lawyer, and thus could be presumed to know the consequences of signing such a form.[63] The average deaf defendant, however, is said to read at a fourth-grade level, and it has been estimated that 60 percent of deaf defendants do not read well enough to understand the *Miranda* warnings in written form.[64]

The normal procedure, therefore, should be to employ the services of an ASL interpreter. Several states have recognized this point, requiring police to obtain a certified or otherwise qualified interpreter before interrogating a deaf person, with any statements made before that time deemed inadmissible.[65] We believe that this should be the rule in all jurisdictions, unless perhaps it can be shown that the deaf suspect is adept at writing or is a native English speaker who lost the ability to hear later in life. Because an interpreter will be needed in any event to conduct the interrogation properly, the burden on law enforcement will be minimal.

Even when there is an interpreter, translating legal concepts into ASL is not always easy. Just as spoken language can be expanded by coining new words, ASL can develop signs for any concept. But that does not guarantee that the average deaf person will recognize the sign, just as a hearing person may not recognize a neologism or technical legal term. Moreover, what does it mean to tell a deaf person that he has the right to remain silent?[66] Police and judges should keep in mind that a relatively literal translation of the Miranda warnings into ASL may not suffice. Interpreters should be encouraged to explain what the rights mean in practical terms that deaf suspects will comprehend.

Interpreters play a critical role here, not only translating the warnings but also helping establish that a defendant understood them. This requires that before actually giving the warnings, the interpreter interact with the suspect to determine his preferred method of communication and his ability to use it. After giving the warnings, the interpreter might briefly question the suspect to determine how well he understands his rights. These steps are especially important with deaf defendants because of their proclivity to sign documents without fully understanding them and to say "Yes" when asked if they comprehend something.[67] Without taking such additional steps, having a deaf defendant sign the standard waiver form is relatively meaningless.

How Can Comprehension Be Improved?

One way to make the Miranda warning better accomplish its objectives would be to have it more explicitly address issues that many suspects seem not to grasp. Recall that Grisso found that people have the most trouble understanding the notion that everything they say can be used against them, as well as understanding the right to counsel. Other research supports these findings. For example, some people who receive the warnings do not realize that oral statements can be used against them just as well as written confessions; one survey of suspects in the Denver County Jail found that 45 percent thought that oral statements were not evidence.[68] People tend to believe that for a statement to have legal effect, you must "get it in writing," and often enough this is true. Wills and contracts relating to land are not valid unless they are written. The same does not apply, however, in the context of interrogation.

Moreover, suspects may not know that they have the right to an attorney at the interrogation, not just at trial, or that the police cannot question them further until a lawyer arrives.[69] The language of the *Miranda* opinion—that a suspect has the right to the "presence" of an attorney—does not make explicit when during the process the suspect has that right. Additionally, suspects may not be aware that the lawyer will be provided at no charge if they cannot afford to pay. The *Miranda* opinion simply states that if a suspect cannot afford a lawyer, one will be appointed to represent him, if he wishes. Thus, though elegant in its simplicity, the language of *Miranda* is incomplete and should not, without more, constitute the entirety of the actual warning read by law enforcement agents.[70]

We realize that the Supreme Court has not been very sympathetic to arguments of this kind. In *Duckworth v. Eagan,* for instance, the defendant pointed out that he was informed by a police waiver form that a lawyer would be provided "if and when you go to court." This formulation suggests that he could not have the assistance of an appointed lawyer during interrogation. The Supreme Court upheld his conviction, stating that "talismanic" adherence to the exact text of the *Miranda* decision was not required. The warnings should not be examined "as if construing a will or defining the terms of an easement."[71]

Much of the difficulty of improving the *Miranda* warnings is that courts can do little more than hold that the language read to a suspect in a particular case was incomplete or misleading, which will usually lead to invalidating his confession and overturning his conviction. Furthermore, it will open the door to many other prisoners claiming that the *Miranda* warnings they received were similarly flawed, potentially resulting in large numbers of convictions being overturned. Most judges would be extremely reluctant to open such a Pandora's box. Change is not impossible, however. Courts can recommend improvements to the language of the warnings without necessarily reversing a slew of cases. For example, the Supreme Court of New Jersey has required trial courts to begin using more comprehensible "reasonable doubt" jury instructions without holding that the old instructions violated the Constitution.[72] Others involved in the criminal justice system might also be able to encourage such changes.

Based on these observations, we recommend a warning along the following lines:

1. You have the right to remain silent. You do not have to answer any questions or make any statements.
2. If you decide to speak with us, anything you say—whether or not it is

recorded—can be used against you in a court of law. [We will videotape our session so that we have an exact record of what was said. The tape can be used against you in court.]

3. You have the right to have a lawyer here during questioning. All you have to do is say, "I want a lawyer." If you do not know where to find a lawyer, we will get a lawyer for you. If you cannot afford to pay, the lawyer will be provided free of charge.

4. As soon as you tell us that you want a lawyer, we will not ask you any more questions until you have talked with the lawyer.[73]

While no warning can be perfect, we believe that one along these lines is a substantial improvement over current practices.

With suspects who do not speak English well, including those who are hearing impaired, providing a qualified interpreter is obviously of paramount importance. Not only does this help ensure that any waiver of rights is done knowingly, but the interpreter can help prevent the subsequent interrogation from being overly coercive. Being questioned and forced to defend oneself in one's native language can be intimidating enough. Doing so in a foreign language is even more so, and the potential for misunderstanding is great.

In addition, as we stated several times in earlier chapters, we believe that police should routinely videotape the administration of the warnings and any subsequent interrogation. Videotape can pick up nonverbal cues, like nodding the head, which may be critical to understanding an oral statement. If a judge or perhaps an expert witness must later decide whether a waiver was knowing and voluntary, a videotape will greatly help in the analysis. We also believe that suspects should be made aware that they are being videotaped. This will help drive home the point that what they say during interrogation will have important consequences. As the costs of the necessary equipment drop, videotaping is becoming more common.[74] We believe that it should be made mandatory.

Finally, people may claim at trial not to have understood their rights, perhaps because they did not receive an interpreter or because the translation was inadequate. In some cases, of course, it may be obvious that the defendant speaks adequate English and that the claim is bogus. In others, the claim may be more legitimate. To decide which is which, judges should have qualified assistance at their disposal. There are various ways in which comprehension can be measured. Asking people whether they understand what they heard, which is routinely done after reading the *Miranda* warnings, is probably the most relied upon but least effective method. Most people are reluctant to admit that they do not understand something, especially when their pride is at stake. On the other hand, defendants may learn that it might benefit them legally if they did not comprehend their rights, and suddenly many may claim ignorance. Self-assessments are notoriously unreliable. We do not assign grades in school based on how well students believe they learned a lesson; instead, we test students to see how well they really understood. Courts should do the same.

Consequently, where comprehension of the *Miranda* warnings is questionable, judges should call on experts to help them determine the validity of a waiver. Methodologies are being developed to assist experts in making these assessments. For instance, Thomas Grisso has developed testing instruments to determine whether juveniles and people with low intelligence or mental problems understand their rights.[75] Similar tests should be developed for use with defendants who are hearing impaired or do not speak English well.

There are doubtless those who would object to the time and cost involved in some of these measures. We hope to have shown, however, that a suspect's own assessment that he understands his rights, perhaps combined with a judge's casual observations of the defendant's linguistic performance, is a poor substitute for a more professional examination. Of course, a full-blown examination of a defendant by a psychologist or professor of Spanish will usually not be necessary. Interpreters might be trained to ask a few follow-up questions to gauge whether their explanation of *Miranda* rights was effective. That should probably suffice for routine cases.

Taken together, these measures would do much to fulfill the original promise of the *Miranda* decision by helping guarantee that when suspects speak to interrogators, they do so voluntarily. Yet as we saw in chapter 4, the reliability and truthfulness of admissions and confessions made during interrogations are separate issues that do not entirely disappear after *Miranda*. Linguistic and psychological coercion during interrogation is problematic not just because it offends human dignity and constitutional principles, but also because it can lead to injustice if it causes someone to confess to a crime that he did not commit, even if that confession is fully voluntary. We therefore conclude this part of the book by considering the impact of *Miranda* on interrogation and confessions.

Conclusion

Although we have focused here on the *Miranda* warnings, our ultimate concern in both this and the previous chapter has been the nature of interrogations and the confessions that they produce. As every criminal lawyer knows from practical experience, and as has been well documented in the psychological literature, confessions have a disproportionately powerful impact on jurors, who have been known to convict even if the defendant has repudiated the confession and physical evidence contradicts it.[76]

Despite the controversy surrounding the *Miranda* decision, suspects still confess. In fact, research indicates that they confess in roughly the same numbers that they did before.[77] At the same time, the *Miranda* warnings have become so familiar to the public, mainly through television, that it is fair to conclude that the vast majority of the adult population in the United States is aware that an arrested person has the right to remain silent and request an attorney.[78] No doubt the warning is at least partially responsible for the fact that the worst abuses during interrogation have disappeared.[79] In that sense the *Miranda* decision has been a success.

On the other hand, there is a shadow side to *Miranda*. Relatively few judicial decisions currently take the time to analyze whether interrogation methods that produced a confession were proper or whether a confession is indeed reliable and true. Instead, the focus has shifted to technicalities regarding the administration of the *Miranda* warnings and the subsequent waiver. Many courts seem to have adopted the attitude that if the warning was properly administered and the defendant signed a piece of paper waiving his rights without overt compulsion, any subsequent confession should be automatically admitted into evidence. The truthfulness or reliability of a confession has moved to the background.[80]

Moreover, the nature of the voluntariness requirement itself has also subtly shifted. Recall that the legal standard used to judge confessions is whether they are voluntary and knowing, rather than whether they are reliable and true.[81] Under *Miranda,* however, the primary focus has become whether the defendant's *waiver* was voluntary. Thus, not only do courts now seem to pay relatively little attention to whether a confession is reliable and true, but they also seem to focus relatively little on whether it was voluntary.

Many judges seem to assume that if a defendant made a voluntary, knowing, and intelligent waiver of his rights, and then confessed to a crime, the confession must necessarily have been voluntary. And it must presumably be reliable and truthful as well because no reasonable person, acting of his own free will, falsely admits to committing crimes that could lead to severe penalties. For the most part, these presumptions seem logical enough, and as a result our criminal justice system appears to work relatively well when dealing with the average adult.

But the fact of the matter is that not everyone in our society is average, nor does everyone think and function in ways that a judge or juror might consider reasonable. It is especially people with mental handicaps or very low intelligence, or those unfamiliar with the English language or American legal culture, or juveniles, who are likely to act in ways that may not appear to be entirely rational to observers. And because of their relative powerlessness, these individuals are more vulnerable than others to various forms of linguistic coercion. They are also more likely to speak deferentially, and thus indirectly, to people in positions of authority, such as police officers.

Therefore, the more vulnerable members of our society are more likely to consent to searches because they are unaware of their right to refuse and thus interpret an officer's "request" as a command. When arrested, they tend not to understand the *Miranda* warnings all that well. If they understand their right to counsel and try politely to invoke that right, interrogating officers may ignore them because they did not make the request directly enough. And as the interrogation continues, they are more likely to give in to indirect threats and linguistically coercive styles of questioning. In some cases—no one knows for sure how many—this process can lead to false confessions.

For most people, therefore, *Miranda* should accomplish what it was intended to accomplish: advise detainees of their rights and thereby reduce the inherent coerciveness of the interrogation process. Yet the warning appears to be less effective when directed at more vulnerable suspects. We therefore believe that in such cases judges should not just ask whether the defendant signed a waiver form and then admit the confession into evidence. Rather, they should look beyond the waiver to the confession itself. The judge need not necessarily convince herself that the confession is reliable and true—this has always been the function of the jury in the American system. But she should look for at least some minimal corroboration or other evidence that supports its truthfulness before allowing it to go to the jury. This requires nothing more than evidence that the suspect knew something about the crime that was not known to the general public, or that the interrogation led police to physical evidence associating the defendant with the crime. A mentally retarded person or a juvenile of low intelligence should not be convicted of a crime when the only evidence that he committed it is a confession that he made during interrogation.

We recognize that in the current legal climate, our recommendation that confessions by vulnerable suspects be corroborated is unlikely to be adopted any time soon as a matter of federal constitutional law. But states may find that such a procedure is required by their state constitution, or judges may impose it on themselves under general principles relating to the law of evidence. More likely, prosecutors may use their discretion to assure themselves that a confession is reliable before pursuing a case. No doubt this happens in many prosecutorial offices now as a matter of good practice.

In fact, there is already a legal principle that requires limited corroboration of confessions. The *corpus delicti* rule, developed many years ago because of concerns over the possibility of false confessions,[82] states that a criminal defendant cannot be convicted merely on the basis of his own confession. There must be corroboration, or independent evidence, that the crime for which the defendant is being prosecuted actually occurred. The *corpus delicti* rule's effectiveness is limited by the fact that it usually requires only evidence that a crime was committed, not that the defendant was involved in it. Nonetheless, it could easily be extended to require some minimal evidence that associates the defendant with the crime. Regardless of the exact mechanism chosen to address this issue, we believe that some degree of heightened judicial scrutiny of confessions made by vulnerable defendants is greatly desirable.

The corroboration approach has an additional advantage. Suppose that a crime has clearly been committed and a juvenile of low intelligence or a mentally retarded adult has confessed after ostensibly waiving his rights. Judges might be reluctant to exclude the confession entirely, which is what happens if they decide that the waiver was not knowing and intelligent. On the other hand, with vulnerable defendants like these, they might have some reservations about whether the defendants fully understood the implications of waiving their rights or whether the confessions are reliable. Our approach allows the judge to admit the confession in such a situation, but only if there is corroborating evidence that it is true.

By now it should be evident that language—often the exact words that someone said—can matter a great deal in the criminal justice system. Only when judges and the legal profession become more sensitive to the nuances of language can we say that justice is more equally available to us all—rich or poor, young or old, hearing or deaf, English-speaking or foreign-born, Nobel prize winner or mentally retarded teenager.

Part 3

Linguistic Evidence in Court

It is no wonder that people love television programs that feature lawyers in the courtroom. Whether it is Perry Mason's precise cross-examination, the shouting matches that occur in *The Practice,* or Rumpole of the Bailey's recitation of Shakespeare to a judge who hates both Rumpole and his client, language games played for such high stakes make gripping entertainment. It is all the more so when the case is a real one, as we all learned from the trials of O.J. Simpson and Louise Woodward, the English nanny convicted of killing the young child of two physicians in suburban Boston, only to be released by a judge who thought the jury had it all wrong.

It is hard to watch these cases—real or fictional—and not conclude that the way language was used has something to do with the outcome. Indeed, many people have written about this phenomenon. We touched on some of this literature in chapter 4 when describing how suspects often use indirect or "powerless" forms of speech when talking with law enforcement officers. The same studies also show that people who hedge, equivocate, and otherwise speak less forcefully tend to be less impressive to a jury, and therefore weaker trial witnesses. Among the leading authors in this area are Robin Lakoff[1] and the team of John Conley and William O'Barr.[2]

Most likely because of their political ramifications and the intense interest they hold for feminist scholars, rape trials have been a frequent subject
of studies of language and power in the courtroom. For example, a recent
book by Gregory Matoesian describes in great detail the ways in which defense counsel used language to evoke cultural biases in the 1991 rape trial
of William Kennedy Smith, the nephew of Senator Edward Kennedy.[3]

To take just one instance, the alleged victim had testified that after
offering Smith a ride home, she accepted his invitation to go inside with
him because she wanted to see the house. The Kennedy estate in Palm
Beach, Florida is a landmark, and obviously a matter of curiosity for those
who might have a chance to see it. Defense lawyer, Roy Black, asked the
following questions:

> So even though it was early in the morning you wanted to see the house?
> All right, even though you were concerned, for example, about your child you
>   still wanted to see the house?[4]

It would hardly matter how the woman answered these questions. The
use of "even though" suggests an incongruity between what one would
ordinarily expect from a person and what this woman did. In fact, her young
child was staying overnight with her mother, making the second question
barely relevant. Andrew Taslitz has written about how lawyers attempt to
evoke cultural stereotypes in cross-examining the alleged victims of rape
by relying on a few classic narratives, such as the woman who is afraid
of sex and then guilt-ridden for having consented to it.[5] Other research
has shown more generally that many legal battles are often fights over
competing narratives, with the use of language by both sides playing a role
in determining which story the jury will accept.[6]

Such studies demonstrate how nuances in the use of language can have
a profound effect on the message conveyed, and perhaps on the outcomes
of trials. It is obviously consistent with the points that we made in part 2
of this book concerning the way police officers and suspects interact, and
the ways in which courts react to their interactions. In the following three
chapters, however, we turn our attention elsewhere. Rather than adding to
a body of literature that is already well established, we introduce readers to
several areas of linguistic evidence that have received little or no attention
in the scholarly legal literature.

Chapter 6, "Exact Words," examines more closely a question raised in
chapters 3 and 4, but rarely asked by the legal system. When the law must
consider spoken language—whether between a police officer and suspect,

a person accused of threatening the life of another, a defendant said to have confessed to a crime, or any of a host of other examples—how can we possibly know what that person said exactly? In chapters 7 and 8 we discuss issues of linguistic identification: speaker identification and identification of authors by the style of their writing, respectively. The impact of linguistic evidence on the legal system will probably never rival that of DNA, and there are some serious problems with its use under the current state of the art. Nonetheless, it has the potential to make a substantial contribution to solving crimes and absolving the innocent.

Chapter 6

Exact Words

I don't know exactly what
he said, but I know he
said he did it.

In chapters 3 and 4 we saw how close examination of language used in legal settings can uncover some of the legal system's hidden assumptions and biases. The law is systematically more concerned with how a suspect asks to see a lawyer than it is with how a police officer asks for permission to conduct a search. In both cases, however, the words of the suspect or police officer matter. For example, such subtleties as using "maybe" in invoking the right to counsel may lead a court to hold that the suspect was merely thinking aloud and not actually asserting his constitutional rights. Legal analysis relies heavily on close inspection of the words that were actually used. Often, however, witnesses can't remember the exact words that were spoken. The inevitable result is that important evidence will sometimes be unavailable and other times will be degraded. How does the legal system respond to this cognitive gap? This chapter will explore how good we are at remembering what was said, and how the legal system deals with the shortcomings we have.

Our recall of the actual words that we read or hear is very poor. Just try to quote verbatim any sentence that you just read on the preceding page. You can't do it, even though you understood it, and even though you read the sentence just a few seconds ago. This means that when the legal system allows a witness to testify to the *substance* of what was said, it is making a compromise: while the testimony may indeed be probative to some extent, it is not an inherently reliable report of what was actually said. Even when a witness tries to testify fully and accurately, all kinds of nuances will have disappeared as the judge or jury hears what was said only as filtered through the testifying witness's memory and worldview.

This issue concerning human memory is not limited to contexts we have already discussed, such as encounters between a suspect and the police. It surfaces any time a witness testifies about what someone has said (including what that witness herself may have said at an earlier time). Because of our inability to recall exactly what was said, the accuracy of testimony is always a legitimate question when it involves reported speech. In criminal cases, the problem may occur when jailhouse informers report that a defendant confessed. It also arises when someone is accused of committing a language crime, such as making threats or false statements of various kinds. We discuss some of these crimes in part 4.

Typically, courts yield to the frailty of human memory and accept testimony about the substance of what was said. Occasionally, however, only exact words will do. For example, a federal statute, the Jencks Act, requires that prosecutors provide defense attorneys with any verbatim statements made by prosecution witnesses concerning the subject matter of the witness's testimony.[1] Prosecutors usually avoid the issue by not having verbatim transcriptions in their files. And in some states, exact words are required in defamation cases.[2]

Just as we saw in the previous chapters, the system vacillates between exhibiting concern for fair play and evenhandedness, and exhibiting concern for seeing to it that police and prosecutors maintain certain strategic advantages in order to avoid acquitting the guilty. Before we get to the law, though, let us see how good we really are at remembering what people said.

Forget about It: Human Memory for Verbatim Speech[3]

We are much better at remembering the gist of what was said than we are at remembering what was actually said. Jacqueline Sachs demonstrated this point in 1967 in an important early study.[4] Sachs read various passages to subjects. One of the sentences in each passage was the target sentence.

After the passage was completed, the experimenter presented subjects with another sentence—the test sentence. The test sentences were either the same as the target sentence, different from the target sentence only in form but not in substance, different in substance, or different in whether the sentence was in the active or passive voice. For example, for the target sentence, "He sent a letter about it to Galileo, the great Italian scientist," the test sentences were:

1. "He sent a letter about it to Galileo, the great Italian scientist" [same substance, same form].
2. "He sent Galileo, the great Italian scientist, a letter about it" [same substance, different form].
3. "Galileo, the great Italian scientist, sent him a letter about it" [different substance].
4. "A letter about it was sent to Galileo, the great Italian scientist" [same substance, passive form].

Subjects were asked to say whether the test sentence was one that they had read in the passage, and how certain they were about it.

When asked to answer immediately after hearing the target sentence (that is, when the target sentence was the last one in the passage), subjects were correct between 85 and 95 percent of the time. But when asked after hearing an additional sixty syllables of the passage, they continued to perform well (about 80 percent correct) only on the test sentence whose meaning had changed (sentence 3 in the examples given above). When 180 syllables of passage intervened between the target sentence and the test sentence, subjects still were correct more than 70 percent of the time in recognizing that the semantically altered test sentence was one that they had *not* heard, but performed only slightly better than chance on the others. This shows that we recall the gist of what we heard pretty well, but cannot reliably recognize the exact words even a few moments later.

A great deal of work on verbatim memory has been conducted by the British psychologist Alan Baddeley, who refers to short-term verbatim storage as a "phonological loop." Baddeley has estimated that verbatim speech remains in memory for two seconds. In one of his books on human memory, Baddeley reports on some very interesting studies that involve the effects of this phonological loop on the scores in IQ tests. One of the subtests in the Wechsler Intelligence Scale is the ability to repeat digits. The more digits the person taking the test can repeat, the higher the score. It had been observed that Welsh-speaking children performed worse on this subtest than their English counterparts. This led to all kinds of speculation about intelligence.[5]

N. C. Ellis and R. A. Hennelly, however, explored a different hypothesis. Welsh vowels are longer than English vowels. Therefore, one can repeat fewer Welsh numbers in the same time it takes to repeat numbers in English. Because of the phonological loop, this could prejudice the test against speakers of languages like Welsh. Sure enough, when children bilingual in English and Welsh were tested in English, the differences disappeared.[6]

Subsequent work by Moshe Naveh-Benjamin and Thomas J. Ayres has shown that the ability to repeat digits corresponds to the mean syllables per digit in the language in which the test is administered.[7] Chinese is the friendliest language in this regard, with English not far behind. "Seven" is our only bisyllabic word for a digit. Spanish and Hebrew have longer words for numbers on the average, with Arabic averaging more than two syllables per word. Not surprisingly, Arabic speakers can retain fewer numbers in short-term memory than can speakers of Chinese.

Of course, we do sometimes remember the precise words that we have heard. If someone says, "Give me your money, or I'll shoot," we are likely to recall those words. But ordinarily, what we remember are snippets of speech that grabbed our attention. Baddeley explains this by noting that we can keep verbatim language in storage by rehearsing it immediately after we hear it, usually by subvocalizing.[8] Moreover, various syntactic phenomena affect recall. For example, Robert Jarvella found that people do much better recalling exact words when asked to do so at the end of a clause within the sentence they are still processing.[9] Baddeley's phonological loop must be revised, in turn, to take such factors into account.

What happens to the words we hear once they "disappear" from short-term memory? Some of what we hear is forgotten altogether. As to the rest, we store in long-term memory only the "gist" of what we heard. Surprisingly, we still know relatively little about how good we are at recalling the gist of what was said after the passage of time. While there has been substantial research on how well people recall events, memory for speech has not received the same attention in the psychological literature. The research that exists, moreover, is not very encouraging. For example, Amina Memon and Daniel Yarmey examined how different interview techniques affect recall.[10] Subjects listened to seven minutes of a monologue recorded on tape. Two days later, they returned to answer questions about what was said, and to try to identify the voice they had heard. As for recollection of what was said, subjects remembered an average number of details ranging from about thirteen to sixteen, depending on the interview technique that solicited their responses. They also erroneously recalled an average of about 1.25 details that were never said. Although the researchers didn't report the total number of details on the entire recording, seven minutes of speech no doubt contains a high number. Thus, although the retention interval was only two days, the authors concluded that witnesses had a difficult time recalling details about a short (seven-minute) monologue.

The research mirrors everyday experience. Recall the last time you had a leisurely dinner with a friend. Now try to recall the conversation. Even if you remember what you talked about, your recollection will be a far cry from complete. In fact, you are very likely not to remember most of the topics you discussed, except for those that remain important to you.

As for the accuracy of recall, we've all had the experience of thinking— or, less happily, of being told,—"You're reacting to what you wanted to hear, not to what I said." Studies confirm this popular perception: people have a hard time distinguishing between what they actually hear and the inferences that they draw from it. In an important early study, Marcia Johnson, John Bransford, and Susan Solomon read subjects a set of short stories. One of the stories went as follows:

> When the man entered the kitchen he slipped on a wet spot and dropped the delicate glass pitcher on the floor. The pitcher was very expensive, and everyone watched the event with horror.

After a brief interval, the subjects were presented with various test sentences and asked whether they had heard each sentence in any of the stories. Some of the test sentences were actual sentences from the stories. Others were not in the story, but contained inferences that one would naturally draw from the actual sentences. For example, some subjects who heard the above story were presented with the following test sentence:

> When the man entered the kitchen he slipped on a wet spot and broke the delicate glass pitcher when it fell on the floor.

Overall, subjects correctly identified actual sentences from the stories 66 percent of the time. But they incorrectly claimed to remember hearing sentences that were not in the story 62 percent of the time when those test sentences, like the example above, contained inferences that people would naturally draw from the actual sentences. They made this mistake significantly less often (22 percent) when the stories were altered so that there was no inferential relationship between the actual sentence and the test sentence.[11] Thus, our memories have trouble distinguishing between what we know from the words themselves and what we know from the inferences that we draw from the words.

This research is consistent with some of the eyewitness testimony literature that shows people often claim to recall having seen things that they never actually saw, but merely inferred from what they saw. In one influential study, Elizabeth Loftus and John Palmer showed subjects a film of a car accident. They then asked some of the subjects to estimate how fast the cars were going when they "smashed" into each other. For the remaining subjects, they substituted other words for "smashed," such as "collided," "bumped," "hit," and "contacted." Questions containing verbs like "smashed" led to significantly higher estimates of speed than did "contacted." But even more notably, when called back one week later, 32 percent of the people who had heard the word "smashed" in the question claimed to have seen broken glass in the film. Of those hearing the word "hit" in the question, only 14 percent recalled seeing broken glass. In fact, there was no broken glass in the film.[12]

This study is interesting for many reasons. For our purposes, it shows that people generally remember more or less accurately not only what they see or hear, but also what they infer from what they see or hear.[13]

Not only do our answers about events depend in part on the questions asked about them, but our recollection of the words used in the question depends in part on the nature of the answer. Psychologists Philip N. Johnson-Laird and Charles E. Bethell-Fox showed subjects a video displaying a series of simple events: a pencil falling against a large jug, a pencil sharpener pushing a pencil onto a cup, and so on. After each event, the experimenter asked the subject a question, the correct answer to which was sometimes "Yes" ("Did the pencil fall against the large jug?"), sometimes "No" because the event asked about didn't happen that way ("Did the pencil fall against the small jug?"), and sometimes "No" because the question contained a false assumption (e.g., the question referred to the pencil, but that isn't what fell in the video).[14]

Immediately after this exercise, subjects were taken into another room and asked to write down all of the questions that they could remember having been asked. They remembered many more questions whose answer was "Yes" (68 percent) than questions whose answers had been "No" because the question misdescribed the event (55 percent). They found it particularly difficult to recall questions for which the answer was "No" because the question contained a false premise (27 percent). In all three categories, subjects made large numbers of mistakes in repeating the question even when they did remember that it was asked. The authors explain this curious result:

> Once listeners have discovered that a question is based on a false assumption, they do not execute any further procedures corresponding to the meaning of the question; their memory for such a question is correspondingly impaired, since they have processed it to a lesser degree than an ordinary yes question.[15]

The broader ramifications are clear: both the quantity and quality of our recollections of earlier conversations depend on how we integrate utterances into a complex set of inferences that we make on the spot.

All of this matters in assessing the accuracy of testimony about reported speech when there is no other evidence of what was really said. We will almost always have to settle for the witness's characterization of the substance of the actual words spoken, or disallow testimony about the speech act altogether. Even on these terms, the testimony will almost certainly be only a partial account of what was said, and in many instances an inaccurate account, for reasons suggested in the psychological literature just described. Trial lawyers display an intuitive sense of the problem when they object to a witness's testifying to "a conclusion" instead of to what the witness saw or heard. When we are threatened, for example, we recall the fact of the threat well, but we may not recall the exact words that were used. A good lawyer will cross-examine a witness to bring out the fact that the witness is testifying only about inferences that were drawn—not about what was said. If the witness can say nothing more than that she was being threatened, there is a good chance that the evidence will be excluded as an improper conclusion from a fact. More likely, however, the witness will be able to provide some sense of what she believes was actually said.

We now proceed to discuss some of the ways in which the legal system has reacted to this limitation of human memory in these and similar circumstances.

The Legal System's Response: Substance Is Good Enough

People do not always have good intuitions about linguistic phenomena. For example, as we will see in chapter 7, we think we are better at identifying people by their voices than we really are. But we have no such illusions about our ability to recall verbatim speech. We know that we can't, and the legal system generally takes this limitation into account. Consider Judge

Richard Posner's comments in response to a witness who made corrections to his deposition transcript:

> The reason given for making the correction was that the original language was "garbled." Garbled it was, though it was not an error in transcription; not only did the court reporter state in an affidavit that Linton's testimony was correctly transcribed, but Linton could not have remembered the exact words that he had stated months before at his deposition. Had he said that "for" was really "versus," it is possible that he might have been correcting an error in transcription. But it is unreasonable to suppose that he remembered that he had said "were associated with the products that had the longest term potential versus" rather than "did we feel have the longest-term potential for." What he tried to do, whether or not honestly, was to change his deposition from what he said to what he meant.[16]

Similar understandings of the frailties of human memory inform judicial reaction to all kinds of testimony.[17] We discuss some of them here, and begin with encounters between suspects and the police.

Police Testimony of What the Defendant Said

We saw earlier that courts are willing to infer a defendant's consent to a search quite broadly, but require defendants to assert *Miranda* rights with clear statements. In most of these cases, especially those involving consent to search, there is no recording of the interaction between the suspect and the police. Courts must therefore rely on testimony, usually by police officers, about what was said.

Consent to Search

In chapter 3, we observed that the law is not very fussy about how the police request consent to make a search, even if most people would interpret the "request" as a command about which they have little choice. Yet the exact phrasing of a question to a suspect, or the suspect's response, can be critical in deciding whether the officer's utterance was more a request or a command. Nonetheless, courts often rule that as long as the police testify reasonably enough that the defendant consented to a search, it doesn't seem to much matter what was actually said. The Seventh Circuit decision in *Maldonado v. United States* illustrates this outlook:

> Both parties acknowledge that Agent Boertlein requested further consent from Maldonado to search the "juicer boxes." However, at the suppression hearing

there were discrepancies in the testimony regarding Maldonado's response to
Agent Boertlein's request. The two DEA agents both testified that Maldonado
affirmatively consented to Agent Boertlein's request to search the juicer boxes;
nonetheless, neither agent was able to recall the specific words used by
Maldonado to express his consent. Agent Krok testified that he did not hear
Maldonado's response because of the background noise from the electronic doors,
but that he did see Maldonado make an oral response and nod his head in a
positive manner. Agent Boertlein testified that Maldonado made an affirmative
response to his request to search the boxes, but Boertlein was unable to recall
the exact words Maldonado used.[18]

Because police are likely to be believed at trial, and because the defendant
often decides not to testify, this standard typically makes police testimony
the only story that the judge or jury hears on the issue of consent, and
makes it quite difficult to accurately determine whether the consent truly
was voluntary.

We do not argue that only testimony demonstrating verbatim recollection should be admitted. That would be unrealistic. But we do, once
again, recommend recording conversations as often as is practicable, so
that courts can evaluate what was actually said, rather than relying on a
witness's characterization long after the fact.

Many police cars now carry video recording equipment. This practice,
however, is not required under state or federal law. It is generally specific to
the local practices of the law enforcement agencies that use such devices.
Because such equipment is not only easily available but has become quite
inexpensive, the burden should be on the prosecution to explain—in cases
where it matters—why an encounter was not recorded when it could have
been. If the criminal justice system is serious about getting at the truth,
it should—now that the means are readily available—strongly encourage
the police to record interactions with the public that are likely to become
the focus of later litigation.

Invoking the Right to Counsel Our observations about consent to searches
also apply to suspects who invoke their right to a lawyer during interrogation. In the absence of a video recording, the only evidence whether the
right to counsel was invoked is what witnesses claim took place. This can
again be problematic because, as we saw in chapter 4, the exact words may
be critical in determining whether a request was made; if there was a request, it would render inadmissible any information elicited subsequently.
Typically the only evidence of what transpired is testimony from a police

officer, who not only is limited in how well she can remember exact words, but is ordinarily inclined to favor the prosecution. At the same time, there are limits as to how far judges will go in taking the word of law enforcement agents in this situation.

In one interesting case, the court suppressed an out-of-court statement by an agent who changed his story about what was said after being coached to do so by a prosecutor. In *United States v. de la Jara,* the defendant had moved to suppress statements that he had made to police officers after he was arrested. The actual words the defendant used were ambiguous. He said in Spanish, "Debo yo llamar a mi abogado." As the court rightly noted, this can mean any of the following:

> Can I call my attorney?
> Should I call my attorney?
> I should call my lawyer. [19]

Without knowing such things as the defendant's tone of voice—something that a recording would reveal—it is not possible to tell exactly what he meant just from reading the words. Nonetheless, the police officer to whom de la Jara spoke reported the defendant's request in the police report as follows:

> I started to close the door slightly when I heard DELAJARA say in Spanish that he wanted to call his attorney. I told the agent who was standing outside the office that it sounded like DELAJARA was invoking his rights because he just asked to call his attorney. The agent asked me if that's what I heard and I said "yes." [20]

Some five months later, in preparation for trial, an Assistant U.S. Attorney drafted a statement for the officer that contradicted his earlier report. The statement, which the officer signed under penalty of perjury, read in part:

> Shortly thereafter I heard the defendant say something about speaking to an attorney. . . . I was unable to hear the exact words which preceded "speak to an attorney," because my attention was directed [elsewhere]. Because I heard the defendant say something about wanting an attorney, I assumed he had invoked his rights and told the officer standing next to me that it "sounded like De La Jara was invoking his rights." I then wrote this statement in a police report. In writing the report, I specified that it "sounded" like the defendant was invoking

his rights because I did not hear his exact words and thus was not positive that he had in fact invoked his right to an attorney.[21]

Incredibly, the district court rejected the earlier, contemporaneous report of what de la Jara had said, and instead accepted the officer's in-court testimony. The court of appeals reversed and suppressed the defendant's admissions made subsequent to arrest. The officer's report didn't just say it "sounded" like an invocation of the right to counsel, it also said, "I heard DELAJARA say in Spanish that he wanted to call his attorney." The officer's initial characterization of what de la Jara said took precedence over both the words themselves (which were ambiguous), and the officer's belated attempt to retract his original interpretation of what he heard. While such evidentiary shenanigans are all too common in civil litigation, they have no place in criminal trials, particularly when committed by the prosecutor, whose duty to find the truth should always prevail over his desire to win. In any event, evidentiary tricks of this sort would be far less common if the original transactions were taped.

Confessions   Confessions are obviously an important type of evidence. When made outside of court, they are also a form of hearsay. The Federal Rules of Evidence define hearsay as "a statement, other than one made by the declarant while testifying at the trial or hearing, offered in evidence to prove the truth of the matter asserted."[22] The rule states that hearsay is "not admissible except as provided by these rules or by other rules. . . ."[23] The definition of hearsay surely would include reported confessions. What could fit the definition better than a police officer testifying, "The defendant told me he committed the crime"? However, Rule 801(d)(2), which governs "admissions by party opponents," excludes admissions from the definition of hearsay: "A statement is not hearsay if: The statement is offered against a party and is . . . his own statement, in either an individual or a representative capacity."[24] Later subsections of the rule, dealing with "adoptive admissions," also exclude from hearsay "statements of which the party had manifested an adoption or belief in its truth . . . ."[25]

One of the rationales for the system of hearsay rules is that hearsay evidence is likely to be unreliable. A treatise on evidence explains: "The hearsay rule seeks to eliminate the danger that evidence will lack reliability because faults in the perception, memory, or narration of the declarant will not be exposed."[26] Testimony reporting admissions of an opposing party is allowed into evidence despite this concern. As the Advisory Committee to the Federal Rules of Evidence noted, "Admissions by a party-opponent are excluded from the category of hearsay on the theory that their admissibility in evidence is the result of the adversary system rather than satisfaction of the conditions of the hearsay rule."[27]

Testimony of reported confessions is admitted into evidence despite the risk of unreliability on the theory that the adversarial system, especially cross-examination, will work toward uncovering the truth. But when witnesses testify about the gist of what was said, cross-examination is necessarily less effective. We can never test the witness's description of the confession against the defendant's style of speech, for example, because the witness has not purported to repeat what the defendant actually said. Compare this situation to that of eyewitness identifications. With all of the problems that lead to false identifications,[28] at least it is possible to compare an out-of-court description of a party with that party's actual appearance, and to judge the credibility of the witness by the extent that the two vary. In fact, the quality of a witness's description of the person being identified is an important factor in determining the admissibility of the identification.[29] Not so when a witness testifies about the substance of a defendant's out-of-court confession. Of course, defendant's counsel can cross-examine a witness on any differences between what he told policemen earlier, and what he says in court. But, once again, the absence of verbatim recollection creates an impoverished record that diminishes the effectiveness of any such inquiry. Moreover, as noted above, a federal statute, the Jencks Act,[30] does not require prosecutors to turn over notes of interviews with witnesses unless the notes contain a verbatim account, which they rarely do.

How do courts handle this problem? Testimony of confessions, based on the substance or gist of what the defendant said, are routinely accepted. Typical are the following descriptions of testimony by two courts of appeals in cases involving police testimony in suppression hearings:

Although Deputy Cuchta could not remember the words Leshuk used in disclaiming ownership, he testified generally that both defendants denied ownership. Furthermore, although Deputy Fluharty could not recall the exact words Leshuk used, he was adamant that Leshuk denied ownership of the property. During cross-examination, Deputy Fluharty agreed with defense counsel's observation that "[t]he impression that [Leshuk] denied ownership is what is left in your mind; is that correct?"[31]

He (Clemons) told me that he didn't trust the C.I. (confidential informant) because he had heard that he was working for the police. And he suggested that

I would—that I leave him alone and didn't have nothing else to do with him. He said that if I wanted to do business with him, that was fine, but he wouldn't do anything else with the C.I. [32]

In both cases, the courts affirmed the admission of the evidence.

In other cases, there is some sensitivity to the problem, but standards of reliability are still very low. For example, in affirming a murder conviction and death sentence, a federal court of appeals noted, "The state introduced Howard's confessions into evidence through the testimony of Agent Battle and Lieutenant Hitchins, both of whom had taken meticulous handwritten notes of their conversations with Howard." [33] Again, the police could have recorded the confessions, but didn't. Cases of this sort are commonplace in the system.

Along these same lines, Roger Shuy writes of police reports that purport to quote the suspect's language in a verbal confession, but that often enough are written in the style of the police officer, using words and syntax that the suspect would probably not have used, but that are typical of law enforcement lingo. [34] Malcolm Coulthard writes of a similar phenomenon in the famous English case of Derek Bentley, which we discuss more fully in chapter 8. Bentley, a mentally retarded young adult, was executed for telling his friend to "let him have it," after a policeman asked the friend to hand over the gun he was holding. An important piece of evidence against Bentley was a signed confession, which the police claimed was merely a transcribed record of what Bentley had said. Coulthard's subsequent analysis showed that it was really written in language commonly used by police officers but considerably remote from that which would have been used by a retarded person. In 1998, Bentley was exonerated posthumously. [35]

These cases only highlight the fact that when a defendant contests the accuracy of a reported confession at a suppression hearing, it will almost always be impossible to prove that the report is wrong unless a recording was made of what was actually said. When credibility is at issue, as when a motion to suppress evidence depends precisely on what transpired between a police officer and a suspect in a drug raid, the police will almost always win. Judges have always been reluctant to find that police officers are not telling the truth unless the evidence of untruthfulness is very strong. Moreover, when a police officer testifies inaccurately at trial, the defendant will have to weigh his right to rebut the officer's testimony against his own right not to testify. The choice is an unhappy one whether the defendant is guilty or innocent.

A related issue is that during an interrogation, police sometimes make indirect threats and promises, something that Richard Ofshe and Richard Leo have pointed out in explaining why suspects sometimes confess to crimes they did not commit.[36] The threats and promises are made indirectly because, if made overtly, they could well lead to a resulting confession being denied admission in court. Consequently, according to Ofshe and Leo, such speech acts are generally made by "pragmatic implication." They also point out, however, that these strategies are very subtle and that suspects cannot reasonably be expected to recall the exact words that an interrogator used. Ofshe and Leo therefore recommend the use of recorders whenever feasible.[37]

Jailhouse Informants

As we noted in chapter 4, as of March 2004 the Innocence Project had identified 143 prisoners exonerated by DNA evidence, including some who were on death row. In an analysis of the first seventy of these cases, the Project found that in sixteen of them the evidence at trial included testimony by cellmates and other "snitches" that the defendant had confessed to committing the crime.[38]

To take one example, in August 2001 the press reported the exoneration of a person who had been sentenced to death. Charles Fain was to be executed for raping and killing a nine-year-old girl in Idaho. His conviction was based on microscopic hair analysis conducted by the FBI,[39] and on the testimony of two jailhouse informants. DNA analysis of the pubic hair that was found on the body of the victim showed that it was not Fain's hair, and he has since been released. But the prosecutor who tried the case eighteen years earlier was unimpressed with the scientific evidence. He was quoted as saying: "It doesn't really change my opinion that much that Fain's guilty. The case was a circumstantial evidence case. There was a myriad of circumstances that pointed in his direction."[40] These remarks, which are not unusual in such cases, show that once the system has reached a decision, it is very difficult to dislodge it, even when there is unassailable evidence to the contrary.

It is easy enough to understand the reluctance of prosecutors to see cases they had won long ago be reopened and possibly overturned. The justification for this reluctance often involves the benefit of finality to the criminal justice system and repose for the victims and their families, both worthwhile considerations. But the situation is obviously much more personal than that. Even if the prosecuting attorney acted with the highest ethical standards throughout the case,[41] it must be extremely painful to deal with having helped to ruin the life of an innocent person while allowing a guilty one to go free. That no doubt explains in part the fact that prosecutors fight so hard to keep defense counsel from obtaining DNA for post-conviction testing.[42] For a variety of reasons, then, the legal system resists efforts to reconsider cases that are officially closed.

The lesson from these false convictions is that when the system relies on jailhouse confessions to other inmates, it is important to ask serious questions about their reliability. Prisoners, nonetheless, are called to testify about a defendant's confession in many cases. We found about 111 published opinions in a recent ten-year period that raise the issue.[43] Since so few cases go to trial, and only a small percentage of those cases lead to published opinions, it is only reasonable to see jailhouse informants as a substantial phenomenon in the criminal justice system. It has been widely observed that heavy reliance on this sort of evidence is problematic because the people allegedly hearing the confessions have reason to lie. Typically, prosecutors make deals with such prisoners in exchange for their appearance and testimony. Here, we would like to emphasize that the reliability of these confessions is reduced even further because the exact words of the defendant are not available.

Our review of a wide range of judicial opinions reveals that cellmates are often called to testify about the substance of the defendant's alleged confession. This is accepted so routinely that the issue of exact words does not arise. Typical is the court's terse discussion in *United States v. Hamilton:* "A cellmate testified that Hamilton confessed to him regarding robbing a bank in the Grand Avenue Mall, noting specifically that Hamilton used the stolen money to buy a leather outfit."[44] Because there is no record of it, there is no analysis of what the defendant actually said. In turn, the absence of the precise language of the confession makes cross-examination far less effective, thereby enhancing the reported confession's influence on the jury.

We recognize that if courts required testimony of exact words, there would be virtually no confessions of this kind admitted into evidence. The legal system has made a decision to admit this relatively degraded evidence. Of course, whatever deals a prosecutor makes will come out at trial. But the compromise is a far more serious one than is generally recognized. The problem is not just that cellmates have a stake in lying. It is exacerbated by the fact that witnesses can do a fairly good job insulating themselves from strong cross-examination by never having to give much detail about what the defendant actually said.

It is not only prosecutors who rely on jailhouse confessions. In *Carriger v. Stewart,* for example, it was the defendant who presented a cellmate's statements that someone else had confessed to a murder for which the defendant had been convicted and sentenced to death. The court of appeals, relying in part on the confession to the cellmate (but also on a great deal of additional evidence), granted the defendant's motion for habeas corpus, and released him.[45] Nonetheless, the use of jailhouse confessions is typically a tool of the prosecutor. For a system whose goal is to determine the truth, this evidence is even riskier than is generally acknowledged.

A partial solution to the problem is for courts to require corroborating evidence when reported confessions are used.[46] Perhaps the law of perjury can serve as a model. Courts have imposed a "two-witness rule" on federal perjury prosecutions. In order to prove that an allegedly false statement is actually false, the government must produce two witnesses or one witness plus additional corroborating evidence.[47] As one court explained the rule:

> Historically, it is founded on the notion that a conviction for perjury ought not to rest entirely upon "an oath against an oath"—that witnesses who are compelled to testify will testify more freely if they know that they will not be subject to prosecution for perjury simply because an equally honest witness may well have a different recollection of the same events.[48]

When it comes to reported confessions, the case for corroboration is at least as compelling.

Language Crimes without the Language

Another area in which the system of criminal justice relies on the gist of what was said involves language crimes. In chapters 9–11, we take a close look at such issues as what counts as a threat, a conspiracy, a solicitation, an agreement to accept a bribe, and a false statement in a perjury prosecution. Here, we look at an evidentiary issue: whether the government must prove what words the defendant actually uttered.

The short answer is no. The government can prove its case through witnesses who testify about the substance of what the defendant said. If it were otherwise, then some sort of surreptitious recording would have to be a prerequisite for many crimes that have been prosecuted since centuries before there were recording devices. Yet this means that people routinely are convicted for saying things that no one remembers verbatim.

Of course, this would never happen in a perjury case today because legal proceedings are recorded. But legal proceedings that can form the basis of a perjury prosecution were not always recorded. In fact, as recently as 1948, a court of appeals upheld a conviction for perjury based in part on a witness's testimony about what the defendant had sworn to, even though there *was* a transcript of the original testimony, which the government introduced into evidence later in the trial. That case, *United States v. Myers,* involved false testimony before a U.S. Senate committee. At the perjury trial, a witness testified as to what one of the defendants had said before the Senate. The court of appeals held this to be appropriate:

> The transcript made from shorthand notes of his testimony was, to be sure, evidence of what he had said, but it was not the only admissible evidence concerning it. Rogers' testimony was equally competent, and was admissible whether given before or after the transcript was received in evidence. Statements alleged to be perjurious may be proved by any person who heard them, as well as by a reporter who recorded them in shorthand.[49]

Myers argued that given the existence of a transcript, the best evidence rule precluded the testimony of witnesses whose recollection may be faulty. But the best evidence rule generally deals with issues such as the admissibility of a copy of a document when the original is available. The court held the rule inapplicable, and disposed of the case. A strong dissent argued that to have allowed this testimony was unfair.[50] But implicit even in the dissent's argument is the assumption that absent a transcript, testimony from recollection is unquestionably admissible. After all, it would be both the best and only evidence of what was said.

In modern perjury cases, we can find no examples in which transcripts are not used as a matter of course when they are available.[51] But there is a closely related crime where oral statements can be prosecuted. Section 1001 of the federal Criminal Code makes it a crime to knowingly make "any materially false, fictitious, or fraudulent statement or representation" in any matter within the jurisdiction of a federal agency.[52] Falsely made oral statements are just as much a crime as falsely made written ones. But by the time the trial occurs, no one really knows exactly what the oral statement was. Government agents testify about the substance of what the defendant said, and that's good enough.[53]

An interesting statement of this rule comes from the prosecution of John Poindexter, President Reagan's National Security Advisor, in connection with the Iran/Contra affair.[54]

Poindexter was convicted of, among other things, violating § 1001 by lying to members of Congress, although he was not under oath when he did so. (The conviction was later reversed because Poindexter was held to have immunity.) While the case raises some interesting issues concerning the relationship between the executive and legislative branches of government, the court had no trouble with the issue of whether oral statements, falsely made, can constitute a violation of § 1001:

> Poindexter also argues that § 1001 should not apply to "private discussions between representatives of the political branches where, as here, no oath is administered and no verbatim transcript is maintained." In such circumstances, "proof literally becomes a matter of one person's word against another, even though neither may have heard or remembered with precision exactly what form of words was used in making an allegedly false statement." We have already held, however, that § 1001 may be applied to "statements [that were] not under oath [and were] not stenographically transcribed." [Citation omitted.] The absence of such formal trappings is relevant, of course, to the difficulty of proving beyond a reasonable doubt exactly what the defendant said and whether he intended to deceive his audience as to a material question of fact; but these are issues of the sufficiency of the evidence in a particular case, not reasons for carving a categorical exception from the statute.[55]

The court understated the problem. It is not merely the case that "exactly what the defendant said" is a material question of fact. Rather, it is also the case that "exactly what the defendant said" is a material question of fact that is not subject to proof. No one can remember.

Thus, it is possible to convict someone of a felony based only on the hearer's perception of what the defendant said. This may be the right balance to strike. But it does compromise the defendant's ability to argue that the statement was literally true, but misunderstood, a standard defense in perjury cases and other cases involving false statements. By the time he can testify, there is no statement to analyze. The defendant's only available recourse is to claim that he didn't intend to say anything false, but he can't prove it, because he doesn't remember exactly what he said either. And he can only do that much at the cost of waiving his Fifth Amendment right not to testify.

We see no way out of this double bind. Our suggestion that police interviews, warnings, and requests for consent be taped cannot possibly apply to every encounter that citizens have with governmental officials. Nor do we wish to suggest that the government be required to surreptitiously tape conversations between citizens before prosecuting for a language crime. This is one situation where cross-examination is the best we have. And it is not very good.

Conclusion

We hope to have shown in this and the preceding chapters that what matters is not just *what* you say, but *how* you say it. This is not just an adage
about everyday life, but is equally relevant in many areas of the criminal
law. Because the language that a suspect uses to consent to a search or invoke his right to counsel can be so critical, our limitations in remembering
the exact words that police officers or a defendant spoke can have serious
implications. The problem becomes all the more serious when testimony is
offered to prove that a defendant admitted having committed a crime.

   We return to these issues in part 4, where we consider crimes of language like bribery, solicitation, threats, and perjury. As we will see, all of
these crimes focus on words that the defendant uttered, so that the issue
of exact words will again come to the fore. Meanwhile, we turn to the issue
of linguistic evidence.

Chapter 7

Who Said That?

Hey, doctor. Over here,
over here.

One of the most notorious crimes of the twentieth century was the kidnapping of the young child of the famous aviator Charles Lindbergh. Hoping to get his son back alive, Lindbergh accompanied Dr. John Condon to St. Raymond's cemetery in the Bronx. Condon's mission was to deliver ransom money to the kidnapper, while Lindbergh waited some eighty to a hundred feet away in the car.[1] Out of the darkness came the words "Hey, doctor. Over here, over here," spoken with a foreign accent.[2] Based in part on Lindbergh's identification of his voice at trial, Bruno Richard Hauptmann was convicted of kidnapping and murdering the Lindbergh baby. He was executed soon thereafter.

Twenty-nine months after the encounter in the cemetery, in September 1934, Lindbergh had told a Bronx grand jury that "[i]t would be very difficult to sit here and say that I could pick a man by that voice."[3] Nonetheless, the district attorney asked Lindbergh later that day, "Would you like to see the man who kidnapped your son?"[4] The next morning, Hauptmann was brought into the D.A.'s office, and asked to repeat the words, "Hey, doctor. Here, doctor, over here."

Lindbergh, who was sitting in the back of the room among a group of detectives, told the prosecutor that he recognized Hauptmann's voice as that of the kidnapper.

At trial, Lindbergh recounted the events at the cemetery.[5] He then testified:

> Q. Whose voice was it, Colonel, that you heard in the vicinity of St. Raymond's Cemetery that night, saying, "Hey, Doctor"?
> A. That was Hauptmann's voice.
> Q. You heard it again the second time where?
> A. At District Attorney Foley's office in New York, in the Bronx.[6]

Lindbergh's lawyer commented: "The minute Lindbergh 'pointed his finger' at Hauptmann, the trial was over. 'Jesus Christ' himself said he was *convinced* this was the man who killed his son. Who was anybody to doubt him or deny him justice?"[7]

Sixty-five years later, Hauptmann's conviction and execution remain controversial. Was he truly guilty of the kidnapping, or was he wrongly convicted, perhaps in part because of the anti-German sentiment then prevalent in the United States? We will not attempt to answer the question of Hauptmann's guilt or innocence. But we will address others that the Lindbergh case raised: Are people really able to remember a voice that they have only heard once? Are three syllables enough of a sample? Isn't twenty-nine months a long time? Does the stress of the situation make memory better or worse? What effect does a foreign accent have on our ability to identify voices? Hauptmann's attorney was in no position to present expert evidence on any of these questions. There was no relevant expertise at that time.

We have, however, learned a great deal since Hauptmann's trial. As we will see, the legal system in the United States all too often overestimates people's ability to recognize voices. Other countries fare no better. In 1995, a Canadian appellate court exonerated Guy Paul Morin, who had been convicted three years earlier of raping and murdering a young girl, in large part based on an identification of his voice. Post-conviction DNA testing excluded him as the perpetrator.[8]

The problems that people have identifying speakers by their voices are similar to those that people have as eyewitnesses. The amount of exposure, the nature of the identification process, and the number of exposures all matter in determining how likely a witness is to be correct.[9] Yet while the reliability of *eye*witness identification has been a focal point in the news media, the scholarly literature, and the courts, the unreliability of *ear*witness identification has gone virtually unnoticed. The reluctance of the legal system to deal with this problem stems from a confluence of rigid adherence to historical positions that are no longer tenable and some interesting judicial missteps concerning the accuracy of "voiceprints" that have made courts unreceptive to voice identification research. Most of all, the U.S. legal system has simply not had easy access to the growing body of research on this issue.

Legal Standards for Identifying Speakers

Whether a voice identification should be admitted at trial has traditionally been mainly a question of the law of evidence. During the past three decades, however, the U.S. Supreme Court has held that the Due Process Clause of the Constitution sometimes imposes additional requirements relating to the reliability of earwitness identifications. We first look at the application of these constitutional requirements. Then we examine a set of cases in which the voice being identified is on tape. There, courts apply rules of evidence governing authentication, and require only minimal familiarity with a voice for an identification to stand. As we will see, courts sometimes pay too little attention to reliability issues in tape cases, and occasionally even apply the minimal standards of tape cases to live identifications.

Due Process Requirements

The *Biggers* Criteria   The seminal case in both eyewitness and earwitness identification is *Neil v. Biggers,*[10] decided by the Supreme Court in 1972. That case involved a crime victim's identification of the defendant at a "show up"—a procedure in which the police march the suspect in front of the victim and ask for identification, without the safeguard of requiring the victim to choose the defendant from among a group of people in a lineup. Officers showed the defendant to a rape victim at a police station approximately seven months after the crime occurred. She had an opportunity to look him over and hear him utter the words "Shut up or I'll kill you." Based on his appearance and voice, she testified at trial that she had "no doubt" that the defendant was her assailant.[11] Like Lindbergh's identification of Hauptmann, the circumstances of this identification were highly suggestive in that the identifier was confronted with a single suspect whom the police clearly thought was the perpetrator.

The Supreme Court, which concentrated on eyewitness aspects of the identification, established a framework for evaluating claims that a defendant's right to due process was violated by a suggestive identification procedure. The focus should be on the risk of a false identification:

> It is the likelihood of misidentification which violates a defendant's right to due process. . . . Suggestive confrontations are disapproved because they increase the likelihood of misidentification, and unnecessarily suggestive ones are condemned for the further reason that the increased chance of misidentification is gratuitous. But . . . the admission of evidence of a showup without more does not violate due process.[12]

The Court then articulated criteria for evaluating the likelihood of misidentification:

> We turn, then, to the central question, whether under the "totality of the circumstances" the identification was reliable even though the confrontation procedure was suggestive. As indicated by our cases, the factors to be considered in evaluating the likelihood of misidentification include the opportunity of the witness to view the criminal at the time of the crime, the witness' degree of attention, the accuracy of the witness' prior description of the criminal, the level of certainty demonstrated by the witness at the confrontation, and the length of time between the crime and the confrontation.[13]

Applying these criteria, the Court held that the rape victim's identification of the defendant as her assailant was good enough to pass muster. It noted that the defendant's appearance was consistent with a description she had given police shortly after the crime occurred. Moreover, she had previously been shown several other suspects and had failed to single out any one of them as the rapist. The Court was also impressed with her level of confidence in the identification.

In a subsequent case, *Manson v. Brathwaite,*[14] the Court elaborated on the decision in *Biggers.* It held that "the corrupting effect" of suggestive procedures must be balanced against indicia of reliability, which is "the linchpin in determining the admissibility of identification testimony."[15] If the identification is reliable, then it should be allowed notwithstanding improperly suggestive procedures. This creates a two-step analysis in cases of this sort. First, a court should ask whether the identification was suggestive. If not, there is no constitutional issue and the identification will usually be admissible. If it was suggestive, the second step is to determine whether the identification was nonetheless reliable under the criteria set forth in *Biggers*.

Although *Biggers* and *Manson* both concentrated on eyewitness identification, it is worth bearing in mind that the victim in *Biggers* was exposed not only to the defendant's appearance, but also to his voice. There is no reason for courts to limit the holdings of these cases to eyewitness identification, and they do not. Thus, *Biggers* and *Manson* set the constitutional standard for admitting voice identification evidence in earwitness cases.

Due Process Analysis in Voice Identification Cases The initial question in a *Biggers/Manson* analysis is whether voice identification procedures were overly suggestive. The surest way to avoid this problem is to use an appropriately constituted voice lineup, where the witness tries to identify the perpetrator from among a set of possible candidates. Consider the description by the Supreme Judicial Court of Massachusetts of a permissible procedure using a five-voice lineup:

> After consulting with the office of the district attorney, the police used a voice identification procedure that adequately protected the defendant's rights. There was no one-on-one confrontation between the victim and the defendant. The victim could not see the participants during the procedure, nor could they see her. The defendant selected the order in which he would read. The participants read the same innocuous passage from a fifth-grade reader. Defense counsel attended the procedure and, although consulted, never objected to it. In addition, we have viewed a videotape of the voice identification procedure, and conclude that the procedure was not impermissibly suggestive. The defendant's voice did not stand out because of his age, nor did any other aspect of the procedure direct undue attention to the defendant's voice. Hence, we conclude that the judge properly denied the defendant's motion to suppress the voice identification.[16]

The Massachusetts procedure was not flawless. For example, there probably should be more than five voices in a lineup. But the court was clearly making a reasonable effort to ensure that fair procedures are being used.

In contrast, one-on-one voice identifications are almost inherently suggestive. For example, in *Yeatman v. Inland Property Management, Inc.*,[17] a federal district court rejected an identification when "[o]nly one tape containing only one female voice was played. Moreover, the witness already knew the critical need to give an affirmative answer to the question that she was being asked, and no opportunity was given to [the opposing parties] to participate in or to monitor the procedure."[18] The court likened the identification process to a "card trick" where "a magician forces on the person chosen from the audience the card that the magician intends the person to select, and then the magician purports to 'divine' the card that the person has chosen."[19]

Similarly, *State v. Johnson,*[20] a New Jersey case, involved a woman who was raped by a man whose face she could not see, but whose voice she heard. She was asked to come to the police station, and through an open door she heard the voice of a suspect talking to a detective. After some initial hesitation, she identified the suspect as her assailant. On appeal, the court noted that the constitutional safeguards that apply to visual identifications "are equally applicable to identification of a voice through auditory senses," particularly because the risks of misidentification "are even more apparent where the identification is by voice alone."[21] It concluded that the identification procedure was suggestive enough to require a *Biggers* analysis of reliability.

Other courts have reached similar conclusions.[22] Some, however, have allowed more questionable identification procedures. One Connecticut case held that a lineup consisting of just two voices was not overly suggestive.[23] The same result was reached in a Louisiana case when a defendant's voice was one of three in a voice lineup.[24]

If the voice identification is found to be suggestive, the next step is to apply the *Biggers* criteria to determine whether it was nonetheless sufficiently reliable. For example, in *Commonwealth v. Marini,*[25] the Massachusetts court, having found identification procedures unduly suggestive, went on to find the identification unreliable when nine months had elapsed between the crime and the identification.

In most cases, however, courts find adequate reliability. *United States v. Duran* is typical. There, the Ninth Circuit affirmed a conviction for bank robbery. Key evidence consisted of the tellers' identification of the defendant's voice at trial. In response to the defendant's argument that the identification was excessively suggestive, the court applied the *Biggers* factors.[26] In doing so, it made some questionable assumptions. For one, it noted that the identification occurred "just" three months after the robbery. But three months may be a long time to remember a voice. For another, the court surmised that the tellers were "likely attentive." The opinion demonstrates a judicial recognition that reliability is an issue, but does not provide much analysis of what makes an identification reliable or unreliable.

A more convincing case for reliability was made in *United States v. De-*

gaglia. Although the Seventh Circuit did not explicitly apply the *Biggers* factors, it took seriously the fact that the agent identifying the defendant's voice testified that he had heard it on several occasions for periods of up to one and one-half hours and that the defendant had a very distinctive voice, which the agent described as "high pitched, raspy, and nasal."[27] Here our intuitions are that the identification is more reliable. Courts, in fact, frequently hold identifications to be reliable when the witness testifies to having heard the voice on multiple occasions.[28] We will see that repeated exposure to a voice really does have significant impact on accuracy in experimental studies.

In summary, when an identification has occurred under suggestive circumstances, courts require as a condition for admissibility some indication that the identification was nonetheless reliable. Nonsuggestive identifications, in contrast, are not subjected to scrutiny of their reliability. That issue is left to the trier of fact.

Voices on Tape

When the voice being identified is on tape, courts often do not engage in the *Biggers/Manson* analysis. They do not consider how suggestive the identification was, nor analyze the indicia of reliability even when the identification clearly was suggestive. Rather, they apply ordinary rules of evidence that permit a witness, often a police officer, to authenticate the tape, and leave the question of reliability to the jury. Most prominent today is Rule 901 of the Federal Rules of Evidence, which provides that "[t]he requirement of authentication or identification as a condition precedent to admissibility is satisfied by evidence sufficient to support a finding that the matter in question is what its proponent claims." It is enough that the witness heard the voice "at any time under circumstances connecting it with the alleged speaker."[29]

The Advisory Committee Notes accompanying the rule make it clear that experts should generally not be part of the process: "Since aural voice identification is not a subject of expert testimony, the requisite familiarity may be acquired either before or after the particular speaking which is the subject of the identification, in this respect resembling visual identification of a person rather than identification of handwriting."[30]

The rule requires only "evidence sufficient to support a finding" that the tape is what it purports to be, and just about anything is sufficient. The lax standard for admissibility set by the U.S. Court of Appeals for the Ninth Circuit is typical:

Rule 901(b)(5) establishes a low threshold for voice identifications offered
to determine the admissibility of recorded conversations. So long as the
identifying witness is "minimally familiar" with the voice he identifies, Rule
901(b) is satisfied. The record reveals that Speziale was present in Anchorage
at Plunk's initial post-arrest interview. The familiarity that he gained through
that exposure was sufficient under Rule 901(b)(5) to support his identification
of Plunk's voice on the tape recorded conversations being offered into
evidence.[31]

The court took it as a given that the witness had gained sufficient familiarity with the suspect's voice to identify it, despite his obviously very limited
exposure.

In many if not most cases, this "minimally familiar" approach to admitting tape-recorded evidence does not appear to create significant risk
of misidentification. For one thing, the identification often *does* have substantial indicia of reliability. For example, sometimes the person identifying
the voice actually participated in the tape-recorded conversation.[32] In other
cases, the identifying witness almost certainly was familiar enough with the
voice to identify it correctly. Experience and research support the intuitions
of judges that people typically can identify the voice of a close relative, or
that someone who has frequently heard a voice is likely to recognize it if
he hears it on a tape.[33]

Moreover, the circumstances under which a tape was made usually provide ample evidence of reliability to reduce concerns about possible due
process violations. When an officer says that he made a tape of a wiretapped conversation between two people as part of an investigation into
the defendant's conduct, and one of the speakers was using the wiretapped
phone at the defendant's residence, and the person thought to be the defendant responded to being called by the defendant's name and said the
kinds of things the defendant often said, there is significant likelihood
that the defendant was one of the speakers. Thus, when the circumstantial
evidence is robust, the risk of error is rather low, even if the identifying
witness's only experience with the voice was when he heard the defendant
speak six months earlier at the defendant's arrest.[34]

Perhaps the most compelling circumstance is the existence of the tape
itself. Of course, it is possible to misidentify a voice on a tape. But the tape
limits the range of plausible identifications and its very existence provides
the defendant with the opportunity to dispute the identification through
witnesses who testify to the contrary. If it doesn't add significantly to the

likelihood of misidentification (an issue to which we return below), then the *pro forma* authentication is efficient and not unfair.

D. Michael Risinger, Mark P. Denbeaux, and Michael J. Saks point to similar issues in the law governing the identification of documents.[35] While the most compelling reason to consider a document to be authentic often involves the circumstances in which it was discovered (in the defendant's desk drawer, for example), the system also requires some formal identification of the defendant as the document's author. The acceptance of handwriting experts grew out of the need to provide such an identifying witness when there was no other witness available. To the extent that courts treat the personal identification as a formality, relying principally on the circumstantial evidence, the issues raised with respect to speaker identification mimic those that arise in the authentication of documents.

When strong circumstantial evidence is lacking, however, the possibility of suggestiveness is more of a concern. Yet few courts have considered the problem of suggestiveness in the context of identifying a speaker on tape. For instance, in *United States v. Degaglia,*[36] the court found nonsuggestive a procedure for identifying a voice on a tape that was very much like a show up. Rather than being presented with a number of candidates from which to choose, the identifier was asked to answer "Yes" or "No" to a single proposed candidate. Almost all courts, as we observed above, would regard this procedure as impermissibly suggestive in the earwitness context and would require a *Biggers* analysis of reliability.

Other courts have accepted similarly unreliable procedures. For example, in a Sixth Circuit case, *United States v. Knox,*[37] the officer identifying the defendant's voice had heard it only once some three years before his testimony at trial. The court upheld the identification as meeting minimal evidentiary standards. Often, it appears that the prosecutor contacts an officer who heard the defendant's voice, perhaps during an earlier arrest, and asks him to identify it on a tape.[38] The reliability of these identifications depends more on the circumstances in which the tapes are made than on the identifications themselves.

Consider also *United States v. Zambrana,*[39] where a government agent identified the defendant's voice as being on a tape recording and the court admitted it under Rule 901. The evidence of suggestiveness was particularly strong. As the agent listened to a tape, he had a transcript that included the defendant's name in the margin.[40] Nonetheless, the court held that this was not overly suggestive because the agent then went on to identify the defendant's voice on additional tapes without a transcript.[41] Clearly the damage had been done. An initially suggestive identification can taint later ones, and that was precisely the risk in this case.

At the same time, it appears that the objections that defendants raise to these identifications are almost always formal ones. A defendant might claim that the procedure did not meet legal standards, but typically provides no reason to conclude that the identification is not accurate, by producing alibi witnesses or witnesses who disagree with the identification, for example. The absence of such evidence tends to support the notion that Rule 901's minimal standards regarding the identification of speakers on tape recordings do not generally result in a serious risk of misidentification.

We therefore agree with most courts that a *Biggers* analysis is generally not necessary as a prerequisite for admission of a tape-recorded voice into evidence. Nonetheless, there are several situations in which we believe the system is far too casual. First, if a defendant comes forward with facts that raise concerns of a mistaken identification, then courts should apply *Biggers* and evaluate the potential for misidentification before admitting a suggestive identification of a taped voice based on minimal exposure to it.

Second, courts should be careful not to admit a suggestive identification of a recorded voice when the circumstantial evidence is not strong. Consider a recorded bomb threat made from a public telephone in a major city. Suppose that police arrest a malcontent whom they suspect to have made the call. Should we allow one of the arresting officers, who heard the suspect say a few words while being booked, to testify that the voice on the tape belongs to the defendant? Not only might the call have been made by any one of millions of people, but telephones transmit only a limited range of acoustic information, and this limited information is even further degraded by a tape recorder.

Third, when there is no tape recording, the *Biggers/Manson* analysis should clearly apply. A recent Fifth Circuit case applied only the minimalist approach of Rule 901 in a case where a police officer identified the defendant's voice as the one he had heard during a telephone surveillance.[42] No tape was made. The facts do not show whether the identification was suggestive enough to trigger application of the *Biggers* criteria, but the issue should have been raised and discussed.

Once a court decides that the identification of a voice was overly suggestive, due process requires that it determine the reliability of the identification. Moreover, in all cases where evidence of a voice identification is admitted, jurors must determine how reliable it was. As we will see, however, people are not all that good at identifying voices, especially under less ideal conditions. And we tend to overestimate how good we are at doing so.

Voice Recognition Research and the Reliability of Identifications

We make mistakes identifying voices even under the best of circumstances. Guy Paul Morin's DNA exoneration in Ontario, to which we alluded above, is a startling reminder. One of the earliest known cases of mistaken identity of a speaker is the trial of William Hulet, who was accused of having executed King Charles I.[43] Once the monarchy was restored under Charles II, one of its first orders of business was to prosecute for treason those involved in the regicide. The evidence against Hulet consisted almost entirely of rumor and innuendo, much of which would be excluded as hearsay today. Especially probative was testimony by Richard Gittens, who not only was a witness to the execution, but belonged to the same regiment as Hulet did at the time. Gittens testified that he heard the executioner beg the king's forgiveness, and that he knew that it was Hulet "by his speech."[44] Cross-examined later by Hulet himself, who asked him how Gittens knew that he (Hulet) had been on the scaffold at the time, Gittens replied, "By your voice."[45] After deliberating for longer than usual, the jury found Hulet guilty of high treason,[46] the punishment for which was a gruesome death. What is interesting about this case is a footnote inserted by the editors. They report that the actual perpetrator was the ordinary hangman, who later confessed, and that the court, "being sensitive of the injury done to [Hulet], procured his reprieve."[47]

Today it is possible to list a number of factors that make voice identification easier or harder. Much of the relevant research has been conducted in Europe, Canada, and Australia, and has thus been less accessible to the American legal community.[48] These studies have found that familiarity with a voice, knowing in advance that one will later have to identify a voice, length of exposure, the language being spoken, foreign accents, and length of the delay in performing the identification are among the factors that play significant roles in the ability to identify voices. Most of these factors are completely absent from any discussion in the case law. In contrast, a witness's confidence in the accuracy of the identification, which courts sometimes consider relevant, does not correlate substantially with correctness of identification. In this section, we look at empirical data that tease out many of these factors.

Familiarity

Just about everyone would assume that people are better at identifying familiar voices than unfamiliar ones. The assumption is largely correct, yet questions remain. How much difference does familiarity make? Does it matter *how* familiar the voice is? What is the rate of error despite familiarity?

Some of these issues have recently been studied by Daniel Yarmey and a group of his colleagues.[49] In one study, sixty-eight people who agreed to participate as "speakers" each recorded a sixty-four-word passage, and then two minutes of spontaneous speech. The speakers were asked for the names of friends and associates who might participate in a subsequent voice identification study. With respect to each friend or associate, the speakers also identified themselves as being a "high" familiar speaker, a "moderate" familiar speaker, or a "low" familiar speaker. The speakers were asked not to discuss the experiment with any of the people that they named.

For each listener, the experimenters were able to select at least one speaker who was a high familiar speaker, one who was a moderate familiar speaker, and one who was a low familiar speaker. The listeners were then presented with passages from four different voices: three that varied with degree of familiarity, and also an entirely unfamiliar voice. Listeners were asked to say who the speaker was, if they could, as soon as they recognized the voice. They then listened to the rest of the passage and were permitted to change their minds if they thought they had initially made a mistake. Some of the results of this study are summarized in table 7.1.

As expected, familiarity does matter. We are pretty good at recognizing the voices of people we know well, not as good at identifying the voices of people we know casually, and even worse at acknowledging that we don't know a voice at all. In addition, many of the errors are "false alarms," where identifiers say they recognize a voice as belonging to a particular speaker, but are wrong.

The Yarmey study is not unique in this finding. Earlier work by Harry Hollien and his colleagues had reached a similar conclusion. They presented subjects with recordings of familiar and unfamiliar voices, and then

Table 7.1. Accuracy (percent) for Identifying Voices of Varying Familiarity

Familiarity	Correct Response Rate	False Alarm Rate
High	89	6
Moderate	75	12
Low	66	20
Unfamiliar	61	36

Source: A. Daniel Yarmey et al., *Commonsense Beliefs and the Identification of Familiar Voices*, 15 Applied Cognitive Psychology 283 (2001).

immediately tested them by asking whether a series of voices matched the one they had heard. The study found that when a normal tone of voice was used in the recording (as opposed to a stressed or disguised voice), subjects identified familiar voices with 98 percent accuracy, whereas accuracy dropped to only around 40 percent with unfamiliar voices, even with almost no lapse in time between the initial exposure and the identification.[50]

These results confirm our intuitions that people are generally good at recognizing familiar voices. Yet they show remarkably high rates of error in identifying unfamiliar voices. Contrary to what most people would expect, fewer than half of the subjects were able to identify a previously unfamiliar voice they had heard only a brief time before. Thus, the presumption made by many courts that a policeman who briefly hears a voice once can later identify it on tape seems questionable, and it becomes more questionable as the number of potential target voices increases.

Amount of Exposure

As we have seen, when a voice is unfamiliar, people have greater trouble identifying it later. This is a significant issue in the forensic setting. Whether we are concerned about a rape victim identifying the voice of her attacker or a police officer identifying the voice of the defendant as the one on the tape, the legal system routinely deals with situations in which the witness is asked to identify a previously unfamiliar voice to which she had only a brief exposure. No doubt this is why researchers have focused their attention on this issue.

In another set of experiments performed by Professor Yarmey,[51] subjects participated in a telephone conversation with the experimenter. The length of the conversation was short (average 3.2 minutes), medium (average 4.3 minutes), or long (average 7.8 minutes). Subjects then received a second phone call and were asked if they could identify the voice they heard in the first call out of a lineup of six voices presented in the second call. Half the subjects heard a lineup that did not contain the first voice at all. The other half heard a lineup that did contain the first voice. Some of the subjects received this second call immediately after the first one (immediate test), some received it two hours later (two-hour delay) and others received it two or three days later (two/three-day delay).

For subjects receiving a lineup that actually contained the target voice, 24 percent who had a short original conversation identified it, while 48 percent who had a long conversation identified it. In addition, the rate of false alarms went up among those receiving a lineup containing the target voice when the initial exposure to the voice was longer (14 percent vs. 35 percent), and was even higher (48 percent, 51 percent, and 44 percent) for all three lengths of exposure when the target was not present. It would appear that individuals asked to participate in a voice identification procedure seem predisposed to identifying someone, even if that means making a mistake.

Other researchers have found that the *number* of initial exposures to a voice (not just the *length*) is of critical importance. Kenneth Deffenbacher and his colleagues[52] report a study in which one group of listeners heard a sixty-second passage to which they were told to pay close attention. When asked to identify that voice two weeks later out of a voice lineup containing nine voices, they were correct 29 percent of the time, made false alarms 14 percent of the time, and the rest of the time didn't know. A second group of subjects heard the same sixty seconds of speech, but it was divided into fifteen- to twenty-second segments and presented to them over the course of three consecutive days. Their hit rate was a perfect 100 percent. The researchers concluded that a witness who hears sixty seconds of speech on one occasion is less likely to later recognize the suspect's voice than someone who hears fifteen- to twenty-second segments on three or four separate occasions.[53]

Interestingly, when subjects heard a passage only half as long, even the three-day distribution did not rescue them from poor performance. Apparently, exposure for thirty seconds is not enough to support recollection two weeks later, whether the passage is heard in its entirely or in separate segments.

The research thus shows that both the number and the frequency of exposures are significant in identifying a previously unfamiliar voice. Consistent with our intuitions, a longer initial exposure will lead to a more reliable identification later. Less intuitively obvious is the finding that frequency of exposure is also relevant, perhaps even more than is duration. As we have seen, the law takes little account of such results. Bruno Hauptmann was convicted of murdering the Lindbergh baby based largely on Lindbergh's being exposed to the speech of the perpetrator for perhaps two or three seconds. Even today, courts sometimes allow an identification of an unfamiliar voice based on a very brief exposure, including in one case the utterance of the single word "Yes."[54]

Delay

We all know that memory deteriorates over time, but research shows that it doesn't happen linearly. It seems that we remember voices quite well for some period of time, perhaps as long as a few weeks, and then our memories fade significantly.

A simple, but elegant, experiment was published in 1937 by Frances McGehee.[55] The experiment, inspired by the Hauptmann trial, aimed to determine how well people can identify unfamiliar voices after extended periods of time. In the study, students listened to a person reading a fifty-six-word passage from behind a screen. The students were asked at various subsequent times whether they recognized any of five voices presented to them at the testing session. The results are presented in table 7.2. In a follow-up study conducted under somewhat different conditions, McGehee found that performance deteriorated to 48 percent after a two-week delay, but stayed more or less steady after that.[56]

Similarly, Deffenbacher and colleagues found significant decay in recollection after two weeks, especially when the listener had only a single initial exposure to the voice. They concluded that "[i]f the initial memory strength of the voice trace is weakly enough established, then, voice identification accuracy will not be very impressive even at delay intervals briefer than those possible in forensic situations."[57]

While the numbers differ somewhat from one study to another, perhaps depending on the length and frequency of the initial exposures, the overall picture is fairly clear. In identifying unfamiliar voices, we perform much better if asked to do so immediately after hearing the voice. If there is a delay beyond that, our memories seem to remain fairly stable for a few weeks, after which performance drops off significantly. Moreover, at least after a rather brief initial period, the amount of exposure to the voice interacts with the length of the delay.

Table 7.2. Effect of Delay on Accuracy of Identification

Delay	Correct Responses (percent)
1 day	83
2 days	83
3 days	81
7 days	81
2 weeks	69
3 weeks	51
3 months	35
5 months	13

Source: Frances McGehee, The Reliability of the Identification of the Human Voice, 17 Journal of General Psychology 249 (1937).

Once again, we have seen little indication that courts making evidentiary rulings take these findings into account, or that jurors do so in evaluating evidence that has been admitted. The twenty-nine-month delay in the Hauptmann case might still be acceptable today in some courts. This is not to say that judges do not consider the issue of time lapse; in fact, they almost always mention it. But they greatly underestimate the extent to which memory for voices decays over time. Consider the New York case in which a court allowed a policeman to identify a voice on tape after a time lapse of fifteen months,[58] or the *Knox* case, where the delay was around three years.[59] We are not claiming that it is impossible to remember a voice for that period of time, but we do believe that the legal system should take this cognitive frailty into account far more than it presently does.

Emotional State and Tone of Voice

Many criminal trials in which voice identification plays a role concern crimes that happen suddenly. This is especially true of violent crimes, such as rape, burglary, and robbery. The victim or other witness may not have seen the perpetrator, but is later asked if she can identify his voice. One question relevant to many of these cases is whether the stress of the experience heightens one's perceptiveness, making it easier to identify a voice later, or whether stress has the opposite affect. Research on this issue concerning eyewitness identification shows that stress makes us worse at identifying faces, despite our intuitions to the contrary.[60] Does the same hold true for the identification of people by their voices?

In an interesting study, Howard Saslove and Daniel Yarmey had 120 experimental subjects engage in what they were told was an experiment on clairvoyance.[61] While an experimenter was conversing with a subject, an angry, hostile voice was heard from a tape recorder in the next room, for about twelve seconds. The experimental subjects were subsequently asked to pick the voice out of a voice lineup of five speakers. All five speakers uttered the same words as the original angry voice. For half of the subjects, the target voice used the same hostile tone. For the other half, she used a calm voice. The results were dramatic. Eighty-five percent of the subjects who heard the angry voice again were able to identify it, but only 22 percent of those hearing the same voice in a calm tone could do so. Warning some subjects in advance that they would be asked to recognize the voice made a difference, suggesting that people who witness crimes but don't focus on the fact that they may have to identify a voice later are at a disadvantage if asked to do so.

The Saslove and Yarmey experiment also suggests that certain voice qualities vary with the emotional state of the speaker. Research shows this to be the case. For instance, our voices' *fundamental frequency,* which relates largely to pitch, increases when we speak under stress.[62] Unfortunately, such changes are not always predictable, which means that to the extent that emotional states like stress lead to changes in voice quality, they complicate the process of voice identification.[63]

Because perpetrators of a crime are likely to be excited or angry, and the victims under stress, these results suggest that voice identification in these circumstances may be difficult. Yet that is precisely the condition, as Saslove and Yarmey state, that "might be considered most similar to the legal setting."[64] It is not at all clear that courts are aware of these findings. One case where it made a difference was *State v. Johnson,* [65] where a man was very calm and soft-spoken while raping a woman. When later exposed to his voice through an open door at the police station, where he was speaking in an angry and abusive tone, the victim could not positively identify him. After he calmed down and spoke more normally, however, she claimed to recognize his voice immediately.

The Problem of Disguise

Even more troublesome for voice identification are attempts by the speaker to disguise his voice or imitate the voice of someone else. The easiest way to disguise a voice is to whisper. Many of the acoustic features that permit us to identify a speaker (like voicing) are absent when people whisper. Thus, the distinction between voiced consonants (like *z*) and corresponding voiceless ones (like *s*) largely disappears when a person whispers. As a result, the words "zap" and "sap" are difficult to distinguish when whispered.

Yarmey and colleagues, in the same set of studies discussed earlier in connection with familiarity, had speakers record a speech sample in a whisper. Recall that the experiments compared people's ability to identify voices based on their familiarity with the speaker. When the passage was whispered, highly familiar voices were identified correctly 77 percent of the time (vs. 89 percent in a normal tone), moderately familiar voices 35 percent (vs. 75 percent), voices with low familiarity 22 percent (vs. 66 percent), and unfamiliar voices were acknowledged as such 20 percent of the time (vs. 61 percent). False alarm rates were also significantly higher. In short, when a speaker wishes to mask his voice by whispering, he has a good chance of succeeding, especially if he is not a very close friend or family member.

of the hearer, and even then he might succeed. Perhaps more disturbing is that independent panelists, when asked how often listeners were likely to be correct in identifying whispered voices, wildly overestimated their capacity to do so, guessing 91 percent for highly familiar voices, down to 74 percent for unfamiliar ones.[66] If jurors have similar misconceptions about our ability to identify whisperers, it is not good news for an innocent defendant accused of having whispered an incriminating or illegal statement.

Studies have reached similar conclusions regarding other types of phonetic disguises. Harry Hollien and his colleagues instructed speakers to mask their voices however they wished. Experimental subjects were able to identify disguised familiar voices 79 percent of the time, but could do no better than 20 percent with disguised unfamiliar voices.[67] And Brazilian kidnappers have been reported to place a pencil between their front teeth, under the tongue, to disguise their voices while making ransom demands. This leads to complex phonetic changes in speech that make the speaker significantly more difficult to identify.[68]

Imitation is an especially pernicious form of disguise. People who are good at imitating the voices of others have the power to cast suspicion on the innocent. How good are people at detecting imitators? A study conducted in Sweden examined how well people could identify in a voice lineup the voice of Carl Bildt, the former Swedish prime minister, which was well known to the study's subjects. In one set of conditions, Bildt's voice was present in the lineup along with that of a skilled impressionist, who imitated Bildt's voice. Happily, subjects almost always knew the real Bildt. But when Bildt's voice was not among the choices, almost all subjects mistook the impersonator's voice for Bildt's.[69] These results suggest that a good imitation can fool people, especially when the actual voice is not present for comparison.

The emerging field of forensic phonetics is making progress in characterizing various ways in which people can mask their voices, but it has yet to produce a systematic approach to the problem.[70] Researchers have begun to determine what features of a speaker's normal voice are likely to remain the same even when he tries to disguise it.[71] Yet disguise remains a problem, both for lay and expert identification of voices.

Other Linguistic Variables

Variation in Talent Some people seem to be born musicians. They can hear a tune once and sing it exactly on key. Others are virtually tone deaf. Do we vary similarly in our ability to identify voices? The research is clear: some people are quite adept at identifying speakers from their voices, whereas others are terrible at it.[72] This should not be surprising. We know from both personal experience and from experimental testing that people differ enormously in their abilities to recognize faces.[73] Why should voice recognition be different? The legal system does not recognize such differences in skill. The rules of evidence certainly do not, and we have never seen a published opinion in which this issue was raised.

Accents and Knowledge of Language   Research has shown that eyewitnesses are generally better at identifying someone of the same race.[74] Are people similarly better at identifying speakers of their own language? In one experiment, Olaf Köster and Niels Schiller investigated how well native speakers of Spanish and Chinese can identify a German speaker by his voice. The experimenters contrasted subjects who knew German as a second language with those who knew no German at all.

Subjects were presented with a five-minute sample of a native speaker of German speaking in that language. They were then asked to identify the speaker from a voice lineup consisting of six native speakers of German. The results show that Spanish speakers who know some German performed significantly better than Spanish speakers who do not know German. The same result held for the Chinese speakers. These findings suggest that results of voice lineups involving speech samples in a language that the witness does not understand should, as the authors note, "be handled with caution."[75] Other studies have come to similar conclusions, while providing some further details.[76]

The fact that it is significantly more difficult to identify someone speaking an unknown language reveals that the term "voice identification" is actually a misnomer. If the task were simply to identify a voice, it would logically make no difference at all whether we understand the language. In fact, it does matter. The reason is that the ultimate task is to identify the *speaker*. The quality of the speaker's voice may be an important clue in this endeavor, but it is not the only one. We also use other linguistic variables that depend on our ability to understand what is said and how it is said. Hollien, for example, lists a number of speech characteristics that listeners use to identify the speaker, including dialect, unusual use of linguistic stress or affect, idiosyncratic language patterns, speech impediments, and idiosyncratic pronunciations.[77]

The effect of general speech characteristics on voice identification has not been extensively studied.[78] Fortunately, some judges seem to have an intuitive notion that foreign accents may present a problem, and have sometimes required expert testimony if a witness is to identify a voice by its accent.[79] Others seem to consider it largely irrelevant that a speaker was speaking Spanish on one occasion and English on another.[80]

Witness Confidence

Among the criteria for predicting reliability that the Supreme Court endorsed in *Biggers* is "the level of certainty demonstrated by the witness at the confrontation."[81] Research shows that jurors, like judges, take statements of confidence seriously. Research also indicates, however, that there is at best a limited relationship between the likelihood of accuracy and the degree of confidence that the witness has in the identification. If people react positively to the confidence of the identifier, and confidence fails to predict accuracy, then we might expect people to overestimate the likelihood that an identification will be accurate. That is just what seems to happen.

Several researchers have studied the relationship between accuracy and confidence in connection with speaker identification. For the most part, the research indicates little positive correlation. Deffenbacher and colleagues, who set out to study the significance of the factors suggested in *Biggers,* conclude from their studies that the Supreme Court was probably wrong on this point. "The safest generalization to make is that earwitness as well as eyewitness confidence are not very reliable indices of identification accuracy."[82] Yarmey's review of the literature led him to reach the same conclusion.[83]

Moreover, jurors are likely to be swayed by confidence levels. A recent study by Amy Bradfield and Gary Wells shows that people pay a great deal of attention to how confident a witness is in his identification in deciding how much weight to give it.[84] This bias can lead to insufficient skepticism on the part of jurors whose job it is to assess the reliability of a witness's identification.

Finally, people seem to have an inflated sense of their ability to identify voices. Yarmey and his colleagues asked a group of experimental subjects to estimate how successful listeners would be at identifying voices from each of the four levels of familiarity. For every level of familiarity, the subjects assumed that identifiers would be more accurate than they actually are.[85] This gap between perception and reality suggests that jurors may be predisposed to giving too much weight to identification by voice.

These results have serious ramifications. Although jury instructions do not use numerical certainty thresholds, people within the judicial system, when asked, estimate that proof beyond a reasonable doubt requires about a 90 percent level of certainty.[86] Disturbingly, Yarmey and his colleagues found that participants in their study generally believed that earwitness speaker identification is correct under most circumstances about 90 percent of the time, whereas in reality, it is significantly less reliable, especially when we are not very familiar with the voice being identified. The legal system's failure to correct this overestimation may, in cases relying heavily on earwitness testimony, result in jurors wrongly concluding that the government has met its burden of proof beyond a reasonable doubt even when the evidence is actually quite uncertain.

Taken together, these facts tell a disturbing story. People rely on an identifier's level of confidence in judging how accurate the identification is likely to be. But that level of confidence correlates only weakly with the likelihood of accuracy. The result is that people tend to place too much credence in an identification. This situation cries out for judicial safeguards, to which we return in the conclusion to this chapter.

Expert Speaker Identification

When the issue is the admission of a tape-recorded voice, someone must determine whether the defendant's voice matches the voice on a tape. We have seen that in the typical case a witness, usually a police officer, is called to identify the voice as the defendant's. The question we ask here is whether training in voice identification, or phonetics in general, is helpful in this task.[87] The question of expert testimony arises in two situations. The first is when phonetic experts are offered to make aural identifications by ear only. The second relates to the reliability of spectrographic analysis (or voiceprints) to identify voices on tape.

Aural Identification by Experts

The question of whether the voice on a tape recording is the defendant's arises in many drug and organized crime cases. As we have seen, some people are better at making this comparison than are others. Here we ask whether linguistic experts specializing in phonetics are typically better than lay people at aural identification. The answer seems to be yes.

Harry Hollien and Reva Schwartz tested people's abilities to identify voices by comparing contemporary samples with noncontemporary ones. All samples were on tape. There were three groups of subjects: people with no background in phonetics, students with some background in phonetics, and experienced phoneticians. The results, presented in table 7.3, suggest

Table 7.3. Effect of Expertise on Voice Identification Skill

Length of Delay	Lay Subjects (%)	Phoneticians (%)	Students (%)
4 weeks	74	89	76
20 years	32	74	33

Source: Harry Hollien and Reva Schwartz, *Aural-Perceptual Speaker Identification: Problems with Noncontemporary Samples,* 7 Forensic Linguistics 199 (2000).

that training in phonetics increases performance on identification tasks, especially after a long delay.

In another study, Niels Schiller and Olaf Köster tested seventeen college students and ten experts in phonetics on their ability to identify voices under ideal experimental conditions. Both expert and lay subjects did very well on this test. Still, the experts performed significantly better (98 percent hits, 1 percent false alarms) than the lay subjects (92 percent hits, 2 percent false alarms). The differences may not look dramatic, but the reduced error rate would certainly be important in a trial setting.[88] These studies suggest that the use of experts may improve the accuracy of voice identification under certain forensic circumstances.[89] Significantly, they highlight the fact that phonetics is an independent field of scientific research, which takes seriously the need to investigate its own strengths and limitations, distinguishing it from other areas of forensic identification, such as handwriting analysis and microscopic hair analysis, which have received substantial criticism in the legal literature for failing to test the reliability of their conclusions.[90]

These results do not mean that the system should *require* expert identification of voices on tapes. But they do suggest that the courts should be receptive to such experts, especially when the admission of the tape into evidence is based on little exposure to the voice, as is sometimes the case when a police officer identifies a voice on a tape based on a brief encounter with the defendant at a much earlier date. Expert phoneticians may also be appropriate when a police officer or other witness becomes familiar with a voice specifically in order to become eligible as an authenticating witness.[91]

Consider *United States v. Drones,*[92] in which the Fifth Circuit reversed the district court's grant of the defendant's petition for habeas corpus based on ineffective assistance of counsel. The case against Drones, who was convicted of various drug crimes in a Texas state court, depended heavily on a police officer's identification of his voice on a tape. His attorney, however, had done nothing to challenge the identification. Later, after new counsel was retained, witnesses who knew Drones listened to the tape and concluded that it was not his voice. In addition, an expert on voice identification opined from both aural and spectrographic analysis that the voice on the tape was not that of Drones. The government also had an expert who debunked spectrographic analysis, but agreed that the voice on the tape did not sound like the defendant's.[93]

The Fifth Circuit held that Drones's first lawyer did not act irresponsibly in not pursuing the lay testimony, which may have opened up other questions about the defendant's background. It also held that it was not irresponsible for that lawyer not to pursue spectrographic comparison of Drones's voice with that on the tape, since courts have not been receptive to such analysis in recent years. But the court never said why the defendant's lawyer should not have had an expert study both the tape and examples of the defendant's voice, and offer his opinion based on aural analysis. At the very least, an expert could have pointed out to the jury ways in which particular sounds differed from one sample to the other, and left it to them to agree or disagree. The case is especially compelling because the government's own expert shared the defense expert's opinion, and because the standards for admitting the original identification were so relaxed.

In fact, as we will see, courts have sometimes permitted expert phoneticians to present opinion testimony on the identity of a voice on tape. Their expertise is parallel to that of other experts who are permitted to assist the jury on questions of identification. For example, expert witnesses are permitted to interpret surveillance photos to point out similarities between the facial features of the defendant and the individual in the surveillance photo.[94] In one case, it was held to be reversible error not to permit the defendant to offer such testimony to the jury.[95] While these experts are not always permitted to offer opinions as to identity, they are routinely allowed to share with the jury detailed observations regarding facial shape and measurement.

At the very least, phoneticians should be permitted to point out similarities and differences between the defendant's voice and that of the person on a tape in order to make them salient to the jury. To the extent that such analysis can be enhanced by comparison of the relevant features of spectrograms, we see no reason why the experts should not be permitted to use that information as well. For example, to enhance her testimony based on aural comparison of two voices, a phonetician may want to show a jury how one speaker's [a] sound routinely appears in one area of the spectrogram, while the [a] sound on the tape that is in evidence appears elsewhere. Most phoneticians use both types of information.[96] This use of acoustic information is quite different from that used by so-called voiceprint experts, whose claims have been a matter of controversy for several decades, an issue to which we now turn.

Spectrographic Evidence

DNA evidence has become an important forensic tool, both for law enforcement agencies and for those who have been wrongly accused. A technology able to compare voices with such accuracy would obviously be a welcome addition to the system of criminal justice. For a time, at least, there was hope that "voiceprints" could play that role. Voiceprints, or technically *sound spectrograms,* are visual representations of the frequencies and amplitude of sounds as represented on a time line. In the forensic setting, spectrographic analysis involves visual comparison of the spectrogram of the questioned voice with one from a known voice, typically the voice of the defendant in a criminal trial. Most of those who conduct this kind of analysis are not phoneticians, but are rather police officers and technicians who have been trained for this task, and who typically have limited backgrounds in acoustics or phonetics. The main issue is whether the methodology produces sufficiently reliable results.

The early history of the debate surrounding spectrographic analysis is both legally significant and interesting in its own right. Sound spectrography was developed in the 1940s by Bell Laboratories for teaching deaf people how to speak,[97] and was quickly pursued for use in military operations during World War II.[98] Then, in 1962, Lawrence G. Kersta of Bell Labs published an article in *Nature* in which he made some extravagant claims about the ability to identify speakers by their voiceprints.[99] He likened the technology to fingerprints, asserting that an individual's voice is similarly unique and identifiable through visual inspection of his voiceprint. The scientific community responded skeptically. For example, the Committee on Speech Communication of the Acoustical Society of America had the following reaction:

> We conclude that the available results are inadequate to establish the reliability of voice identification by spectrograms. . . . Procedures exist, as we have suggested, by which the reliability of voice identification methods can be evaluated. We believe that such validation is urgently needed.[100]

Prominent phoneticians, including Peter Ladefoged of UCLA, went on record as opposing the use of spectrography in the courtroom because it had been inadequately tested.[101]

During the late 1960s and early 1970s, U.S. jurisdictions were divided on the issue of spectrographic evidence. Some courts rejected the methodology as not widely enough accepted within the scientific community.[102] Typically, these jurisdictions applied the *Frye* test, which stated that for expert opinion testimony to be admitted, "the thing from which the deduction is made must be sufficiently established to have gained general acceptance in the particular field in which it belongs."[103] Other appellate courts reached the opposite conclusion, holding that it was within the discretion of the trial judge to admit the testimony because the technology showed indications of being sufficiently reliable.[104]

At this same time, Oscar Tosi, a Michigan State University professor, published studies that purportedly demonstrated great accuracy in the identification of speakers by visual inspection of voiceprints.[105] Tosi's design overcame the most serious problems of Kersta's study, which had used a closed set of possible voices and contemporaneous recording under laboratory conditions. Tosi's study, in contrast, compared noncontemporaneous recordings in both fixed and random contexts, an approach more in tune with forensic settings. Tosi's results were impressive. There were approximately 6 percent false alarm errors and 13 percent false elimination errors.[106] He conjectured that the error rate could be reduced further if the examiner is permitted to answer "I don't know" if he did not reach a high level of certainty.

The Tosi study led Ladefoged to moderate his opposition to the use of voiceprints, though he was still not prepared to offer a ringing endorsement. Ladefoged expressed his position in a 1971 letter to the President's Science Advisor.[107] There he expressed concern that the Tosi study did not deal with the problem of people in the same community, say a gang of high school dropouts, who might have very similar speaking styles and mutually confusable voices. He also expressed concern about the lack of standards governing voiceprint experts and their work. In an introductory text to phonetics dating from that same period, Ladefoged explained that it was his "best guess" that experts using spectrograms were wrong in about one case out of twenty, which meant that it was a useful but limited law enforcement tool. Ladefoged went on to characterize as "completely irresponsible" the assertions of witnesses in court that "[t]he voice on the recording is that of the accused and could be that of no other speaker."[108]

While the scholarly community gave the Tosi study mixed reviews, it was compelling enough to convince some courts that voiceprint analysis was sufficiently valid for courtroom purposes. The federal and state law reports contain a number of cases in which voiceprint analysts were permitted

to testify over the objection of the opposing party, typically for the prosecution in criminal trials.[109] Other courts continued to reject spectrographic
evidence. The standard for admissibility under *Frye* was whether a procedure or methodology had been accepted in the scientific community, and
the debate under *Frye* often centered around the question "Whose community?" In Tosi's community of supporters, voiceprint analysis was widely
accepted. In the broader community of acoustic phoneticians, it was not.
This difference explains, at least in part, the divergent court rulings.

Then, in 1975, the Federal Rules of Evidence were adopted. Its standard
for admissibility of expert testimony was that the expert "will assist the
trier of fact."[110] This standard would seem to leave more opportunity for a
court to admit spectrographic analysis through experts. In 1979, however,
an influential report by the National Research Council, usually referred to as
the "Bolt Report," questioned the ability of voiceprints to produce accurate
results under forensic conditions with sufficiently low rates of error.[111] The
report summarized its findings in the introduction:

> The Committee concludes that the technical uncertainties concerning the
> present practice of voice identification are so great as to require that forensic
> applications be approached with great caution. The Committee takes no position
> for or against the forensic use of the aural-visual method of voice identification,
> but recommends that if it is used in testimony, then the limitations of the
> method should be clearly and thoroughly explained to the fact finder, whether
> judge or jury.[112]

The Committee later explained:

> The degree of accuracy, and the corresponding error rates, of aural-visual voice
> identification vary widely from case to case, depending upon several conditions
> including the properties of the voices involved, the conditions under which the
> voice samples were made, the characteristics of the equipment used, the skill
> of the examiner making the judgments, and the examiner's knowledge about
> the case. Estimates of error rates now available pertain to only a few of the
> many combinations of conditions in real-life situations. These estimates do not
> constitute a generally adequate basis for a judicial or legislative body to use in
> making judgments concerning the reliability and acceptability of aural-visual
> voice identification in forensic situations.[113]

It is important to note that the committee did not dispute Tosi's findings. In fact, Tosi was on the committee. Rather, the report complained

that findings supporting the use of voiceprints are too limited. They fail to consider important real-life variables that would be necessary to draw valid conclusions about forensic use of voiceprints.

Subsequently, Peter Ladefoged reached similar conclusions. A Hawaii court quoted him as making the following points in 1985:

> Dr. Ladefoged proposes the following safeguards: (1) two plus minutes of each speech sample; (2) a signal to noise ratio where the signal is higher by 20 decibels; (3) a frequency of 3,000 hertz or better; (4) an exemplar in the same words, the same rate, in the same way, spoken naturally and fluently; and (5) a responsible examiner. Dr. Ladefoged believes there is general acceptance given his safeguards, and "he believes there is now more agreement."[114]

Rarely will all these safeguards be met, which on this standard would make visual voiceprint analysis of limited evidentiary value. For this reason, some linguists continue to express serious doubts about the reliability of this technology in a forensic setting. Indeed, one phonetician has called it "a fraud being perpetrated upon the American public and the Courts of the United States."[115]

Throughout the 1980s and early 1990s the published opinions, albeit in smaller numbers overall than before, continued to be split on the issue. Decisions to admit voiceprint evidence were reached during that period by the U.S. Courts of Appeals for the Sixth and Seventh Circuits, a federal district court in Hawaii, the supreme courts of Ohio, Maine, and Rhode Island, and a lower court in New York. But during roughly the same time, voiceprints were held inadmissible by the high courts of Arizona, Colorado, Indiana, Louisiana, and New Jersey.[116] Clearly, the courts are seriously divided.

This disagreement has not abated, despite significant legal developments over the past decade. In 1993, the U.S. Supreme Court clarified the standard for admissibility of expert testimony in federal courts when it decided *Daubert v. Merrell Dow Pharmaceuticals, Inc.*[117] *Daubert* prompted courts to focus on their gatekeeping function in screening out expert testimony not determined to be scientifically valid. No federal court has ruled on the admissibility of voiceprints since *Daubert*. However, one state court, the Alaska Supreme Court, ruled voiceprint testimony admissible under *Daubert* in 1999, while the U.S. Court of Appeals for the Fifth Circuit expressed a great deal of skepticism about the technology in 2000. It is instructive to compare the two cases.

As the Alaskan court noted in *State v. Coon,*[118] some published reports support the use of voiceprints in court. Because the approach of the Federal

Rules, under which *Daubert* was decided, is to deal with controversy by presenting both sides of an argument (rather than by excluding evidence altogether), the court placed as much or more emphasis on studies sponsored by police officials that advocate for the use of voiceprints as it did on publications from the independent scientific community.[119]

Compare *Coon* to *United States v. Drones*,[120] the Fifth Circuit habeas corpus case discussed earlier in connection with expert testimony of aural voice comparison. In that case, a defendant convicted of drug offenses in Texas argued that his lawyer had not effectively represented him at trial because he failed to hire a forensic phonetician to compare the voice on a tape to his voice. In support of his motion, Drones enlisted the help of an expert named Steve Cain, the voiceprint expert whose testimony was allowed by the Alaska Supreme Court in *Coon*.[121] Cain "reached a finding of 'probable elimination,' meaning that at least 80 percent of the comparable words in the samples were dissimilar aurally and spectrographically."[122] In response, the government called Bruce Koenig, a former FBI employee, who had been one of the early developers of sound spectrography. Koenig testified that "almost nobody" in the relevant scientific community uses spectrographic voice identification because there is no theoretical basis for the proposition that an individual's voice is truly unique and identifiable.[123]

In reversing the lower court's granting of the habeas corpus petition, the appellate court characterized spectrography as "a dwindling science," not widely accepted in the scientific community. It quoted Koenig's testimony to the effect that the number of practitioners of forensic voiceprint analysis had dwindled from about fifty or sixty to roughly a dozen, as a result of judicial scepticism of the methodology's scientific basis.[124]

While the court in *Drones* mentioned the Alaskan decision in *Coon*, it left out the most significant irony: the scientific evidence upon which the court permitted Cain to testify in Alaska was a 1986 article that Koenig had published in the *FBI Crime Lab Digest*.[125] In fact, a close reading of Koenig's article suggests that the Alaska court misstated Koenig's position. In the article, Koenig indeed said that the rate of error in the FBI's use of voiceprints was extraordinarily low (0.31 percent for false identifications and 0.53 percent for false eliminations). However, he also said that "meaningful decisions were only made in 34.8 percent of the requested comparisons."[126] Koenig concluded:

> Spectrographic voice comparison is a relatively accurate, but not positive technique for comparing an unknown voice sample with known verbatim voice exemplars. Present use of the technique is limited to a relatively small number

of examiners who confront legal barriers to acceptance, limitations in accuracy and no universally recognized examiner qualifications and examination criteria. Its forensic future may shift to testimony where the judge and jury are advised of the technique's probable accuracy or to nontestimonial use as an investigative aid for law enforcement.[127]

It now appears that just about everyone has jumped ship. Voiceprint analysis can be reliable in a limited number of cases, but the scientific community has not adequately established criteria that define those cases in advance. And the underlying philosophical question—whether each individual's voice(print) is indeed unique—has never been answered.

It is true, of course, that voiceprint analysis may well be as reliable—perhaps even more reliable—than lay witness identification of voices on tape, the limitations of which we discussed earlier. Voiceprints might appear useful to bolster an unconvincing aural identification or to counter such an identification. The problem with admitting such evidence is that scientific (or quasi-scientific) jargon and data tend to have a strong impact on the jury. In this sense voiceprint analysis is not unlike the use of lie detectors. Whatever usefulness they might have is generally outweighed by the misleading impression of infallibility that they convey.

Consequently, we do not currently advocate the use of voiceprint analysis to identify speakers, although we do not object to phoneticians using acoustic information to enhance aural comparison of voices. Forensic phonetics is a vibrant and productive field that has much to contribute to law enforcement and the judicial process. But, as most of the phonetics community recognizes, voiceprint evidence alone, in which speakers are identified by looking at pictures of their voice signals, is presently too unreliable to allow an individual's freedom to depend on it, at least if not bolstered by considerable confirming evidence.

We expect in the near future to see improved technology in this area, including the introduction of forensic applications of automatic voice recognition devices currently being developed for academic, commercial, and military purposes.[128] A recent article by a group of researchers from North Carolina reports promising preliminary results using a computer to generate probability functions based on ten acoustic features.[129] A. P. A. Broeders, a Dutch researcher, reports a growing use of automatic and semi-automatic voice recognition technologies by law enforcement agencies around the world.[130] Broeders cautions, however, that considerably more work must be done to make any of these technologies reliable enough to meet evidentiary standards.

Especially encouraging are the high standards that researchers in this area have imposed. The National Institute of Standards and Technology (NIST) undertakes an annual evaluation of automated speech recognition systems, with laboratories from around the world participating.[131] Both misses and false alarms are recorded for each participating group under a variety of conditions, some ideal, others more in keeping with forensic settings. Recent results are quite encouraging, although more progress is needed before these technologies can meet reasonable evidentiary standards.[132]

In the meantime, it is of crucial importance that both lay and expert identification of voices be admitted in court only with appropriate safeguards. We therefore turn now to some recommendations for improving the treatment of speaker identification in the courts.

Conclusion

The legal system could take a number of measures to address some of the problems that we have identified in this chapter. Elsewhere we have laid out these recommendations in detail; we only summarize them here.[133]

Because jurors tend to give great credence to witnesses who were at the scene, a faulty identification can lead to a wrongful conviction. It is therefore of great importance to avoid the problem of suggestive identifications in the first place. Thus, we should ensure that if a witness is to identify the perpetrator at trial, the witness's memory should not be compromised beforehand. The solution, whenever feasible, is to present the witness with not just a single voice, but with a properly constituted voice lineup, analogous to a visual lineup. Appropriate procedure governing eyewitness lineups has received a great deal of attention,[134] and many of the same considerations apply to voice lineups.[135]

With tape-recorded evidence the issue is somewhat less clear. Nonetheless, several adjustments, some in the alternative, seem appropriate. Courts should start making serious inquiries into suggestiveness when the authentication of a tape is challenged, including when the identifying witness is a police officer. Otherwise, no analysis is possible. Most of the time, no doubt, the court will find that the circumstances, taken as a whole, support admitting the tape into evidence. But at least the inquiry will be focused on the relevant issues. Alternatively, courts may wish to apply *Biggers* analysis when the defendant has raised a legitimate question about reliability or when the circumstantial evidence is weak. When there is no tape, *Biggers/Manson* must apply.

We also urge that jurors not receive transcripts of covertly recorded conversations that contain names identifying speakers, unless the issue of identity is conceded or for some other reason is incontrovertible. In fact, transcripts should not be admitted into evidence. Courts should admit only the tape recording itself and make it clear to the jury that the transcript, if provided at all, is merely an aid to understanding the tape.

Another issue is that the *Biggers* factors do not provide a sufficient basis for evaluating the reliability of voice identification. As we have seen, the research reveals that people are better at identifying the voice of someone who was previously familiar to them. Also, the number of exposures to a voice is at least as important as the length of exposure in predicting reliable recall. Changes in tone of voice are also highly significant: a speaker who is under stress or who is very emotional may speak quite differently from her normal tone of voice. Overall, the criteria that courts use to determine whether a voice identification is reliable should be updated to take this and similar research into account.

Once an identification is admitted into evidence, the question goes to the jury. Unfortunately, jurors have little idea how to determine whether a voice identification is likely to be reliable. Several jurisdictions presently provide an instruction that gives some guidance in the case of eyewitness identification.[136] In contrast, courts seldom, if ever, give an instruction on earwitness identification. In one federal case the trial judge refused to instruct the jury that the "value [of the voice identification] depends upon the opportunity the witness had to hear the offender at the time of the offense and later make a reliable identification."[137] The Seventh Circuit affirmed the refusal, holding that "[a]s long as the basic requirement of familiarity with the voice is met, lay opinion testimony is an acceptable means for establishing a speaker's identity."[138] This misses the point. The defendant did not ask that the jury be instructed to ignore the identification. Rather, the request was to advise the jurors that they should "value" the identification only to the extent that they believe it to have been reliable.

The jury's ability to make this evaluation is typically given as the justification for having such a low threshold for admissibility. Yet as we have seen, voice identification is probably even more difficult than eyewitness testimony. We see no reason for refusing to give an instruction that could help jurors more analytically decide how much weight to give an identification.[139] Where voice identification evidence has been admitted, the jury should be instructed on how to evaluate that identification.

An increasing number of courts permit expert testimony at trial on the reliability of eyewitness testimony under appropriate circumstances.[140]

Courts have also been allowing "educational experts" to point out the short-comings with other methods of identification, such as identification by handwriting experts, to demonstrate the limits of those techniques.[141] We believe that courts should do the same when it comes to earwitness identifications. In contrast to jury instructions, which tend to be quite generic, experts can explain to jurors exactly how research into voice identification is relevant to the case at hand. Such testimony has been admitted in some cases.[142] While courts should tailor such testimony to the issues raised in a particular case,[143] it should certainly not be excluded in principle.

We remain skeptical of expert testimony based solely on spectrographic analysis, or voiceprints, largely because it creates the illusion of being more reliable and accurate than it really is. Nonetheless, expert testimony can and should sometimes play a role in identifying speakers. In fact, Professor Hollien has testified in this capacity in several cases.[144] Experts tend to perform better on voice identification tasks than do nonexperts. Of course, when experts testify in such cases, they should be competent in fields like acoustics, phonetics, and linguistics, all of which are fields of serious inquiry that exist independent of the forensic setting.

So, was Bruno Hauptmann guilty of kidnapping and killing the Lindbergh baby? Did Captain Hulet chop off the king's head? We really don't know, but we do know that Guy Paul Morin was falsely convicted of raping and murdering a young child. Questions of guilt or innocence are left to the judge or jury. Yet when the evidence for guilt or innocence includes the identification of the defendant's voice, the legal system must take into account what we have learned over the past half century. Only then can we be confident that the decision made by the judge or jury is the right one.

Chapter 8

Who Wrote That?

You can't eat your cake
and have it, too.

Shakespeare was big news in his own time, and remains so today. Debate over whether he wrote a poem entitled "A Funeral Elegy" has made headlines twice in the past decade. The first time was when Donald Foster, an English professor at Vassar College, determined Shakespeare to be its author. As Foster put it in his book *Author Unknown,* "the whole planet had come to view 'Shakespeare discoveries' as a phenomenon not unlike Elvis sightings."[1] The book describes stylistic similarities between Shakespeare and the author of "A Funeral Elegy," making his conclusion seem entirely plausible.

Foster's pronouncement quickly created controversy in both the scholarly literature and the popular press. Jonathan Bate, a Shakespeare scholar in England, was skeptical of Foster's claim:

> What makes one suspicious is not that the Funeral Elegy is bad, but that it sounds like an imitation of early Shakespeare, yet it was written at the very end of Shakespeare's career—at a time when he was so popular that all sorts of works by other people were appearing with his name on the title-page in order to

boost sales. Furthermore, Foster was unable to establish any connection between Shakespeare and the family of William Peter [the person about whom the elegy is written].[2]

Other scholars suggested that the actual author was John Ford, author of "Tis Pity She's a Whore." Significantly, Ford was a friend and neighbor of the Peter family in Devon. In fact, there now seems to be agreement among literary scholars that Ford—not Shakespeare—wrote "The Funeral Elegy." In 2002, Gilles Monsarrat, a professor at the University of Burgundy, published his findings to that effect. Foster graciously acknowledged his error, again making headlines.[3]

The scholarly debate over the Shakespeare elegy may seem esoteric to many people, but it raises an important question for the criminal justice system, a question that is our topic in this chapter: How good are people, both experts and nonexperts, at identifying an author from the style of her writing? Authorship disputes occur in many kinds of cases. As this book goes to press, law enforcement officials continue to grapple with the question of who wrote the letters that accompanied the distribution of anthrax in 2001. Investigators frequently encounter issues of this sort. When a victim receives a threatening letter or when the family of a kidnapped child receives a ransom note, how can we tell who wrote it? Sometimes serial criminals leave written messages as part of their scheme. Again, how can we tell who wrote those messages? Among the cases we discuss are the Lindbergh case (once again), the Unabomber case, and the JonBenét Ramsey investigation.

Law enforcement organizations use a variety of tools and techniques in the effort to answer these questions. They create statistical models based on earlier cases and then create profiles of the prototypical bomber or kidnapper or terrorist.[4] They examine and compare the handwriting of the perpetrator with known samples of the handwriting of a suspect. And they analyze the substance of the offending documents, comparing them to known samples of a suspect's writing with respect to style, content, and allusions to personal history, among other things. When these analyses lead the police to believe that a particular individual committed the crime, there is typically other evidence available. Frequently, according to our discussions with the law enforcement community, confronting a suspect with the similarities between his earlier writings and the document involved in the present crime will result in a confession, or at least a plea bargain.

Of course, there is a danger to all this. Law enforcement agents can be mistaken about who committed the crime, despite the similarities between the suspect's style of writing and that of the perpetrator. A simple answer to this objection is that this is why we have trials. We do not have to accept the judgment of the police. But additional questions immediately come to mind. How good are jurors at drawing the right inferences from these comparisons? Are the methods currently used reliable enough to form the basis of expert opinion at trial? We look first at how the legal system has addressed these issues.

Hauptmann and the Document Examiners

It is difficult to find contemporary published cases in which stylistic evidence of authorship was admitted.[5] Evidentiary standards since *Daubert*[6] raise serious questions about whether existing methods of author attribution have reached sufficient reliability to be admissible in court. In contrast, it is relatively simple to find older cases that permitted expert stylistic comparison with little scrutiny, if any. This is largely because for a time, a group of experts called "questioned document examiners," typically handwriting experts, were routinely permitted to testify in court. Their testimony was not limited to handwriting, but included analyzing similarities in misspellings, word choice, and so on.[7] Currently, questioned document examiners define their expertise as fitting within a limited domain: "the analysis and comparison of questioned handwriting, hand printing, typewriting, commercial printing, photocopies, papers, inks, and other documentary evidence with known material in order to establish the authenticity of the contested material as well as the detection of alterations."[8]

Opinion testimony about handwriting is now under serious attack in the scholarly literature,[9] and handwriting experts have been receiving less support from the courts in light of their inability to meet *Daubert* criteria, such as the requirement that they provide known rates of error.[10] While handwriting experts still occasionally testify about spelling errors, such testimony does not seem to be the norm today, at least as far as we can glean from published opinions.[11] But before this skepticism took hold, questioned document examiners testified quite broadly.

Among the most celebrated cases in which they participated was the trial of Bruno Hauptmann for kidnapping and killing the Lindbergh baby, discussed in chapter 7. That case also included a battle over whether Hauptmann wrote a series of ransom notes. The prosecution called a host of questioned document examiners, each of whom primarily testified on the similarity between Hauptmann's handwriting and the handwriting in the notes. But they also testified about such matters as misspellings and style.[12]

For example, Eldridge Stein began his testimony by reporting his credentials as an "examiner of disputed documents, including questions of handwriting, typewriting, inks, paper, and those things that enter into the physical makeup of documents."[13] But when it came time for Stein to offer an opinion, he testified at length about similarities in spelling errors between Hauptmann's known writings and the ransom notes.[14] Only later in his testimony did he opine about handwriting.

A number of the experts in the case also mentioned punctuation. Both the ransom notes and Hauptmann's documents used the hyphen in words like *New York*. However, one of the experts, John F. Tyrrell, admitted that this spelling was not uncommon at the time among Europeans writing in English.[15] Differences between Hauptmann's writing and that in the ransom notes were sometimes attributed to failed attempts by Hauptmann to disguise his identity.[16]

In his book *The Lindbergh Case*, Jim Fisher discusses the testimony of these experts, focusing on that offered by Harry M. Cassidy, a questioned documents examiner employed by the Chesapeake and Ohio Railroad Company in Virginia. Like the other experts, Cassidy relied heavily on spelling errors that the ransom notes had in common:

> Now if this was one of those ordinary anonymous letter cases, like I handle every day or every few days down there in Virginia on the road, I wouldn't hesitate to say the same person wrote both sets of writings, I wouldn't care if they was written on the typewriter, because the same person—the possibility or probability of two people spelling all those words wrong in the same way is so improbable that I would say that it is entirely negligible. Now, that's my honest opinion and I am giving it to you; but this is a serious case here. It is too important to decide it, I would say, just on that alone. I would decide an ordinary case on the strength of those eight misspelled words, but I don't feel like I should do it in a case of this importance. So if you will just bear and be patient with me for just one more illustration, I will get to it.[17]

Cassidy then displayed two charts containing handwriting comparisons, and concluded that the ransom notes were written by Hauptmann. He stated that he had given careful consideration to all of these things, "weighed them individually and collectively, and I hoped weighed them in connection with each other. Regardless of the seriousness of this charge, I feel that I am obliged to say that the person that wrote those request writings or standard writings, or conceded writings as they call them, is the same person who wrote all those ransom notes."[18]

Among the misspellings in the ransom notes were "mony" (money), "polise" (polise), "gut" (good), "boad" (boat), and "anyding" (anything),[19] and, as gleaned from our review of the transcript, examples such as "tit" (did), "note" (not), and "affrait" (afraid).[20] On appeal, the Supreme Court of New Jersey affirmed the conviction, relying in part on the handwriting analysis and on "[t]he peculiarities of expression and spelling common to all these notes and admittedly genuine writings by Hauptmann."[21]

The question that the Supreme Court of New Jersey failed to ask, the very question that *Daubert* now mandates that courts must ask, is "How do you know?"[22] Whoever wrote the ransom notes was probably a native speaker of German, or a similar language in relevant respects. As we noted in chapter 2, in German voiced stops (*b, d,* and *g*) cannot occur phonetically at the end of a word. Instead, German speakers pronounce the written letters *b, d,* and *g* as their voiceless equivalents (*p, t,* and *k*) when they occur in word-final position. Thus, the *d* in *Bad* ("bath") is pronounced as a *t*. As a result, many German speakers have trouble with the difference between voiced and voiceless consonants at the end of English words.

Many of the misspellings in the ransom notes reflect this confusion: the word "boat" is spelled *boad,* "afraid" is written *affrait,* and "good" is rendered *gut.* But unless we know how common such misspellings were among European immigrants with similar education at that time, we can have no informed opinion as to how likely it is that those ransom notes were written by Hauptmann. All we can tell from the misspellings is that the writer is likely to be a speaker of German or another language (like Dutch) that has final devoicing.[23] Compare the chatty style of Mr. Cassidy's testimony with the statistical analysis so much a part of DNA evidence today, which often includes probability estimation. It is not hard to see why in today's more quantitatively oriented world Cassidy's testimony would be less welcome.

Leaving It to the Jury

Courts today recognize the problem that the *Hauptmann* court ignored. Experts typically do not testify about such matters as mistakes in spelling. This, however, creates an irony, as the leading case of *United States v. Clifford*[24] brings to light. Russell Clifford, former police chief of Saltsburg, Pennsylvania, was prosecuted in a federal court in Pennsylvania for mailing threatening letters to his successor. The letters were printed in block style to make handwriting comparisons difficult, if not impossible. As part of its case, the government wanted to bring to the jury's attention similarities in the spelling, abbreviation, syntax, and paragraph structure between the threatening letters and letters known to be written by Clifford. As the court described it, "Those similarities included misspellings of 'figure' as 'figuar' and 'explosives' as 'explodsives,' the inconsistent use of either circles or dots for the letter 'i,' the lack of indentation or space between paragraphs, the use of certain abbreviations such as 'Chas' for 'Charles,' and the presence of long sentences in both sets of letters."[25]

The government did not call an expert to testify as to these similarities. Instead, it wanted the jurors to be given the opportunity to make the comparison for themselves. The defense objected, claiming that jurors had no expertise in such comparisons and might not draw valid inferences. The judge held a hearing on the matter, at which the principal witness was Murray S. Miron, a professor of psycholinguistics at Syracuse University who had consulted with the FBI on this and other cases about forensic document comparison. Miron testified candidly about the limits of forensic linguistic analysis for the purpose of author identification. The court described his testimony:

> [Dr. Miron explained that] forensic linguistic analysis is the process of matching stylistic similarities in different documents and then of assigning weight to those similarities according to their distinctiveness and frequency of occurrence. He further stated that such an analysis could not provide a positive means of identifying the author of an anonymous document. He indicated that the results of forensic linguistic analysis could be probative in establishing authorship but could not prove that one person, to the exclusion of all other possible authors, had written a document.[26]

The FBI special agent assigned to the case and the FBI analyst who had written a report on the linguistic issues in the case testified similarly.

When later quizzed by the judge about the ability of jurors to draw appropriate inferences by comparing documents without the help of an expert, Miron was skeptical:

> The judge then asked Dr. Miron whether a jury, without the aid of an expert, could analyze the various similarities and "draw valid and certain conclusions beyond a reasonable doubt." Dr. Miron stated that an expert could help a jury to decide just how unusual or distinctive certain similarities are and thus how much probative weight to assign to those similarities. Dr. Miron further indicated that the jurors "might not draw the proper conclusions if not assisted in how they are to interpret the evidence."[27]

The result is in part a no-win situation. While useful to law enforcement, forensic author identification is not a precise enough science to form the basis of an expert opinion in court. But jurors are even less likely than experts to know how much to make of stylistic similarities and differences. Recognizing this fact, the trial court decided that the documents known to be authored by Clifford would not be admitted into evidence for the purpose of allowing the jury to compare their style to that of the threatening letters.

The court of appeals agreed with the trial court's decision not to permit an expert to testify.[28] In fact, the government did not even ask the court to allow their expert to offer an opinion about authorship. But the appeals court reversed on the issue of presenting Clifford's known writings to the jury. Likening this issue to that of handwriting comparison, which juries are permitted to do, the court saw "no reason . . . why jurors cannot merely examine the documents for themselves and consider the similarities between the documents along with the rest of the evidence presented by the government."[29] As the appellate court pointed out, there is a long-standing legal tradition in the United States of allowing jurors to make authorship identification decisions by looking at known and questioned documents and deciding how much weight to give to the similarities.

Addressing the problem that led the trial court to exclude the documents altogether, the appellate court suggested that the defendant can cure defects in the system through "effective rebuttal."[30] This may include pointing out the differences among the documents. However, unless that rebuttal includes testimony from an expert who can advise the jury of the pitfalls of relying too heavily on the similarities, it is not clear how effective the rebuttal can be.

The problem is that people are not adept at integrating base rate information into their reasoning. The classic demonstration of this limitation was made by psychologists Amos Tversky and Daniel Kahneman.[31] Here is the puzzle:

A cab was involved in a hit-and-run accident. Two cab companies, the green and blue, operated in the city. You are given the following data:

(a) 85% of the cabs in the city are Green and 15% are Blue.
(b) A witness identified the cab as Blue. The court tested the reliability of the witness under the same circumstances that existed on the night of the accident and concluded that the witness correctly identified each one of the two colors 80% of the time and failed 20% of the time.

What is the probability that the cab involved in the accident was Blue rather than Green?

Tversky and Kahneman found that most people say that the witness will be right about 80 percent of the time. But that is not the correct answer. The answer lies in the following table:

Says	Green	Blue
Is		
Green	68	17
Blue	3	12

Assume there are one hundred cabs, eighty-five green ones and fifteen blue ones. When the cab was really green, the witness will correctly say the cab was green sixty-eight times (80 percent of eighty-five green cabs), and he will incorrectly say that it was blue seventeen times. When the cab was really blue, he will get it right twelve times (80 percent of fifteen blue cabs), but will incorrectly say that it was green three times. That means he will be right twelve of the twenty-nine times that he says the cab was blue, which is an accuracy rate of 41 percent. Work by other psychologists confirms that people have trouble taking into account underlying base rates in making probabilistic judgments.

Returning to our lay witness, it is all too easy to note some similarities between documents and then conclude that the same person authored both of them, without recognizing that an important piece of information is missing: the frequency with which any particular stylistic peculiarity occurs. Only when the base rate problem is obvious do we notice it and account for it in our thinking. For example, since we know that everyone uses the word "the" in their writing, we would sensibly not draw inferences of co-authorship just because that word appears regularly in two documents. The solution may lie in part with permitting experts to educate jurors about this problem, but it does not lie in allowing experts to take the stand and ignore the base rate problem in their opinions.

This brings us back to the ruling in *Clifford:* forensic stylistic analysis is not admitted for the purposes of author identification, although juries are permitted to make their own comparisons without the help of experts and without any independent knowledge of relevant base rates. As we said earlier, this state of the law is unsatisfactory. Admitting expert evidence without proof of reliability should be avoided. Letting jurors decide questions of authorship without adequate basis for comparison is just as bad.

The solution, we believe, lies in improving the field of author identification so that it does become reliable. In the past few years, some very promising research, which we discuss later in this chapter, has been conducted. But first, we will describe some recent cases—including some high-profile cases—that have reopened debate on the status of expert forensic stylistic analysis as it now exists.

The Return of the Experts?

The Identity of "Anonymous"

In 1996, a journalist named Joe Klein published a novel entitled *Primary Colors* under the pseudonym Anonymous. A fictional account of Bill and Hillary Clinton's conduct during a political campaign, the novel drew attention in part because the book is very entertaining, and in part because the author and publisher kept the identity of Anonymous secret.

New York magazine approached Donald Foster, who had recently identified Shakespeare as the author of "A Funeral Elegy," and asked if he would attempt to uncover who Anonymous was. He agreed, and the magazine supplied him with the names and substantial samples of the writings of thirty-five "suspects." When Foster got to Joe Klein, a columnist for *Newsweek,* comparison of Klein's known writings to *Primary Colors* began to bear fruit. At the heart of Foster's methodology is a comparison of unusual words, spellings, syntax, and content that appear in the known and questioned writings. He later explained, "No single word or group of words could establish Klein's authorship of *Primary Colors,* but once the computer pointed me in the direction of Joe Klein and I began to compare his work with that of Anonymous, the affinities between *Primary Colors* and Klein's *Newsweek* column emerged across the spectrum."[32] In February 1996, Foster's article identifying Klein as Anonymous appeared in *New York,* and his discovery was broadcast widely in the press. Foster was not the first to suggest that Klein was the author, but he certainly was the first to claim that he had demonstrated it.

Foster's list of similarities is impressive. Most involve word choice, such as the use of uncommon adjectives like "elusive," "flagrant," and "lugubrious." Others involved the use of punctuation, especially the colon, in peculiar grammatical positions in the sentence. As for the rest of Foster's presentation, the shear volume of similarities, combined with a very limited number of "suspects," convinces us that he must be right. Like Foster, however, we have no way of determining which, if any, of his observations would be important to us if less information were available and if the number of possible authors had not been limited. For months after Foster identified him as Anonymous, Klein continued to deny it. Eventually, *The Washington Post* obtained a copy of the manuscript containing Klein's handwritten notes, causing Klein to capitulate.[33]

The JonBenét Ramsey Case

Donald Foster's prowess as a "linguistic sleuth" quickly attracted the interest of the law enforcement community, and he responded. But an early, inauspicious application of his skills in a forensic setting serves as a reminder of just why courts have been reluctant to embrace expert stylistic analysis. JonBenét Ramsey, a six-year-old girl who often won child beauty pageants, was murdered on Christmas night in 1996 at her home in Boulder, Colorado. The JonBenét case has remained one of the most notorious unsolved mysteries in recent American history. Among the many open questions is who wrote the ransom note that was found on the scene. The answer to that question would most likely solve the mystery.

In the spring of 1997, Foster had apparently reached the conclusion, after reviewing certain documents, that he could identify JonBenét's killer.[34] On June 18, 1997, he wrote to JonBenét's mother, Patricia Ramsey, who was one of the suspects in the case, "I know that you are innocent—*know* it, absolutely and unequivocally. I would stake my professional reputation on it—indeed, my faith in humanity."[35] He elaborated by saying that the note "appears to have been written by a young adult with an adolescent imagination overheated by true crime literature and Hollywood thrillers."[36] According to the Ramseys, Foster had concluded that the young adult who killed JonBenét was John Andrew Ramsey, the son of John Ramsey by an earlier marriage.[37] He further concluded that John Andrew Ramsey was communicating over the Internet using the name "Jameson." It turned out, however, that Jameson was really a woman named Susan Bennett, who had been following the case and making numerous postings on the Internet. Foster altered his theory to the effect that Susan Bennett was involved with John Andrew Ramsey, allowing him to use her computer.

Subsequently, the Boulder police consulted with Foster. After a far more thorough analysis, Foster decided that it was actually JonBenét's mother who had written the ransom note. We do not have Foster's report to the Boulder police, but a former detective who worked on the case wrote a book in which he likewise concluded that Mrs. Ramsey was the killer. He does not present a detailed description of Foster's evidence, except for one recurrent detail of handwriting: the way that both the ransom note and Mrs. Ramsey wrote the letter "a." Foster claimed that at the time of the murder, both Ramsey and the author of the ransom note preferred the upright "a" to the cursive "a."[38] The Ramseys disputed this by offering a document in which Mrs. Ramsey used the cursive "a" more frequently.[39] We have no idea who killed this poor little girl. But we can certainly understand why, according to a detective who worked on the case, the prosecutors had decided that they could not use Foster: "The defense would eat him alive."[40] Moreover, recent analysis by Gerald McMenamin, also an expert in forensic stylistics, concludes that Patricia Ramsey did not write the ransom note.[41]

These missteps and disagreements provide a compelling argument for developing techniques for author identification that are both accurate and replicable. On the one hand, Foster demonstrates considerable insight with his analyses, as anyone reading his book *Author Unknown* must acknowledge. These insights continue. In a 2003 magazine article, Foster argues convincingly that the government has dropped the ball in its investigation of the 2001 anthrax mailings.[42] Nonetheless, the lack of tested methodology is indeed troubling. As we have seen, it can lead to error, even if Foster is right most of the time. The Supreme Court was not off the mark when it listed the ability to articulate a known rate of error as one of the criteria for determining whether a method is sufficiently scientific to meet evidentiary standards. But this approach to scientific evidence comes with a cost: the absence of a provably reliable methodology can result in the legal system's not taking advantage of important insights even when they are right. Had it gone to trial, the Unabomber case, which we next discuss, might have ended that way.

The Unabomber Case

At the same time that Foster was analyzing the writings of the various parties in the Ramsey case, another high-profile murder investigation had finally achieved a breakthrough. For years, an individual whom law enforcement agents were calling the "Unabomber" had been first delivering and later mailing explosive devices to corporate executives and to academics involved in the development of technology.[43] From May 9, 1979 through April 24, 1995, the Unabomber sent a total of sixteen explosive devices to various people around the United States.[44] Not all of them exploded, but most did, killing three people and causing serious injury to many others. The bombings made national headlines and were a top priority for the FBI.

The Unabomber's undoing was writing and demanding publication of his "Manifesto," a lengthy document subtitled "Industrial Society and Its

Future," which the *Washington Post* published in cooperation with the *New York Times* in 1995.[45] David Kaczynski and his wife, Linda Patrick, happened to read about the manifesto and were struck by similarities it had with views earlier expressed by David's brother, Ted, a disaffected former mathematics professor who was living in a remote cabin in Montana. David and Linda already had a "nagging feeling" that Ted might be involved in the bombings, based on his connections to the various locales from which the bombs had been mailed or where they had been delivered.[46] David contacted a private investigator, who was a family friend. She had the texts of various documents analyzed and then called a lawyer to seek advice. Eventually, David spoke with the lawyer, who entered into negotiations with the FBI. Beginning in early 1996, David began providing law enforcement officials with information about Ted, including where he lived, information about his past, and samples of his writing.

Based largely on information and material provided by David, the government filed an application for a warrant to search Ted's cabin in Montana. The government asserted that the sixteen bombings contained enough notable similarities to support the conclusion that the explosives were distributed by the same person or the same group of people, and that there was probable cause to believe that Ted Kaczynski was behind the entire operation.

In support of its claim of probable cause, the government made a number of arguments. First, Ted had ties with the places from which bombs were mailed. Second, the FBI was able to conduct a comparison of DNA material from postage stamps found on an envelope used to mail a copy of the manifesto to Dr. Tom Tyler (then a professor at the University of California, Berkeley) with a postage stamp from an envelope containing a letter that Ted had sent to his brother David. According to the FBI, the probability that someone besides Ted had sent the letter to Tyler was "3 percent of Caucasians, 3 percent of Blacks, 5 percent of Southeastern Hispanics and 2 percent of Southwestern Hispanics."[47]

The third reason for concluding that Ted Kaczynski was the Unabomber involved a stylistic comparison of documents known to have been written by Ted with documents known to have been written by the Unabomber, including the lengthy manifesto and various letters that the Unabomber had sent. The comparison was conducted by James Fitzgerald, a supervisory special agent of the FBI. Fitzgerald's report was attached to the application for a search warrant and summarized in the supporting affidavit.[48]

Fitzgerald's report consists of a lengthy list of expressions and non-standard spellings used by both Kaczynski in his known writings and the

Unabomber. Many of the comparisons are content-based. For example, a lengthy 1971 essay by Ted and the manifesto both speak of technology "narrowing our sphere of freedom."[49] The report also notes that, in their various documents, both Ted and the Unabomber used common words and phrases: "edible" plants and roots, "technical progress," "technological progress," "propaganda," "mass entertainment," "educational psychology," the "elite," "superhuman" or "superintelligent" computers, "rules and regulations," "large organizations," "power-hungry types," "genetic engineering," "primitive man," "manipulation," "intellectuals," "time studying," "mind-altering drugs," the "rapidity" of social change, "wilderness," "hunting," "the Industrial Revolution," the ozone layer, "anarchism," "art forms," "conservatives," the "water supply," "anger," mental or behavioral "aberration," and "the average man." In addition, both sets of documents alluded to some of the same scholarly books, some of which were known to have influenced Ted earlier in his life.[50]

The two sets of documents also used similar phrases and grammatical filler expressions, such as "more or less," "presumably," "gotten," "in practice," "on the other hand," "in spite of," "by no means," "a matter of," "greater or lesser," "take the liberty of," "clearly," "mere," "on the contrary," "moreover," "namely," and "at any rate." And both used certain words in common, although their contexts differ. For example, Ted referred to a "driver's licence" serving as identification. The Unabomber's manifesto reads, "You need a licence for everything and with the licence comes rules . . . ."[51] Other examples include "refrain from," "apologize," "sneer," "sucker," "crippled," "travelling," "isolated," "guts" ("if you hated my guts" vs. "SOME leftists do have the guts to oppose . . ."), "theorists," "types" (e.g., "intellectual types" vs. "leftish types"), "exclusive" ("exclusive rights" vs. "exclusive superiority"), "thoroughly contemptible," and "more effectively."

Both Ted and the Unabomber used unconventional spellings for certain words: "licence," "analyse willfully," and "instalment" instead of "license," "analyze willfully" and "installment."[52] The *American Heritage Dictionary* characterizes "licence" as chiefly British, and in our experience the same is true for "analyse" and possibly also "instalment."

Perhaps most interesting, both sets of documents contained the expression "eat one's cake and have it" instead of the conventional "have one's cake and eat it."[53] Prior to studying this case, neither of us can recall having heard the former expression. However, as defense counsel pointed out in their critique of the government's stylistic comparison,[54] the adage originally developed the way that both Ted's documents and the Unabomber's documents used it, and it is occasionally used that way in the press today. Our own LEXIS search even found it in a "Dear Abby" column.[55] The co-occurrence of this unusual diction certainly has intuitive appeal, but from a scientific perspective, without information about frequency of use among highly educated people, it is not easy to know just what to make of it.

Based in part on the Fitzgerald Report, the court issued a search warrant, and Kaczynski's cabin was searched on April 3, 1996. The search yielded definitive evidence that Kaczynski was indeed the Unabomber, including incriminating documents and bomb-making materials. Based on the search, an arrest warrant was issued the next day.

In 1997 Kaczynski's lawyers moved to suppress the evidence seized at the cabin, arguing, among other things, that the stylistic comparison conducted by the FBI was flawed. The motion was denied. Much of the motion concerned the nonlinguistic grounds for obtaining the search warrant. However, the disagreement between experts on the issue of author identification highlights two very different perspectives on what constitutes acceptable methodology.

As part of his motion to suppress, Kaczynski submitted an affidavit from Robin Lakoff, a linguist at the University of California, Berkeley. Lakoff found a number of the FBI's inferences flawed.[56] The problems she identified included the following: many of the words that co-occur in the Unabomber's and Kaczynski's documents are common words, and others are common among academics writing about such matters; when two people write about the same thing, the words they use are likely to overlap; some of the words are used in very different senses by the Unabomber, on the one hand, and by Kaczynski, on the other; and the use of unusual, but acceptable, spellings and idioms is not enough to prove identity of authorship.

In response, the government produced a declaration from Donald Foster.[57] Foster wrote of having been contacted in late 1996 by lawyers for Kaczynski, and having reviewed various documents in response to that request, including the manifesto and Kaczynski's lengthy 1971 essay. Foster stated in his declaration that "the FBI had done a remarkably careful job in setting forth evidence of common authorship," and told Kaczynski's lawyer, "It was unlikely she would find an attributional scholar willing to assail Fitzgerald's text-analysis, except perhaps in a few minor particulars."[58] He concluded:

> The evidence of authorial identity rests not in any one instance of similar thought or language, but in a collocation of shared linguistic habits that extends to spelling, rare diction, grammatical accidence, syntactical habits, shared source

material, and shared ideology, together with internal biographical evidence that likewise points to authorial identity.[59]

Foster also accused Lakoff of taking particular examples out of context, missing the point of the analysis.

Lakoff filed a reply declaration in which she noted that "if as the defendant claims a great many of these 'shared linguistic habits' turn out to be unremarkable for various reasons, then the claimed 'collocation' (juxtaposition across texts) breaks down as evidence of 'authorial identity.'"[60]

Who is right? Both sides are. As Foster notes, the similarities between the Unabomber documents and the Kaczynski documents in both content and the use of unusual expressions are striking. In view of their number and frequency, it would be irresponsible to ignore them. But Lakoff is right too. Pointing out the similarities between documents without taking into account the likelihood of such overlap, especially by people in the academic community, and without any analysis of the differences between the authors, is not good science. Moreover, without taking base rates into account, it is impossible to know how much to make of each observed similarity.

Perhaps a disagreement between FBI agent Terry Turchie and David Kaczynski best illustrates the problem. In an affidavit filed in support of a motion to suppress evidence seized when Kaczynski's cabin was searched, David accused the FBI of overstating the extent of his suspicions. Agent Turchie had declared in an affidavit that "David stated that he recognized substantial similarity between the ideas, concepts and expressions contained in his brother's 23 page essay and the UNABOM manuscript."[61] David responded that this characterization was unfair:

> I did provide a copy of my brother's essay to the investigators. However, this paragraph attributes to me a conclusion that was exactly opposite of what I told the investigators. I told the investigators that after reading the copy of the essay, in my opinion there were substantial similarities and *dissimilarities* between the essay and the Unabom Manuscript. I told the investigators that based upon my reading of the essay, as opposed to my memory of it, I felt less suspicious of Ted being the Unabomber.[62]

In fact, there are differences, both in spelling and style, between the manifesto and Kaczynski's known writings, as the defense pointed out in a "Critique" of the Fitzgerald Report filed with the motion to suppress.[63] For example, Kaczynski used the spelling *clorate*, but the Unabomber wrote *chlorate*. There were also differences between *skilfully* and *skillfully; guarantee* and *guaranty*.[64] The Kaczynski documents used many split infinitives, but the Unabomber documents used a split infinitive only once.[65]

Obviously, in this case the similarities outweigh the differences. And the probable cause standard for issuing a search warrant is substantially less rigorous than that for admitting expert evidence at trial. When the nonlinguistic evidence is added to the mix, there certainly seems to have been good reason to issue a search warrant. But when it comes to admitting expert testimony, our rules of evidence are not wrong for requiring some tested, replicable basis as a prerequisite for expressing an opinion. Ultimately, it will be up to the scientific community to produce procedures that demonstrate the validity and reliability of the methodology if expert testimony on author identification is to be permitted at trial. We describe some promising work in that direction later in this chapter.

Van Wyk and the Half-a-Loaf Approach

To the best of our knowledge, the only published judicial opinion in the past several decades to permit forensic stylistic expert testimony on the issue of author identification is *United States v. Van Wyk*,[66] a federal case from New Jersey decided in 2000. Roy Van Wyk had been accused of writing numerous threatening letters to women with whom he had become obsessed, but who rejected his advances.[67] To prove the identify of the author of the letters, the government offered as an expert FBI supervisory special agent James Fitzgerald, the same agent involved in the Unabomber case. Fitzgerald had compared the nine threatening letters with fourteen of Van Wyk's known writings (also mostly letters)[68] and had reached the conclusion that Van Wyk was the author of the threatening letters.

The defense objected to Fitzgerald's testimony, asserting that forensic stylistics has not been shown to be reliable. The defense further argued that Fitzgerald should not be permitted to point out similarities in style between the two sets of documents, proposing instead that the jurors should be permitted to do so on their own, more or less as in *Clifford*. The court agreed with the defense that Fitzgerald should not be permitted to offer an expert opinion on who wrote the threatening letters, but allowed him to testify about the similarities that he had found in the sets of documents. Among these similarities were the following:

Punctuation. Both the author of the threatening letters and Van Wyk sometimes failed to use spaces in typewritten documents after a period or a comma. The report concluded: "Two separate authors having this same carelessness or ignorance of typewritten spacing rules would be highly unlikely."[69] Both Van Wyk and the author of the threatening letters also sometimes made mistakes in using the apostrophe in typewritten documents. This mistake occurred in all of Van Wyk's typed documents, and in two of the five threatening letters. Both Van Wyk and the author of the threatening letters used similar abbreviations (*N.J.*, but not *New Jersey* or *NJ; Ave.*, but not *Avenue*, etc.). Finally, and perhaps most significant, neither author used commas or other punctuation to separate independent clauses in a compound sentence. As we will see below, recent research suggests that syntactically analyzed punctuation decisions may have significant power in author identification research.

Spelling. Both Van Wyk and the author of the threatening letters spelled the word "released" as *realeased* on one occasion in a typewritten document. Van Wyk spelled "lying" as *lieing* in one document, and the author of the threatening letters spelled the word "liar" as *lier* in one document.

Grammatical Accidence. Van Wyk wrote *here* for "hear" in a handwritten document, and the author of the threatening letters did so in a typewritten document. Both authors spelled the word "you're" as *your* on a number of occasions.

Miscellaneous Observations. Both authors capitalized the word "Police" even when it was used as a common noun. Van Wyk ended one handwritten document with a drawing of the peace sign, and the author of the threatening letters ended one typewritten letter with the word "peace." One of the threatening letters made reference to Roy, and two used vulgar expletives. Some of the letters showed a great deal of familiarity with the personal life of the recipient. This feature is not linguistic at all, but is perhaps the most incriminating. Also suspicious is that various of the threatening letters made reference to Van Wyk, portraying him as a victim. Without the need for expert testimony on stylistics, the content of the letters suggests that Van Wyk was their author.[70]

The court held that the FBI's analysis failed to meet *Daubert* standards of reliability:

> Although Fitzgerald employed a particular methodology that may be subject
> to testing, neither Fitzgerald nor the Government has been able to identify a
> known rate of error, establish what amount of samples is necessary for an expert
> to be able to reach a conclusion as to probability of authorship, or pinpoint
> any meaningful peer review. Additionally, as Defendant argues, there is no
> universally recognized standard for certifying an individual as an expert in
> forensic stylistics.[71]

The only scholarly work on which the analysis relied was that by Gerald Mc-Menamin, who candidly admits in his writing that "[f]rom the researcher's perspective, the obligation to explain his or her method and findings leads to conclusions that are 'not so much objective as they are 'intersubjective.'"[72]

Thus, as in *Clifford*, no expert opinion on the question of the identity of the author of the letters was permitted. The judge concluded that "[b]ecause of the lack of scientific reliability of forensic stylistics, the Court is not satisfied that the jury would benefit from Fitzgerald's testimony as to his subjective opinion that the questioned writings were written by the same individual and that that individual is Defendant Roy Van Wyk."[73]

We agree with this holding. As suggestive as the comparisons might be, there is no scientific basis for drawing clear inferences. Moreover, there is no analysis in the FBI report of the differences between the two sets of documents, the inconsistencies within any particular document, such as the ratio of correct use of the apostrophe to omission of the apostrophe, or the frequency of any of these errors based on a comparison with an appropriate reference set (e.g., informal documents written by people with the defendant's educational and cultural background).

But the court then departed from *Clifford* and permitted Fitzgerald to point out to the jury the various similarities between Van Wyk's known documents and the threatening letters, as long as he did not actually state an opinion on the identity of the author. The court reasoned that forensic stylistic analysis was more or less on a par with handwriting analysis:

> Various judicial decisions regarding handwriting analysis, while not identical to text analysis, are instructive because handwriting analysis seems to suffer similar weakness in scientific reliability, namely the following: no known error rate, no professional or academic degrees in the field, no meaningful peer review, and no agreement as to how many exemplars are required to establish the probability of authorship.[74]

As we noted earlier, however, the admissibility of expert handwriting opinion evidence has become controversial[75] and recent challenges to its lack of scientific foundation have begun to gain influence. Some courts have excluded the opinions of handwriting experts, although they do permit them to testify on the similarities between two sets of handwriting samples.[76]

Moreover, as noted in chapter 2, the Supreme Court's decision in *Kumho Tire Co., Ltd. v. Carmichael*[77] closed a loophole that some lower courts had used to continue admitting handwriting experts: since *Daubert* was a case concerning scientific expertise, and handwriting analysis is more an art based on experience than a science, these courts held that the failure of handwriting experts to meet *Daubert* criteria should not disqualify their testimony.[78] In *Kumho Tire,* however, the Supreme Court held that the *Daubert* approach should be used to evaluate all offers of expert testimony, whether based on science or on practical experience.

The *Van Wyk* court was not wrong to liken the then-current state of forensic stylistic analysis to handwriting analysis. No doubt there is something to both endeavors, and those who practice these skills are right much of the time. But significant problems remain to be addressed before stylistic analysis should be routinely admitted into evidence.

First, an important goal for stylistic analysis is determining how to weigh intra-author and inter-author similarities and variations. Different authors writing about the same thing might use the same words; German immigrants without much education might misspell final consonants, as we saw earlier in our discussion of the *Hauptmann* case; some typos and misspellings may be more common than others, but we do not know how common, or among whom they might tend to be more common, and so on. Without this additional analysis, any expert description of the similarities between known and questioned documents will necessarily lack scientific validity, which is what precluded the expert from offering an opinion in the first place. Unless the expert points out not just similarities, but also differences between two sets of documents, and concedes that we cannot yet draw a scientifically based conclusion on authorship and explains why, the testimony will necessarily be misleading. Neither the FBI report nor the court's order in *Van Wyk* contains any reference to such further analysis. As we will see, some very promising work is moving toward addressing these issues.

One can argue, as did the court in *Van Wyk,* that these problems can be cured by vigorous cross-examination. In addition, the defense can rebut testimony on similarities by calling its own expert to point out differences, or perhaps by calling "educational experts" to describe to the jury the limits of stylistic analysis and the reasons that no opinion on the ultimate issue of authorship was given by the government's expert.[79] These are certainly partial solutions. But *Daubert* does not suggest that one party to a litigation should be able to call an expert whose methods have not been proven valid simply because the opposing party can call another witness to explain to the jury why the first expert's position is not sufficiently reliable.

Moreover, the issue should not be viewed in a vacuum. Recent work shows that the government is a large consumer of unproven expertise.

According to the Innocence Project, bad forensic science is high on the list of factors that underlie false convictions. For example, in the first seventy post-conviction exonerations based on DNA evidence, microscopic hair analysis had been introduced in twenty-one cases, false serology included in forty, and what the authors call "defective or fraudulent science" in twenty-six.[80] *Daubert* and *Kumho Tire* caution us that scientific evidence must be shown to be valid before we can be wholly confident of its usefulness.

This suggests that the courts should become stricter, not more accommodating, in admitting expert identification testimony in criminal cases, a point that the court in *Van Wyk* missed in its analogy between stylistic and handwriting evidence. If handwriting analysis were a new field seeking admissibility for the first time, it is highly doubtful that courts would accept it. It seems ironic for a court to allow the government to call an expert to point out similarities in the context of stylistics because that is the practice with handwriting analysis, when the latter is currently being challenged as insufficiently scientific.

Finally, there is no empirical evidence showing a different effect on the jury when an expert testifies to his ultimate conclusion on the identity of an author, as opposed to merely listing the similarities between documents or handwriting samples and then stepping down. In the first instance, the expert's opinion is obvious enough. In the second, having someone identified to the jury as an expert who is then allowed to point out similarities between documents will strongly suggest to the jury that the expert believes that the same person produced those documents, implicitly identifying the defendant as the author. This "half-a-loaf" approach may actually give the government a whole loaf while pretending not to do so.[81]

Unfortunately, the alternative is also far from ideal. Following in the footsteps of *Clifford,* most courts will allow a defendant's known writings to go to the jury, along with questioned documents such as threatening letters. This leaves it for the jury to decide whether the defendant wrote the questioned documents. To do so, they must identify the similarities and differences between the sets of documents, something virtually none of them is trained to do. And as Dr. Miron pointed out to the trial court in *Clifford,* jurors may not draw proper conclusions from such comparisons without expert assistance.

The only real solution to this conundrum is to do the research that is needed to determine how authorship identification can be done with sufficient reliability. Such research was difficult in the past, because it involved a tremendous amount of tedious work that all had to be done by hand. But it has become increasingly feasible with the advent of computers, the development of online databases, and the gathering of collections (or "corpora") of texts written by ordinary people. We therefore conclude this chapter by discussing some promising work that is moving in the direction of making author identification welcome in courts of law.

Some Promise for an Improved Science of Authorship Attribution

In chapter 7 we discussed the ironic fact that because linguistics in general and phonetics in particular are serious academic fields apart from any forensic application, voiceprint analysis has been subject to testing more exacting than have other methods of forensic identification.[82] In fact, some "sciences" like microscopic hair analysis have never been subjected to rigorous testing; they continue to be deemed admissible only because practitioners assert they produce good results and cite the long history of admissibility.[83]

Author identification research is now evolving from an unproven art to a testable set of procedures. Over the past several years, the National Institute of Justice, the research arm of the U.S. Department of Justice, has funded research in the area of author identification as part of a series of projects designed to improve the quality of law enforcement.[84] Similar studies have been underway at universities ranging from the United States to England to Poland.

In a recent article, linguist Carole Chaski describes some of that work, as well as presenting results of her own study of the issue.[85] Chaski collected a number of writing samples from people who had similar educational backgrounds and who were from the same region of the United States. The samples were all relatively short letters. She then chose four of these writers as "suspects." A writing sample of one suspect was removed from the set and designated the "Questioned Document," as though it were a threatening letter or a ransom note that was the subject of an actual case. In reality, the Questioned Document was written by Suspect 16 among her set of writers. She then asked the following question: Would various proposed methods of author identification force the correct conclusion that all four suspects are different people, and that the Questioned Document was written by Suspect 16?

Many traditional approaches to author identification failed this test. For example, it has been suggested that authors can be distinguished based on their *type-token ratio,* which measures the richness or density of their vocabulary.[86] In a document of five hundred words, one author may use three hundred different words, while another might use only half that many. In this case, the type-token ratios would be .60 (300/500) and .30 (150/500), respectively. The higher the ratio, the richer the vocabulary. For the type-token ratio to succeed in Chaski's study, the four suspects should vary significantly from one another in their type-token ratios, and the Questioned Document should have a type-token ratio that matches that of Suspect 16. But that is not what happened. Suspect 16's ratio was significantly higher than that of the Questioned Document (.39 vs. .55), but other suspects had ratios very similar to each other. For example, Subject 9 had a ratio of .37, almost identical to the .39 of Suspect 16, who really was the author of the Questioned Document. This means that someone using this methodology would incorrectly eliminate Suspect 16 as the author of the Questioned Document, and wrongly conclude that Suspects 9 and 16 were the same person.

Chaski found that other methods with intuitive appeal also do a poor job in distinguishing authors with similar backgrounds. For example, in our earlier discussion of the *Van Wyk* case, we saw that the FBI made much of similar spelling errors in the known and questioned documents. Comparison of spelling errors was also at the heart of the expert analysis in the trial of Bruno Hauptmann. Chaski found the following spelling errors among her four Suspects:[87]

Suspect 2:   *behide* (behind)
              frount (front)
Suspect 11:   *aroud* (around)
              beyound (beyond)

If we were looking at these documents as members of a jury, we might be inclined to guess incorrectly that the same person made these peculiar errors. Both leave off the *n* or change the vowel in a word-final sequence of *n* followed by *d* or *t*.

Similarly, what is sometimes called "grammatical accidence," did not work. Many subjects confounded such homophones as "they're," "their," and "there"; "it's" and "its"; "then" and "than"; and others.[88] We saw this method used as part of the FBI's analysis in the *Van Wyk* case. Clearly, these errors are so common that they have very little predictive value.

Measures of readability also failed to distinguish authors accurately,[89] as did other measures of vocabulary richness[90] and semantic content.[91] These findings are important because the expert analyses in the cases discussed earlier are peppered with observations about these sorts of phenomena.

What Chaski did find significant were the relative frequencies of various syntactic structures. Using syntactic theory developed by linguists over the past thirty years, Chaski parsed the sentences of each document with respect to the use of every major part of speech: verbs, nouns, adjectives, and so on. She then computed the ways in which each of these categories was used. For example, the typical prepositional phrase in English consists of a preposition followed by a noun phrase, as in [after [the ballgame]]. But, less typically, prepositional phrases can also consist of a preposition followed by other types of phrases, as in [after [watching the ballgame]].[92] For each of her subjects, Chaski looked at the ratio of more frequent versus less frequent syntactic features. She found that only Suspect 16 and the author of the Questioned Document failed to show statistically significant differences. This is exactly the right result, and the only method she tested that yielded exactly the right result.

Chaski also found that punctuation is a promising identifier of authors, although there are higher error rates. She tested two hypotheses. First, she examined whether the frequency of use of particular punctuation marks distinguishes discrete authors from each other, while at the same time clustering authors in common with each other. The analysis did indeed identify Suspect 16 as the author of the Questioned Document, but it also incorrectly identified Suspects 9 and 80 as the same author. She then enhanced the analysis by looking not only at the punctuation marks used, but also at their syntactic roles. For example, commas between members of a list were considered separately from commas that separated two clauses of a compound sentence. The results were similar, although not quite as good. Punctuation analysis, then, provides a promising avenue for future research.

Of course, as Chaski recognizes, a single study is not enough to prove that this analysis will always work.[93] With only one set of subjects, it is not possible to tell whether the results generalize. Nonetheless, courts have been receptive to this approach, especially if its limitations are acknowledged openly. More research is needed, however, both to determine with greater confidence the validity of this methodology and to explore other avenues. Here, we offer a few observations that we hope will guide additional research.

First, the statistic that Chaski used, the chi-square, asks whether the actual number of occurrences is significantly different from the expected number of occurrences. If so, then we can reject the null hypothesis, which is that the authors were the same. Put into everyday English, when $p <$ .01, we can say, "Statistical analysis reveals that there is only a one in one hundred chance that the same person wrote both of these, and therefore I can confidently eliminate Suspect X as an author." But what can we say when the chi-square is not significant? In Chaski's successful analysis, the one based on syntax, p was less than .05 for all parings except the paring between Suspect 16 and the Questioned Document. For that paring, $p = .2295$.[94] The statistic does not tell us that we should be certain that the same person authored both documents; it only tells us that we cannot conclude with confidence that different people authored them. Therefore, this method does a better job eliminating suspects than it does proving identity. The approach is also somewhat inconsistent with the burden of proof falling on the government to prove identity. Given this limitation, it would be a good idea to look at other statistical models, as Tim Grant and Kevin Baker point out in their critique of Chaski's work.[95]

Second, forensic analysts who use the types of methods that Chaski rejected might cry "foul." What was convincing about the stylistic comparisons in the Unabomber and *Van Wyk* cases, for example, were the number of similarities. Spelling, diction, and grammatical choices all seemed to coalesce. Perhaps it should mean something when so many factors accumulate into a large group of similarities.

In fact, some of Chaski's own data suggest some promise for this eclectic approach. One of the hypotheses she tested and rejected is the presence of grammatical errors. The ones present in the documents she tested were sentence fragments, run-on sentences, subject-verb mismatch, tense shift, wrong verb form, and missing auxiliary verb.[96] None of these has independent predictive force. For example, the Questioned Document and three of the four known authors all used run-on sentences, whereas only two authors used the wrong verb form. However, as Chaski observes, only Suspect 16 and the author of the Questioned Document displayed exactly the same constellation of grammatical errors and non-errors. Both used sentence fragments and run-on sentences, but made none of the other errors. This fact suggests that it may be fruitful for researchers to look systematically at clusters of phenomena in this way, and to analyze both what writers do wrong and what they do right. Gerald McMenamin's recent book, *Forensic Linguistics,* suggests this kind of approach and proposes statistical analyses that may be useful in analyzing data.[97] Validation studies to determine which clusters of phenomena reliably distinguish between authors when the statistics are significant would be especially useful here.

A recent doctoral dissertation by a Polish linguist, Krzysztof Kredens, lends support to Chaski's approach and also suggests some avenues for future research.[98] Kredens conducted a comparison of the speech patterns of two British rock stars (Robert Smith and Steven Morrissey), who are about the same age and have similar educational backgrounds. He examined the transcripts of several press interviews of each musician. Like

Chaski, Kredens found that various traditional methods, including type-token ratios, average word length, the use of hapax legomena (words used only once), and the presence of contracted forms and lexical sophistication were not significantly different, and therefore could not distinguish between speakers.[99] In contrast, the differential use of adverbs and discourse markers were both highly significant, again, using a chi square test. Also significant were the use of adjectives and relative clauses. Thus, Kredens's study supports Chaski's finding that analysis of various syntactic and lexical categories is a fruitful area for future research.

The differential use of discourse markers is interesting for an additional lesson that it teaches. "You know" and "actually" are used similarly by both individuals, while the other markers are used differently. Not surprisingly, these data show that it is considerably easier to draw inferences of distinct authorship than it is to draw inferences of common authorship. Kredens's findings are summarized in table 8.1.

Basic research of this kind is invaluable and is moving us toward far more sophisticated methods of analysis. We fully support additional research along the lines of Chaski's and Kredens's into the usefulness of syntactic markers in author identification. We also support research into more eclectic approaches that characterize Foster's work in the Unabomber case and Fitzgerald's in that case and *Van Wyk*. The stylistic analysis that they and others use may well be demonstrably relevant in determining authorship. In fact, some promising work conducted by Moshe Koppel and Jonathan Schler of Bar-Ilan University's computer science department suggests that this is so.[100] Statistical modeling will have to be used to determine how significant each of these features is and how predictive clusters of particular similarities are of common authorship. Efforts to combine the sorts of syntactic regularities on which Chaski relies and various idiosyncratic features considered by other researchers may also be fruitful.

Table 8.1. Number of Occurrences of Discourse Markers in Speech Samples of Two Musicians

Discourse Marker	Smith	Morrissey	Significance Level
"you know"	17	10	.274
"I mean"	16	4	.009
"actually"	9	7	.839
"kind of/sort of"	9	0	.009
"like"	14	0	.001

Source: Krzysztov Kredens, Forensic Linguistics and the Status of Linguistic Evidence in the Legal Setting (2000), Ph.D. diss, University of Lodz.

Some Easier Cases

The eclectic methods of document comparison that we saw applied in actual cases suffer from a common problem: a failure to take base rates into account. Unless we know how many people leave out the apostrophe in possessive constructions altogether, and how often most apostrophe users leave it out by random error even if they are ordinarily good spellers, we really cannot know what to make of the fact that the defendant and perpetrator are both apostrophe omitters. One solution to this problem is to establish a reference corpus of relevant usage from which comparisons can be made. Recent work by Gerald McMenamin is moving in that direction.[101]

Alternatively, what if we narrow the universe of possible suspects from infinity to two? Let us imagine, for instance, that Roy Van Wyk had claimed that his neighbor wrote the threatening letters, while the government claimed that Van Wyk wrote them, and no one thought that anyone else could possibly have written the letters. Let us further imagine that Van Wyk's neighbor never made any of the mistakes that both Van Wyk and the author of the threatening letters made, but made other errors that Van Wyk did not make. In that case, the FBI report would seem more convincing. The only question would be whether random variation within an individual's writing could account for all these differences. The more samples analyzed, the less plausible that explanation becomes. Recall that both Chaski's and Kredens's work suggest that reliably eliminating a suspect is sometimes feasible, even with current methodologies, when the pool of subjects is small enough and the sample size large enough.

Two types of recurring cases involve only a limited number of possible authors. In some of them, like our hypothetical one, the parties make specific claims that limit the possibilities to two suspects. In another set of cases, the police say that a suspect made a statement that purports to report accurately what the suspect said during an interview or interrogation, but the suspect claims that the police wrote the statement and bullied the suspect into signing it. In both of these situations, there is less need to worry about the base rate of occurrence in the larger population, since the analysis only has to eliminate one individual.

Robert Eagleson reports on an Australian case in which there were only two possible authors of a disputed document.[102] A woman was reported missing, and her husband presented the police with a six-page farewell letter that he claimed his wife had written before running off with another man. The letter had been written on the family typewriter. The police suspected that the husband had killed his wife and had written the letter

Table 8.2. Summary of Comparison of Three Sets of Documents

	H	F	W
Spelling			
Errors in individual words	+	+	—
Capitals with common nouns	+	+	—
Small letters with proper nouns	+	+	—
Intrusive apostrophe	+	+	—
Morphology			
The verb: present tense	+	+	—
The verb: past tense	+	+	—
Syntax			
Sentence structure	+	+	—
Disrupted structures	+	+	—
Punctuation			
Comma with clauses	+	+	—
Comma in series	+	+	—
Asides	+	+	—
Capitals after full-stops	+	+	—

Source: Robert Eagleson, *Forensic Analysis of Personal Written Texts: A Case Study,* in *Language and the Law* 362 (John Gibbons ed., 1994).

himself. They obtained samples of writing from both the husband and wife, and asked Eagleson to perform an analysis. His results are presented in table 8.2, where *H* represents the husband's known writing, *W* refers to those of the wife, and *F* is the disputed farewell letter.

Many of these errors correspond to categories that Chaski found significant, especially syntactically driven analysis of the punctuation used. In fact, most of the syntactic errors also involve punctuation. What Eagleson terms "sentence structure" is largely the use of run-on sentences in which what should be at least two sentences are written as one without the use of a period.[103] "Disrupted structures" are ones in which syntactically required words are omitted, such as the infinitival "to" or "of" in the noun phrase "hundreds of dollars." Other errors, the sorts of phenomena relied on by those using an eclectic approach to stylistic analysis, have not yet been systematically researched and validated.

Whether Eagleson's analysis would be admissible through an expert in an American court applying the *Daubert* standard is an open question. His methodology, after all, is essentially the same as that used by Foster and Fitzgerald. Yet we believe that if appropriately circumscribed, it might well be admitted. In our opinion, the best strategy would be to focus on the differences between the farewell letter and the wife's writings, and then to rely on the research that demonstrates that a number of these differences distinguish the writings of one author from those of another. Because there are only two possible authors, it is not necessary to prove that the husband wrote the letter, but merely that the wife did not. In the actual case, after the husband was confronted with this analysis, he conceded that he had killed his wife and pleaded guilty to manslaughter.

The second situation in which authorship is frequently at issue, but in which there are really only two possible authors, involves cases in which police claim that a signed confession was obtained by writing down the defendant's own words, while the defendant alleges that it was really the police who wrote the confession. The defendant further contends that he was then pressured to sign the police's characterization of what happened. Some of the cases are very sad. Roger Shuy reports of one case in which a mentally disabled boy claimed to have signed a confession because the police promised him that if he did, they would let him go home and see his mother.[104] Shuy was consulted on the case about language issues, but was not permitted to testify at trial about his findings.

The English linguist Malcolm Coulthard has discussed interesting examples of this phenomenon in some high-profile cases. In one celebrated case, Coulthard provided an analysis of a confession by Derek Bentley, who was hanged in London in 1953 for participating in the shooting of a police officer.[105] The case received a great deal of attention, and spawned a movie entitled *Let Him Have It*. Bentley was nineteen years old and mentally retarded.[106] It was undisputed that his friend, Chris Craig, had killed a police officer. But Craig was too young to receive the death penalty under English law at that time. In a signed confession, Bentley admitted that he knew they had gone to break into the building where Craig shot the policeman, but did not know that Craig would shoot anyone.[107] Moreover, Bentley admitted that he shouted something to Craig, but could not recall what he had said. Other testimony at Bentley's trial revealed that he had said "Let him have it, Chris." There is still controversy over whether Bentley really uttered those words and, if he did, whether he meant "Shoot the cop" or "Give him your gun, Chris." In any event, the jury convicted Bentley and he was later hanged.

As part of an effort to obtain a posthumous pardon for Bentley several decades later, Coulthard addressed the question of who really wrote the confession. At trial, Bentley had claimed that the police had "helped" him to write it. The police swore under oath that the confession was simply a verbatim transcription of Bentley's own words. Coulthard focused on the use of the word "then." The 582-word confession contained that word ten times, seven of which used it after the subject of the sentence, as illustrated by the following two examples:

Chris *then* jumped over and I followed.
Chris *then* climbed up the drainpipe to the roof and I followed.

To Coulthard, this diction sounded a lot more like the writing of a policeman than like the spontaneous speech of a young mentally retarded person in custody. To test this hypothesis, he looked at three samples of actual witness statements (930 words in total), and three police reports (2,270 words). The word "then" occurred only once in the witness statements (that is, once in 930 words), but twenty-nine times in the police reports (once every seventy-eight words). To test the fairness of this representation, Coulthard also checked the use of "then" against a reference corpus of 1.5 million words of ordinary spoken language and found that it occurred 3,164 times (once in 474 words). Thus, we have the array of data as shown in table 8.3.

Even more telling, the other witness statements never use the word "then" after the subject of the sentence, while the police statements use it nine times out of 2,270 words in total. In Bentley's testimony at trial, he used the word "then" twice—both times at the beginning of the sentence, which is more indicative of everyday discourse. In contrast, one of the police officers used the unusual construction twice in his trial testimony.

Finally, Bentley's confession contained words and phrases one would expect the police to use, but not a mentally retarded teenager:

We hid behind a shelter arrangement on the roof.
A plainclothes man climbed up the drainpipe . . . .

Table 8.3. Occurrences of the Word "Then"

Speaker	Size of Corpus	Number of Occurrences	Rate of Occurrence
Confession	582	10	1/58
Police	2270	29	1/78
Witnesses	930	1	1/930
Corpus	1,500,000	3,164	1/474

Source: Malcolm Coulthard, *On the Use of Corpora in the Analysis of Forensic Texts*, 1 Forensic Linguistics 27 (1994).

A policeman in uniform came out . . . .
Behind the brickwork entrance to the door . . . .

In fact, there were many references to plainclothes versus uniformed policemen, something that the police might find important, but which is far
less likely to be the focus of a young, mentally retarded man being accused
of murder.

Coulthard's efforts proved convincing. In 1998 the English Court of Appeal quashed Bentley's conviction, referring to Coulthard's analysis as well
as to legal errors made in the trial judge's summing up.[108]

We anticipate that this kind of analysis would be admitted today by
American courts applying *Daubert,* especially if statistical tests were performed to establish the likelihood of the various differences in rates of
occurrence of "then," both in total and in particular grammatical constructions. Coulthard's method of comparing the occurrence of certain salient
aspects of diction to relevant reference sets is an attractive methodology
when the universe of possible suspects is small enough to permit the relevant inferences to be drawn.

Conclusion

It is interesting to compare the cases involving author identification discussed in this chapter with the cases involving speaker identification discussed in chapter 7. In neither situation are experts routinely welcome.
While jurors are typically not in a position to compare voices themselves,
they must assess the credibility of lay testimony, generally without the benefit of an expert to educate them about the limits of our ability to identify
voices. In author identification cases, jurors typically look at the documents and make their own decisions, again without much education as to
what can properly be inferred from similarities and differences. Fortunately,
there seems to be progress in both fields. New technologies are developing
to make mechanical voice recognition more accurate, and new approaches
to author identification, combined with testing of existing methodologies,
seem quite promising.

Whether our optimism is warranted is something that only time can
tell. Ultimately, how reliable identification of voices and authorship can
be depends on how distinct our voices and writing styles really are. That
question has yet to be answered.

Part 4

Crimes of Language

Some crimes are committed partially or entirely by means of language. Among them are bribery, conspiracy, extortion, perjury, solicitation, and threats, all of which we will explore in this part. We do not have the space to discuss other crimes where language plays a central role, such as fraud, or less common linguistic crimes like larceny by trick, criminal libel, and sedition.

Because these are crimes of language, the meanings of utterances and communicative intentions of the speakers play an essential role. This is obviously an area that falls within the expertise of linguists. It raises the issue of whether, and to what extent, an understanding of language and linguistics can be useful in deciding cases of this sort. We hope to show that it is.

Crimes of language can be committed by a variety of speech acts. Recall from chapter 3 that the same language that conveys a request can also be understood as a command, depending largely on the relationship between the speaker and the hearer. Leaving even more room for drawing inferences from context, both of these speech acts are most often performed indirectly. The same holds true for language crimes.

Chapters 9 and 10 look at a variety of linguistic crimes. As we will see, whether a crime has been committed at all often depends on how we categorize the speech act in question. An utterance like "If you do that, you're going to regret it" can be a threat, of course, but it might also be a warning or a prediction. Courts generally recognize this problem, and they typically acknowledge that speech acts are often made indirectly. In many cases, the law protects defendants against remote inferences being drawn about their intent by requiring corroborating evidence. Nonetheless, hard cases remain.

Chapter 11 is about perjury. There, courts require that a statement be literally false before a conviction can occur. We explore what it means for a statement to be false and apply our analysis to the facts underlying the impeachment of President Clinton. This involves applying some advances in the psychology of word meaning to legal situations. We also discuss why reference to the literal meaning of an utterance is more appropriate in cases of perjury than it is in many other crimes of language. As we will see, the debate about whether Clinton lied closely mimics a long-standing debate among linguists, psychologists, and philosophers about how we understand concepts and categories.

It is not our goal to demonstrate that the legal system must engage the help of an expert linguist every time it considers the language of a criminal statute or the meaning of something a defendant said or wrote,[1] although we do hope to show that linguists can occasionally be helpful. Instead, our goal is to show how generalizations about language operate beneath the surface, and can offer explanations for how courts approach these cases. To the extent that our legal system has embedded within it recurring, but unnoticed, generalizations about how human language works, it is only by bringing these to the surface that we can decide whether the system is responding realistically to the events in the world it purports to regulate.

Chapter 9

Solicitation, Conspiracy, Bribery

My wife needs to die.

Solicitation

Not only is it illegal to commit a crime, but people can also be punished for asking or inducing someone else to do so. This is the crime of solicitation. Usually, the law punishes only the solicitation of more serious crimes. The state must usually prove that the solicitor intended the crime to be committed, although the crime does not actually have to be carried out. What is essential, at least under federal law, is that the solicitor "solicits, commands, induces, or otherwise endeavors to persuade" someone else to engage in the crime.[1] The essence of solicitation is language.

The speech act that the defendant must have performed is a *request,* or perhaps an *offer* or *command.*[2] We are familiar with these speech acts from earlier chapters. Unlike consensual searches, where we found the difference between the speech acts of requesting and commanding to be critical, here the distinction is less important. The crux of the matter with solicitation is not so much the specific speech act used (in linguistic terms, the *illocutionary act*), but more the *goal* of the speech act (the *perlocutionary act*). All of the above speech acts, in differing ways, can have the goal of inducing or persuading someone else to engage in a crime.

People accused of solicitation often argue that they were not making a sincere request, but were instead joking about robbing a bank, or were trying to make a political point. A Mr. Rubin of the Jewish Defense League once held a press conference, waved $500 in the air, and offered it to anyone who killed or injured a member of the American Nazi Party. He argued at trial that his words did not constitute solicitation, but should rather be considered a type of political speech protected by the First Amendment.[3] If his offer were really nothing but hyperbolic political oratory, that argument would be persuasive. If, on the other hand, he was truly requesting people to kill Nazis, the First Amendment would offer him no comfort. Repeatedly, the courts have emphasized that although language crimes literally involve "speech," they are not covered by the Free Speech Clause of the Constitution. The sincerity of Rubin's request was therefore critical.

It is worth observing that Americans, and perhaps people of other nationalities as well, tend to talk very casually about killing people. This is especially true of children, who can be heard saying things like "I'll kill you if you tell my parents." Even adults comment that they could "kill" someone for a comment the other person made. Most utterances of this kind are hyperbole. In the *Rubin* case, however, the court noted that Rubin had himself said that he was "deadly serious." Moreover, he emphasized his seriousness by offering a specific amount of money. In his defense, it might be pointed out that he made the comment during a press conference, which supports his argument at trial that his speech was political exaggeration. And it was not made to any particular person.

Suppose that Rubin was not sincere in requesting people to kill Nazis. Could we nonetheless say he made a request, or would we have to conclude that he did not request at all? In other words, is sincerity essential to performing a speech act?

Linguists and philosophers of language generally agree that sincerity is not required to perform a speech act successfully (although sincerity is expected as a matter of morality, of course).[4] If you say to your mother that you promise to stop swearing, you have made a promise even if you secretly do not intend to abide by it. The law recognizes this point in the tort of *promissory fraud*. Someone who enters into a contract and then breaches it, and who at the time of making the contract did not intend to keep it, can be sued not only for breach of contract, but also for fraudulently inducing the other party to enter into the agreement in the first place. In other words, making an insincere promise is a wrongful act, but it is a promise nonetheless.

Yet while actual sincerity is not essential, the person making the promise must intend it to be taken seriously as a promise. If not—for instance, if it is an obvious joke—it is not a promise at all. Thus, the issue is not so much whether Rubin subjectively wanted people to kill Nazis, but whether he *appeared* to be sincere. The court decided that the question could go to the jury, which is probably where it belonged.

More often, the issue will be whether the defendant actually made a request as opposed to some other kind of speech act. Sometimes there is very little doubt. An interesting case involved Sheik Omar Abdel Rahman, a blind Muslim cleric from Egypt who had been living for some time in the United States. He and a group of radical followers were convicted of being involved in the 1993 bombing of the World Trade Center in New York, the murder of Rabbi Meir Kahane (a militant pro-Israel activist), and a conspiracy to murder Hosni Mubarek, the president of Egypt. After a lengthy trial, Sheik Abdel Rahman was sentenced to life imprisonment. He appealed his conviction on various grounds, including that there was insufficient evidence to find him guilty of soliciting the crimes in question.[5]

The appellate court rejected his claims. A number of recorded conversations made it quite clear that the sheik was counseling or advocating his followers to engage in acts like the planned murder of President Mubarek. For instance, he told someone who turned out to be a government informer that he "should make up with God . . . by turning his rifle's barrel to President Mubarek's chest, and kill[ing] him." Referring to the pending visit of Mubarek to the United States, Abdel Rahman counseled another follower, "Depend on God. Carry out this operation. It does not require a fatwa. . . . You are ready in training, but do it. Go ahead."[6] These statements are clearly requests. In fact, they may even be commands. Either way, the speech acts constitute solicitations because the goal is to induce someone to commit a crime.

Another relatively obvious example of a request involved Robert Crandall, the president of American Airlines. Crandall was accused by the federal government of soliciting Howard Putnam, president of Braniff Airlines, to engage in an attempt to monopolize the airline business in the Dallas–Fort Worth area. Both airlines had their hub at the Dallas–Fort Worth airport, and competition between them was intense; as a result, neither airline made much money. One day, Crandall telephoned Putnam about the problem:

Crandall: I think it's dumb as hell for Christ's sake, all right, to sit here and
   pound the **** out of each other and neither one of us making a ****
   dime.

Putnam: Well—

Crandall: I mean, you know, goddamn, what the **** is the point of it?

Putnam: Nobody asked American to serve Harlingen. Nobody asked American to
   serve Kansas City, and there were low fares in there, you know, before. So—

Crandall: You better believe it, Howard. But, you, you, you know, the complex
   is here—ain't gonna change a goddamn thing, all right. We can, we can both
   live here and there ain't no room for Delta. But there's, ah, no reason that I
   can see, all right, to put both companies out of business.

Putnam: But if you're going to overlay every route of American's on top of over,
   on top of every route that Braniff has—I can't just sit here and allow you to
   bury us without giving our best effort.

Crandall: Oh sure, but Eastern and Delta do the same thing in Atlanta and have
   for years.

Putnam: Do you have a suggestion for me?

Crandall: Yes. I have a suggestion for you. Raise your goddamn fares twenty
   percent. I'll raise mine the next morning.

Putnam: Robert, we—

Crandall: You'll make more money and I will too.

Putnam: We can't talk about pricing.

Crandall: Oh bull ****, Howard. We can talk about any goddamn thing we want
   to talk about.[7]

Did Crandall "request" Putnam to violate the antitrust laws by conspiring to
set prices? Or is this merely a "suggestion," which is what Crandall himself
labeled it, and which would not be criminal?

According to linguist Anna Wierzbicka, who has studied the semantics
of English speech act verbs, if I *suggest* something to you:

1. I say that I think that it would be a good thing if you did the suggested act;
2. I say this because I want you to think about it;
3. I do not know whether you will do it;
4. I do not want to say that I want you to do it.[8]

We can see from this semantic description that Crandall may have made
more than just a suggestion regarding prices. To be exact, Crandall's statement about raising fares meets the first three elements of a suggestion. But
it probably fails on the fourth; it appears that Crandall *does* want to say

that he wants Putnam to raise his fares. If Crandall's statement was just a suggestion, it would not be a crime. But it might well be more.

Could the statement be a *request* (which would qualify as solicitation)? Crandall certainly made his desire clear, which makes it more like a request. Moreover, a request typically benefits the speaker in some way, while a suggestion is usually for the benefit of the addressee.[9] Here, it would benefit both airlines if the two companies could coordinate their prices and strategies. It seems, then, that Crandall was making a request followed by a promise: he requested that Putnam raise his prices, and probably promised implicitly that if Putnam did so, he would do the same. If so, Crandall solicited Putnam to engage in the crime of agreeing to monopolize the airline business in the Dallas–Fort Worth area. That solicitation would itself be illegal, even if the underlying crime—as here—never occurred. Like Abdel Rahman, Crandall was not afraid to speak directly.

Yet it may not always be so easy to determine whether a person has actually engaged in solicitation. In chapter 6, we suggested that the legal system would do well to require corroboration of speech act evidence when there is good reason to doubt its reliability. We used the "two-witness rule" in perjury prosecutions as the model. In fact, built into the federal solicitation statute is a requirement of strongly corroborative evidence:

> Whoever, with intent that another person engage in conduct constituting a felony . . . in violation of the laws of the United States, *and under circumstances strongly corroborative of that intent,* solicits, commands, induces, or otherwise endeavors to persuade such other person to engage in such conduct, shall be imprisoned . . . .[10]

To see how important the corroboration requirement can be, let us consider the case of another Arabic-speaking immigrant with a name remarkably similar to that of the sheik, Jawdat Abdel Rahman, who also found himself in trouble with federal authorities for allegedly soliciting a crime. This Rahman was a storekeeper in Chicago. His son and son-in-law had purchased a large amount of stolen merchandise, which they had entrusted to a man named Haik, never to hear from him again. At one point, Rahman offered $5,000 to an acquaintance named Samara to find Haik, after which Rahman would personally "put a bullet in [Haik's] head." When Samara couldn't locate Haik, he reported back to Rahman with a concocted story that Haik had moved to Michigan. Samara, who turned out to be an FBI informant, also informed the FBI. The FBI then arranged for an undercover agent named Henke to pose as a potential "hit man."

Henke would offer his services to Rahman, to see whether he would snap
at the bait.[11]

When Henke met with Rahman, the conversation did not go as the FBI
had planned. It seems that Rahman was far more interested in retrieving
the goods or payment for them than he was in killing or injuring Haik:

> Rahman (to Henke): I wanna pay nothing ok. If you get it this guy, ok, get
> it the merchandise ok from him the money, ok, I give you, if you take
> thirty thousand dollars, I give you ten thousand dollars. . . . If you get
> nothing. . . .
> Henke: I kill people for a living. Now [Samara] here tells me you want somebody
> dead, is that right? Yes or no?
> Rahman: Uh huh yes. . . .
> Samara (to Rahman in Arabic): If this guy says that he'll get him for you, then
> he will.
> Rahman (in Arabic to Samara): What do I need with him? All I want is my
> money. . . . Now if he brings his head, what am I going to gain? I want my
> rights, he [Haik] cheated me, he [Henke] can have the third, a third of the
> amount that he retrieves. . . .
> Henke: How do you expect to collect the money? What do you want me to do to
> the guy? Uh? You want me to break his legs? You wanta kneecap him? You
> want me to beat him up, break a few ribs, what do you want me to do? . . .
> My standard fee is five thousand dollars to kill somebody, not to collect,
> to kill.
> Rahman: I don't want to kill.[12]

Yet, as the conversation continued, sometimes in Arabic, sometimes in English, a few potentially incriminating snippets emerged. For example:

> Rahman (to Henke): Excuse me. If you break her leg . . . or break her har [sic]
> arm or, something from her body, that's sixty thousand dollars.
> Henke: Alright.
> Rahman: Talk to the police, you call the police, is that money from eh,
> somebody else, you call somebody, you break my neck or break arm, just . . .
> after I get it the money.
> Henke: Oh, I see.
> Rahman: I want die.
> Henke: Alright. Alright. Now we're, ok.
> Rahman: I, I don't wanna to break her neck, if I broke . . .
> Henke: Ok.

Rahman: If I go . . .

Henke: So you want me to get the money and then kill him as soon as he gives
   me . . .

Rahman: Uh get the money . . .

Henke: Alright.

Rahman: . . . kill him.[13]

For the most part, though, Rahman showed no interest in the plan. Henke left it that Rahman was to get back to him about paying $2,500 for the killing. But Rahman never did, and he and his family expressed surprise when Henke returned to say that he had kidnapped Haik. (Actually the kidnapping was staged by the FBI, who had found Haik and "turned" him.) At that point, the family seemed frightened, and was more interested in convincing Henke not to behave violently.

Nonetheless, Rahman was convicted of soliciting theft by means of violent acts. Perhaps all of Henke's talk of murder, combined with Rahman's malevolent bluster, led the jury to believe that he really had solicited violence. Linguist Roger Shuy, who has analyzed many conversations of this kind, points out that tape recordings of violent talk and transcripts based on them have a particularly strong influence on the jury. People sometimes recall the substance of the conversation without paying adequate attention to who said what.[14] For this reason, it may be useful to admit expert testimony in order to point out the structure of a conversation, so that the jury can keep clear which party introduced potentially incriminating topics and which party actually made the potentially incriminating statements. Such testimony will not often be necessary, but when it would be helpful to the jury it should be allowed.

The court of appeals reversed, deciding that there was insufficient evidence to support the conviction, a relatively rare ground for reversal because appellate courts tend to defer to factual determinations of the lower courts. Nonetheless, the court held that

> no reasonable jury could have based a conviction on a strict literal interpretation of a few words of Rahman's rudimentary English. Rahman had a tendency to answer Henke's questions by simply repeating what Henke said. Furthermore, after Rahman answered, "Uh huh yes," to Henke's question, "you want somebody dead, is that right?," Rahman immediately turned to Samara and explained in Arabic that he did not want the hit man to kill Haik. The record as a whole overwhelmingly contradicts the contents of these few fragments taken literally.[15]

Although the court regarded Rahman's conduct as "reprehensible," it observed that "there was scant evidence to show, let alone meet the statutory requirement to strongly corroborate, Rahman's intent to have Henke rob and extort Haik through violence."[16]

Other courts have found the distinction between actually requesting that someone engage in a criminal act and simply talking about it to be more elusive. Consider the case of a Colorado man named Hood who—in a tale oft told in films and books—had an affair with another woman and decided to kill his wife. Of course, a divorce would have been less messy, but it would also have been less lucrative because it would have prevented him from collecting on his wife's life insurance policy.

After deciding that he needed to dispose of his wife, Hood met with a friend, Michael Maher, and began to discuss his unhappiness with his marriage, aggravated by the fact that his wife had lupus. As Maher later testified at trial, Hood concluded that his wife was "better off dead." Hood went on to describe several schemes he had considered to kill his wife, such as causing a car accident. Hood had also contemplated staging a robbery, during which his wife would meet an untimely demise, but added that he needed a third person to "pull the trigger." Maher's reaction was that Hood should seek psychological help, to which Hood retorted: "No, she needs to die." Maher testified that Hood seemed quite serious. When Maher commented that Hood had obviously thought about this a lot, Hood replied, "Oh yes, I have." Hood later induced his girlfriend to commit the act and was convicted of conspiring to murder his wife and also of soliciting both the girlfriend and Maher to commit it.

But did Hood really request that Maher kill his wife? He seems to have sincerely wanted her dead, but that is not enough. Maher testified on cross-examination that Hood never directly asked him to kill his wife. Nonetheless, Maher assumed that when Hood suggested he needed someone to "pull the trigger," he was referring to Maher. After all, Maher was the only person in the room. The jury agreed, and the Colorado court of appeals affirmed.[17]

It is true, as we have seen, that requests are often made indirectly. Recall the *Bustamonte* case in chapter 3, where the policeman's ostensible question "Does the trunk open?" was understood as a request or command to open the trunk. Likewise, we hope to have shown in chapter 4 that statements like "I need to talk to a lawyer" should be viewed as requests for counsel. However, we also saw that such statements are most likely to be interpreted as requests, or perhaps commands, when the person making them has the right or power or authority to make a request or command to the addressee, and where the addressee is able to fulfill the request or command. If you drive to a tire store and declare that you "need" to have four new tires installed on your car, specifying the brand and model, you have probably requested or ordered the tires. Yet if, when discussing your car, you tell your hair stylist that you "need" new tires, you are probably not making a request.

Consequently, if Maher was a known hit man, Hood's statement that he needed someone to pull the trigger might well have been a request. It appears that Maher was just a friend, however, which suggests that Hood may just have been telling him about his problems and how he intended to solve them. Only later did he carry out his plan with his girlfriend. However morally repulsive it may be, simply intending to violate the law, or telling someone that you plan to do so, is not a crime.

It is certainly easy to understand why the jury convicted Hood of asking Maher to murder Hood's wife. Later events revealed that he was deadly serious. In fact, the appellate court found that the subsequent solicitation of Hood's girlfriend provided the corroboration of intent that was required to demonstrate that he also intended to solicit Maher. Nonetheless, it strikes us that it would be hard to reach this conclusion beyond a reasonable doubt.

At the same time, it is undoubtedly true that when people talk about committing crimes, they tend to do so very indirectly. The cases of Sheik Rahman and Robert Crandall are exceptional in how openly they discussed violating the law. Criminals commonly use code and argot to conceal their illegal plans.

Consider the case of a Mr. Talley, who was arrested by an FBI agent for engaging in various illegal acts. Shortly after being arrested, Talley contacted a close friend named Tyler and mentioned the FBI agent and a government informant, both of whom were critical witnesses against him. Talley told Tyler to "take 'um out and pop 'um." Tyler understood this to be a request for him to kill the two potential witnesses. Quite properly, Tyler reported the incident to law enforcement officials, who arranged for Tyler to secretly tape-record a subsequent conversation with Talley in an effort to memorialize incriminating statements:

Tyler: All right. So I know what me and you's [sic] already talked about.
Talley: Right.
Tyler: And I know then . . .
Talley: (Unintelligible), yeah.
Tyler: Listen, listen . . .
Talley: Call it the thing.
Tyler: Huh?

Talley: Call it the thing.

Tyler: Call what?

Talley: What me and you talked about.

Tyler: What the pop?

Talley: Yeah.

Tyler: All right. We'll call it the thing then. All right.[18]

Talley was right to be cautious, although his clumsy efforts at secrecy failed when he revealed the code word over a telephone line that was being tapped. The point is that people who are engaged in criminal activity will usually speak very circuitously about what they are doing, especially when they suspect that someone may be eavesdropping or recording the conversation.

The tendency of individuals engaged in criminal activity to speak indirectly or in code or in languages other than English, combined with the high standard of proof in criminal cases, makes it more difficult to obtain convictions. We manage to communicate remarkably well using human language, but a great deal of ambiguity and uncertainty regarding the communicative intentions of others is virtually inevitable. The higher burden of proof in criminal cases resolves linguistic ambiguities in favor of the individual and thus helps avoid the danger that people will be convicted on the basis of an overly literal interpretation of what they said.

Solicitation does not require that the person solicited agree to commit the crime.[19] Recall the alleged attempt of Mr. Crandall to solicit Putnam, a proposal to which Putnam plainly did not agree. Crandall could nonetheless be prosecuted for solicitation. If the person solicited does agree, however, the result may be a conspiracy, which is the topic of the next section.

Conspiracy

A conspiracy is an agreement by two or more people to commit a crime. Where there is an explicit agreement, one party will generally have proposed or suggested a plan, with which the other party agrees. Or they will hammer it out together. Although obtaining explicit evidence of such agreements is relatively rare, conspiracy is a favorite among prosecutors because the planned crime does not have to be carried out—it is illegal simply to agree to commit it. The judge or jury can infer agreement from the actions of the parties to the conspiracy. In fact, evidence that the defendant acted to promote the objectives of a conspiracy allows the jury to presume that the defendant was a knowing participant.[20] This means that the agreement can be proven by circumstantial evidence. Indeed, it almost always is.

In addition, many jurisdictions require that the agreement be followed by an *overt act*. The additional requirement of an overt act in furtherance of the conspiracy appears to be aimed at ensuring that the conspirators are serious, as well as providing concrete evidence that the conspiracy did indeed exist.

Of course, sometimes two or more people simply commit a crime together without necessarily having agreed to do so. Thus, the fact that one person sells illegal drugs to another may support drug-related charges against both of them, but is not in itself evidence of a conspiracy to violate the drug laws.[21] The same issue arises under the antitrust laws, especially where a conspiracy to fix prices is alleged. If one gasoline station raises its prices and the other nearby stations follow suit, there is not necessarily a conspiracy to fix prices. It is normally legal to raise prices, and as long as each station acts independently, no crime has been committed. On the other hand, if they agree to follow each others' price increases, there probably is a conspiracy.[22] Therefore, it often matters a great deal whether parties are acting independently or in accordance with a tacit or express agreement.

Many times there may be linguistic cues from which a jury can infer that there is either an agreement or not. Linguist Georgia Green analyzed a case where the defendant, an athlete, was invited to the apartment of a drug dealer to autograph an athletic program. Also at the apartment was a government agent, who was covertly recording the meeting. The government later accused the athlete of being involved in a conspiracy with the dealer to sell cocaine. Green points out, however, that when the dealer talked about selling drugs, he used the singular pronoun "I" rather than the plural "we."[23] This is strong evidence that the dealer considered himself to be acting in an individual capacity, rather than being a member of a conspiracy. The athlete was acquitted.

In contrast, use of the plural pronoun "we" helped establish the presence of a conspiracy to rig bids at auctions and to avoid the payment of federal income taxes. Part of this conspiracy involved the participants' buying and selling property among themselves, generally paying each other in cash to avoid having the transactions come to the attention of income tax authorities. A critical statement by one of the conspirators, captured on tape by an informant, was that "we don't want any check writing between us. If we get caught by IRS, we'll be dead."[24] This suggests not only knowledge that the scheme was illegal, but that the participants were acting in concert.

On another occasion, a Mr. Gerenstein was accused of conspiring with someone named Harden to kill Gerenstein's wife. Harden went to the police, who persuaded him to wear a body wire in an effort to gather additional evidence on tape. References to the proposed killing were indirect, but at one point the men began to discuss the type of weapon to use. Gerenstein remarked, "[T]hen don't use a gun. . . . A blade and that's what I would do. I wouldn't use a gun or I wouldn't leave the knife. I would do the job or I would use a rope and cut her head off. But you don't have to listen to me. You do it your way. But I don't want to talk about it no more."[25] Although there is, again, no direct evidence of an agreement to kill Mrs. Gerenstein, the discussion of weapon types is certainly incriminating. Combined with the admonition not to talk about it any more, it suggests that the conspirators were quite serious. Even then, of course, one might argue that the men might merely have been at the stage of talking over the possibilities. But Gerenstein's comment to "do it your way" is strong evidence that he actually intended the goal of the conspiracy—murdering his wife—to take place. Fortunately, his wife was never killed, but Gerenstein was convicted of both conspiracy and criminal solicitation.

As with solicitation, people engaged in conspiracies often suspect that they may be overheard or recorded by means of wiretaps or other devices. They therefore tend to use street slang and codes. Street slang, of course, is language that is generally known in the community, or a subpart of the community. Codes, on the other hand, are a type of private language, usually agreed on between the parties and intended to keep conversations secret. Because conspiracies involve a longer-term relationship among the conspirators, and because participants have an interest in keeping their communications secret, they are especially likely to develop codes. A consequence is that inferences from language that a conspiracy exists are more difficult to make because the conversations of participants may be almost incomprehensible to outsiders.

For example, in proving that Antjuan Sydnor was involved in a conspiracy to distribute crack cocaine, the government introduced a recording of a telephone conversation in which the ringleader, Gibbs, told another participant that he had "done something" for Sydnor. An FBI agent with extensive experience in drug enforcement testified that "doing something" means turning cocaine into crack. Gibbs continued, "It was one funny looking jawn and I gave it to him. [It] . . . came out to . . . eight seven five and nine the other one came out like eight . . . twenty three. . . ." The FBI agent interpreted this to mean that the "jawn," alleged to refer to cocaine, had a funny color. He also testified that the numbers referred to two half-kilograms of the drug, which weighed 875 and 823 grams after Gibbs had cooked them into crack.[26]

Clearly, someone has to explain to jurors what terms like "doing something" and "jawn" mean. There are several potential problems, however. One is that the interpretation is typically done by a law enforcement officer, perhaps someone involved in investigating and arresting the suspects. That officer may be one of the few people who understand the argot or code being used by the suspects, but he also has a strong interest in securing a conviction and is usually convinced that they are guilty. Observer bias plagues even the most well-intended scientific research. It is all the more problematic when an expert is not a scientist doing disinterested research, but rather an individual with an institutional stake in the outcome of the case.[27]

Moreover, the agent in this case went beyond explaining what individual words and phrases meant, often discussing what he believed to be the plans and intentions of the speakers. We have no doubt that "doing something" could be used to refer to cooking crack, and—if it is clear that this is a code phrase—it would be appropriate for the agent to explain this to the jury. But this phrase also has a vastly more ordinary meaning that could lead to a more innocent interpretation.

On another occasion, Gibbs was recorded while apparently discussing a plan to hurt or kill someone who had shot him:

Gibbs: I was um, telling T, you know, when he getting ready to go inside that, that, club his pants be down, you know what I mean.

Fluellen: That's, that's what we trying to find out now. . . .

Gibbs: They pull his pants down to go in there cause they don't play that in there, you know.

Fluellen: That's what I, I tryin' to find out which jawn he go to.

Gibbs: Yeah. . . . Right here, before when you get out of there he gotta take it and leave it in there with him in there, you know what I mean.

Fluellen: A huh.

Gibbs: It'll be in the wheel.

Fluellen: Ah huh.

Gibbs: I might you know that's like the perfect place and shit.

Fluellen: Yeah I know. Ok, that's what "E" was talkin' bout then.[28]

During the trial, the FBI agent explained that Gibbs was saying that the club at Forty-seventh Street and Woodland Avenue had a metal detector so that guests could not enter with a gun. Although "jawn" can apparently refer to almost any noun, the agent stated that here it referred to a nightclub. Also, when people have "their pants down" they are unarmed, and "in the wheel" means "in the car." The agent also testified that Gibbs was apparently suggesting that they allow the victim to enter the club, where he would necessarily be unarmed, and then shoot him when he came out.[29]

The FBI agent here is not merely interpreting. He gives content to the virtually contentless word "jawn," which seems to be just as general and vague as terms like "thing" or "stuff" or "crap."[30] The plan that Gibbs had in mind is nowhere stated expressly. Although the agent's educated guess about what they plan to do seems reasonable in light of other evidence, making such inferences is a typical jury function, not the job of an expert witness. In fact, the court of appeals decided that the agent had at times overstepped the bounds of proper expert testimony, but concluded that the error was harmless in light of other evidence.[31]

A further problem with street slang and coded language is that it casts suspicion on those who use it, suggesting that they are involved in criminal activity. This is not unlike the assumption that anyone who wears baggy trousers must be part of a gang, whose members often wear such trousers, even though gang-like clothing is considered fashionable in some urban areas. In a Texas case, the court cited evidence that the defendant used terms like "longs," "shorts," and "apples,"—which refer to a gram, a half-gram, and an ounce of cocaine, respectively—as evidence that he was involved in a conspiracy to sell drugs.[32] By the same token, it certainly did not help Antjuan Sydnor that he was recorded speaking street slang and code with the ringleader. The court of appeals specifically noted his familiarity with coded drug language when affirming his conviction.[33] Sydnor was obviously involved in illegal drug transactions with members of the conspiracy, for which he seems to have been properly convicted, but the decision that he conspired with others to sell drugs on a wider scale may have been more a matter of guilt by linguistic association.

Bribery

Giving someone an item of value with the intent to induce that person to act in a particular way in her official capacity can constitute bribery. Conversely, the act of taking or receiving the item of value is also a crime. Bribery also has a mental component: the item of value must be "corruptly" offered or received for the purpose of influencing official action.[34] Thus, there must be an act (giving or receiving), accompanied by the proper mental state. An additional requirement is that the recipient of the bribe must belong to a specified class of people, typically someone who can influence government action. This includes not only government officials, but generally also witnesses in court cases.[35]

Bribery can be accomplished by the physical acts of giving or receiving, or—and this will be our concern—through words alone. The briber might simply *offer* something of value, rather than actually giving it immediately. Under common law, bribery was analogized to contracts, so the crime was not complete until the offer was followed by acceptance. Today, acceptance is not required; it is illegal to make the offer regardless of acceptance. It is also illegal for government officials to *request* a bribe or to *agree* to accept one. There are thus at least three different speech acts that can be involved in bribing: offering, requesting, and agreeing.

Because bribery is a criminal act, it is generally done surreptitiously. Thus, the language of bribing, as one might expect, may be indirect. We have already seen that requests are often made indirectly, usually for reasons of politeness. Requests for bribes are equally indirect, though for a different reason. People involved in bribery hope to achieve what politicians have come to call *plausible deniability*. With reference to bribes, plausible deniability means making a bribe in such a way that one can later claim that it was not a bribe at all.

Consider the California case of *People v. King*, in which a juror approached one of the parties to a lawsuit and said that it was "down the drain" but that "for peanuts" it could be "turned your way." The court held that this was a request for a bribe.[36] Likewise, for an official to suggest that a bidder on a government project should "take care of him" or make a "gesture" toward him has been held to constitute a request for a bribe.[37] Although both of these phrases are relatively vague, it is worth noting that expressions relating to making or giving someone a "small gesture" conventionally accompany the presentation of a gift or tip. Additionally, bidders on a government project do not normally "take care of" or make "gestures" to officials unless they intend to offer a bribe. In this context, therefore, any suggestion by an official that he should receive something extra from a bidder could probably be taken as a request for a bribe.

According to press reports on corruption among elected officials in Chicago, aldermen have been known to indirectly accept a bribe by saying in response to an offer, "It's not really necessary." One of the interviewed aldermen described this as "a different language, a different code, how to say no and yes at the same time." Interestingly, they use this code—just like drug dealers—in case somebody is listening in on the conversation.[38] Note that "It's not really necessary" is commonly said by a person who receives an unexpected gift, and who means to say, "You didn't really have to give me this gift, but I thank you and accept it."

Both offering and accepting bribes can be done not just indirectly, but nonverbally. While living overseas, one of us (Tiersma) was told about an official in the local immigration office who, when he felt a gratuity might be appropriate, would open a drawer in his desk. The applicant was expected to slowly place banknotes into the drawer. When the official felt that the offered amount was sufficient, he would close the drawer. True or not, it is a nice illustration of how both the request for the bribe, as well as accepting it, can be accomplished without saying a word. The same holds for offering bribes, which can be accomplished by placing money in a passport or driver's license that is handed over to government officials.

Sometimes the nature of the speech act of *promising* is also relevant in a bribery case. A federal bribery law, for example, requires that the money given to a public official must be in exchange for a promise by the official to engage in some future act.[39] This requirement was an important issue in the Abscam investigation and trials that took place in the late 1970s and early 1980s. Briefly, several members of Congress were approached by a government agents posing as representatives of wealthy Arab sheiks with large amounts of money to spend. What the agents of the pretended sheiks sought from the congressmen was a promise that they would help the sheiks with possible immigration difficulties in the future. In exchange, the congressmen were to receive thousands of dollars in cash.

Congressman Myers from Pennsylvania readily walked into the trap, as evidenced by a videotaped meeting between Myers and the representatives. When the representative mentioned possible immigration problems, Myers responded, "Absolutely. Where I could be of help in this type of a matter, first of all, is private bills that can be introduced . . . if I wanta keep somebody in the country, all I do is introduce a private bill." At the end of the meeting the sheik's representative handed Myers an envelope with $50,000 in $100 bills. "Spend it well," he said. Myers replied, "Pleasure."[40]

It certainly seems that the sheik's agent offered Myers a bribe, and that Myers readily agreed to, and did, accept it. Denying the obvious would have been a poor defense strategy. Instead, Myers and several other Abscam defendants claimed that they were only "playacting." Although it is clear that Myers accepted the money he was offered, he claimed that he never promised the sheik anything. In other words, he was not sincere when making what seemed to be a promise.[41] If the congressman never really promised to do anything in exchange for the cash, the money he received would simply have constituted a gift. The defense was allowed to make this argument at trial, but the jury—based on their guilty verdicts—rejected it.

It appears from the facts recited in the appellate court's opinion that Myers seemed to be quite sincere when he told the sheik's representative that he could, if necessary, introduce a private bill. Accepting the money that the sheik offered confirms that conclusion. Myers appeared to be making a valid promise, albeit indirectly. Recall from our earlier discussion that a promise that appears to be sincere counts as a valid promise even if the speaker secretly does not intend to carry it out. Myers thus successfully performed the speech act of promising, despite his later claim to have been doing otherwise. The court of appeals agreed, holding that Myers could be convicted of bribery for making promises to people he believed were offering him money to influence his official actions, even if the promises were secretly not sincere.[42] The critical point is that, despite any secret reservations he may have harbored, he intended his promise to be taken seriously.[43]

The crime of bribery is similar to solicitation and conspiracy in that they all involve multiple participants who somehow act together—willingly or not—to accomplish an illegal act. The critical speech acts are usually requesting and agreeing, two actions that are inherently cooperative. In the next chapter we turn to threats, which depend on compulsion rather than cooperation.

Threats

I am going to get you,
bitch!

Threatening people is generally considered bad form, but threats are usually not criminal in and of themselves. An employer has not committed a crime if she tells one of her workers, "If you make one more obscene gesture at a customer, you'll be fired." Threats become illegal, however, if they are made to accomplish certain goals, or if they are directed at certain people. It is illegal under federal law, for example, to threaten federal officials or the U.S. president.[1]

Similarly, to ask a person on the street for money is usually nothing more than begging or panhandling; there may be restrictions on when and where a person can solicit money, but it is not normally a crime. But if the request or demand is accompanied by a threat that causes the victim to hand over property against her will, the action may constitute robbery. Threats are also an intimate part of the crimes of extortion and blackmail, where the victim consents to give money or property to the extortionist, but only because of his threat to do something bad to the victim in the future.[2] Likewise, using threats to cause another person to engage in sexual intercourse is generally considered rape.

Crimes like robbery, extortion, and rape often involve using physical force to overcome the will of the victim. Force typically involves actual violence. Threats provide a basis for criminal liability if they instill fear of violence as retribution for failing to comply with a demand. Obtaining money, property, or sex from someone is a crime if it is done against the will or without the consent of the giver, or if the giver consents only under duress. Whether such actions are accomplished by actual violence or the threat of violence is usually immaterial. In contrast, threats that do not instill fear are not likely to be considered crimes.

Thus, while threats are not essential in committing crimes like extortion, robbery, or rape, they are frequently used to accomplish them. Rather than dealing with each of these crimes separately, we here consider the nature of threats in general.

What Constitutes a Threat?

Threats are similar to warnings and predictions in that all three concern events or states of affairs that are likely to happen in the future. Threats must therefore be carefully distinguished from these other speech acts. Linguist Bruce Fraser posits that to make a threat, a speaker must

1. express an intention to personally commit an act, or to be responsible for having an act occur;
2. believe that the act will lead to an unfavorable state of affairs to the addressee; and
3. intend to intimidate the addressee through the addressee's awareness of the speaker's intention.[3]

An additional requirement is that a threat, like most other speech acts, must be intended to be taken seriously.

The first of Fraser's requirements implies that threats deal with matters that will happen in the future. In this sense, they resemble *predictions*. Yet there is an important difference. When we predict that something will happen, we simply state that we believe that a certain state of affairs will come about in the future. When we make a threat, on the other hand, we express our intention to bring about or cause the state of affairs to happen. This distinction was important not long ago in a labor dispute. During an election by factory workers deciding whether to be represented by a union, plant officials stated that unionization would lead to increased costs of doing business and intimated that as a result it might become necessary to close the plant. Was this a threat to shut down operations (which would have been illegal under these circumstances) or merely a prediction? The answer depends on whether the employer was stating or suggesting that it intended to bring about this future state of affairs (a threat), or was simply saying that this state of affairs was likely to come about if the workers voted to unionize (a prediction). The court held that the statements did not constitute a threat to close the plant in case of a union victory.[4]

Just as requests and commands can be hard to distinguish from one another, threats can be hard to distinguish from predictions. Both types of verbal acts tend to use the future tense. Consider the plight of an impetuous youth who sent a letter to the White House during the presidency of Ronald Reagan. It read, "Ronnie, Listen Chump! Resign or You'll Get Your Brains Blown Out." Below these words was a drawing of a gun with a bullet emerging from it. The sender, David Hoffman, was convicted of threatening the life of the president and sentenced to four years in prison.[5] Was this merely a prediction, as the dissent argued on appeal, or a real threat, as decided by the majority? Hoffman used the future tense, which could signal either a threat or a prediction. The critical issue, as noted above, is whether he communicated his intent to bring about this state of affairs (that is, to kill Reagan or have him killed), or whether he was simply predicting that, given the mood of the country, someone else out there was likely to commit the deed. The jury concluded that he had done more than speculate about the future, and the appellate court affirmed. The dissent pointed out that Hoffman used the passive voice ("You'll Get Your Brains Blown Out"), which suggests that he did not plan to be personally responsible for the killing.[6] When combined with evidence that he had psychiatric problems, one wonders whether he was really making a credible threat.

In another case, a man made a potentially threatening statement about the future to a woman whom he had dated in high school. She had since married and started a family with someone else. At some point the man wrote her this letter:

> Your Husband, David Goldstein will have his health take a turn for the worse this Christmas Season and you will be widowed in 1990. I am truly sorry that this is the "Kay Ser Ra Ser Ra" scenario that has to take place. However you will always be the foci of my desires as I remember you to be the most exuisite [sic] creature that has ever taken me in. I'm always grateful that we have had the moments given to us and I will be there should you ever desire me again. I can say with all sincerity, I Love You.[7]

Does this letter contain merely a prediction that the husband will die? The trial court held this and similar communications to be so ambiguous that it granted the defendant a judgment of acquittal before the case went to the jury. The court of appeals, however, reversed the lower court's decision and sent the matter to trial. It pointed out that the defendant had a twenty-year history of stalking and harassing the woman and her family. Against this background, what might seem like a prediction (regarding a bad state of affairs that might happen in the future) could quite reasonably be viewed as a threat: a bad state of affairs that the speaker intended to bring about.[8]

A second requirement for a threat is that the speaker believe that the future state of affairs will be bad for the addressee. Someone usually does not threaten you by saying that he intends to *give* you a million dollars. It might be a threat, on the other hand, if someone tells you that he intends to *take* money from you.

In this respect threats resemble *warnings,* which also refer to a bad future state of affairs. Sometimes, in fact, threats are made in the guise of warnings, as when a known thugs says, "Just a friendly little warning— if you date my girlfriend again, you're dead meat." But if a friend tells the amorous young man that he should stop dating the thug's girlfriend, it would be a warning. Warnings are typically aimed at protecting the addressee from a potential harm caused by natural forces or someone else.[9] We can warn someone against a harm that we cause ourselves, but in that case the injury would have to be unintended ("Get out of the way! My brakes are failing!").

A relevant incident occurred in the Santa Ynez Valley in California, which is an increasingly popular wine-producing area. Some local residents have become concerned about ancient oak trees being cut down and natural areas being plowed over to make way for more vineyards. An article in the magazine *Earth First!* declared that if vintner Kendall Jackson, which had cut down many oak trees to allow planting of vineyards, "doesn't remove their newly-planted grapevines and irrigation pipes in a prompt and orderly fashion, perhaps some brave midnight warriors will have to do it themselves, the old fashion way."[10] Is this a prediction, a warning, or a threat? Law enforcement officers took it as a threat, and promptly told area vintners to be on the lookout for midnight eco-warriors. The critical issue is whether this statement was aimed at alerting Kendall Jackson to a potential danger caused by others, or whether the article suggested that the magazine's supporters would do the act themselves, which would make it a threat. The phrase "will have to" certainly lends some weight to finding it a threat rather than a warning.

Similarly, people often use the word "promise" to issue what are actually threats. Like threats, promises express an intention to engage in an act or create a certain state of affairs in the future. Typically, however, a promise involves an act or future state of affairs that will benefit the addressee, while a threat portends something harmful. Thus, saying to someone, "Lay one hand on my car, and I promise you'll regret it" is a threat, whether or not it is also a promise.

The third of Fraser's criteria for a threat is that the speaker must intend to *intimidate* the addressee through the addressee's awareness of the speaker's intention. The intent to intimidate can be critical when prosecuting hate crimes. The government can generally prohibit threats of racial violence. Even though such threats are technically a type of "speech," the Supreme Court has repeatedly held that they are not protected by the Free Speech Clause of the First Amendment.[11]

Consequently, when someone burned a cross near an apartment building that was experiencing racial tensions, he could be prosecuted for violating a federal statute that prohibited threatening or intimidating people who are exercising rights guaranteed by the Constitution or federal law. Ultimately, whether he actually threatened residents would be up to the jury to decide, but the fact that the cross-burning took place near a specific apartment building would support the conclusion that it was meant to intimidate the occupants of the building, rather than merely making a political statement.[12] In contrast, burning a cross as part of a political rally at a remote location would be less likely to threaten any person in particular.[13] In light of American history, the message of hate conveyed by cross-burning is quite frightening to most people, but the context of a political rally would usually prevent it from being taken as expressing an intent to cause a specified harm to a particular person. Here, it seems correct to regard it as more of a political statement, not a threat.

The intent to intimidate was also an issue in the prosecution of a student named Baker who was accused of making a threatening communication through interstate commerce, which is a federal crime.[14] Using a computer in Ann Arbor, Michigan, Baker exchanged email messages with someone named Gonda in Ontario, Canada. The men exchanged messages describing some violent fantasies about sexual acts that they would like to commit on young girls, such as the following:

I highly agree with the type of woman you like to hurt. You seem to have the same tastes I have. When you come down, this'll be fun! Also, I've been thinking.

I want to do it to a really young girl first. 13 or 14. Their innocence makes them so much more fun—and they'll be easier to control. What do you think?[15]

This is certainly offensive, but probably not criminal. As the trial judge observed, describing fantasies or desires does not necessarily rise to the level of actually expressing an intent to commit those acts.

This was not the end of the matter, however. Before long the men seem to come much closer to expressing an intention to carry out their morbid fantasies, as the following exchange of emails reveals:

> Baker: Just thinking about it anymore doesn't do the trick. . . . I need TO DO IT.
> Gonda: My feelings exactly! We have to get together. . . . I will give you more details as soon as I find out my situation. . . .
> Baker: Alrighty then. If not next week. or in January. then definitely sometime in the Summer. Pickings are better than too. Although it's more crowded.[16]

It sounds as though the men have moved from fantasizing to actually planning to carry out their fantasies. But did they intend to intimidate the addressee through the addressee's awareness of their intentions? Because this was private email correspondence between two individuals, the answer clearly is no. Baker obviously did not intend to intimidate Gonda, and no one else was aware of the messages. As the court of appeals observed, "Even if a reasonable person would take the communications between Baker and Gonda as serious expressions of an intention to inflict bodily harm, no reasonable person would perceive such communications as being conveyed to effect some change or achieve some goal through intimidation."[17] Repulsive as this young man's messages might be, they did not constitute real threats.[18] Of course, it would have been another matter entirely if Baker had sent his messages to a potential victim, or if he were being prosecuted for participating in a conspiracy.

A final requirement, common to many speech acts, is that a threat must appear to be *sincere*. In chapter 9 we saw that someone who makes what seems to be a promise, while secretly not intending to carry out the promised act, will be understood to have made a promise nonetheless. The same is true of threats. People often jokingly make statements that might be considered threats if taken literally, but that are evidently not meant to be taken as such. In one case a firefighter claimed that his superior threatened him by saying, "I should just shoot you." In light of the circumstances and the firefighter's own testimony that he did not take the comment seriously, the court held that the statement was merely intended as a joke.[19]

It is important to emphasize that to make a threat, the speaker does not *actually* have to be sincere, but need only *appear* sincere. To be more exact, the speaker must intend the hearer to believe that the speaker intends to carry out the threatened act.[20] If a robber approaches you in a dark alley, shows you a gun, and tells you that he will kill you unless you give him your wallet, it does not matter that the robber might have absolutely no intention of carrying out his threat. He has made a threat nonetheless, because his intention was to appear sincere and thereby intimidate you into handing over your money. The question of sincerity is often an important issue surrounding politically motivated utterances, a subject that we address in greater detail toward the end of this chapter.

Indirect and Ambiguous Threats

Threats—like other speech acts in general and like crimes of language in particular—tend to be made indirectly. Alternatively, they may be phrased in ambiguous terms to give them plausible deniability. As with other speech acts, pragmatic factors count for a lot in determining whether an utterance is a threat or something else.

Sometimes threats can be made by gestures. A man who placed his hands around the victim's neck was held to have threatened her with violence in a rape case.[21] Burning a Vietnamese fisherman in effigy, in an area where there was hostility by native fisherman to competing immigrants from Vietnam, has been held to communicate a threat.[22] A defendant who made hand gestures in the shape of a gun to a prosecution witness entering the courtroom was also held to have made a threat.[23] In each of these cases, the defendant expressed—in gestural form—an intention to commit an act; the defendant apparently believed that the act would lead to an unfavorable state of affairs to the addressee; and finally, the act was intended to intimidate the addressee through the addressee's awareness of the speaker's intention.[24] There is no doubt that in the proper circumstances, gestures that mimic acts of violence, and are not understood as a joke, can be threatening.

Even when expressed verbally, threats are frequently indirect or intentionally ambiguous. Suppose that a person tells someone, "You make one move[,] you big ugly motherfucker[,] and I will put a hole in you."[25] Just what the speaker means by this comment might, in isolation, be somewhat obscure (although it does not sound like a pleasant prospect, to be sure).

The context and surrounding circumstances—that the speaker is furious at the addressee and is holding a gun—clearly makes this a threat.

Is it a threat for someone who had accosted a woman and meets her later, perhaps believing that she had reported the incident to police, to tell her that "I am going to get you, bitch"?[26] The word "get" has a number of meanings, most quite innocuous. Yet among the myriad meanings of "get" in the *American Heritage Dictionary* is one that appears especially applicable here: "[to] take revenge on, especially to kill in revenge for a wrong."[27] Under the circumstances—the woman had escaped his earlier assault and presumably reported the incident—the interpretation that the defendant was threatening her with revenge seems apt. Observe that in both this and the previous case, the use of abusive epithets ("bitch," "ugly motherfucker") underscores the threatening nature of the utterance.[28]

What if the perpetrator of a crime tells witnesses that if they say anything to the police, "something [is] going to happen to them?"[29] Normally, the fact that "something" will happen is not all that menacing; the speaker does not directly state that he is going to commit an act of any kind, nor is there any particular suggestion that "something" would be unfavorable to the addressee. The circumstances, again, make all the difference. Here, the court's decision that this was a threat seems justified by the context.

Consider also a case where an accused rapist told the victim, "I don't want to hurt you." Taken in isolation or in the context of a loving relationship, this could mean that the man is concerned about the woman's welfare and does not want the act of sexual intercourse to injure her. This is the view that the court seems to have taken, holding that these words were not threatening enough to constitute duress, thus deeming the intercourse consensual.[30] But the court may have been a bit too literal, perhaps even patriarchal. Would the judge have reached the same conclusion if the defendant had approached the woman in a dark alley and said, "Give me your purse—I don't want to hurt you"? We doubt it.

Overall, however, most courts are less generous to defendants who make what are arguably threatening statements, at least judging from recent published appellate opinions. In *People v. Hunt*, for instance, the defendant drove a young woman to a remote area, where she apparently consented to engage in sex. The defendant did not explicitly threaten her. Nonetheless, he was convicted of rape. The court of appeals affirmed, noting that threats may be inferred from conduct. Specifically, the man had refused the woman's pleas to turn the car around, and the jury could reasonably have concluded from her testimony that she was genuinely afraid for her safety.[31] In another case a man was convicted of rape when he took a woman to a hotel on the pretext of finding her a job. When she hesitated to enter the room, he pushed her and said that she would not get out until she undressed and went to bed with him. The appellate court held that her apparent consent was induced by threats and upheld the conviction.[32]

We have seen in previous chapters that a question can sometimes be a statement, and that a statement can be a question. For example, "Didn't you say I had a right to a lawyer?" may be equivalent to "I request a lawyer," and "It sure would be too bad if one of those disabled children found that shotgun" can, in the proper circumstances, constitute a question: "Where is the shotgun?" Not surprisingly, a question can also constitute a threat. A woman in Nebraska received harassing telephone calls from a man and reported it to the police, who charged the man with making intimidating calls. A month later the man again called the woman, informed her that he had been forced to pay a fine, and continued by asking, "What should I do to retaliate?" Even though, on the surface, this was no more than a question, the court had no trouble concluding that the statement could be viewed "as promising punishment, reprisal, or distress."[33] The threat exists in the presupposition. Asking what he should do to retaliate presupposes that he intends to retaliate. Communicating this intention to the victim can reasonably be considered a threat.[34]

An illustration from California involved a litigant with little success in the courts. He wrote a letter to some of the judges asking, "Are all the windows insured?" The court of appeals held that this question, in context, could be a threat:

> The concluding words of his letters to Judges Swain, Smith and Huls are not such as to be a simple inquiry into the status of the insurance on their respective windows. We think that the words (are all windows insured?) as used in context with the remaining parts of the letters and considering all of the other facts and circumstances could well be adapted to imply a threat to do damage to the respective judges or to their property.[35]

When it comes to threats, then, courts for the most part find indirect or obscure expression to be quite natural. Regarding extortion, which is often accomplished by threats, the California Supreme Court wrote over a century ago that "[p]arties guilty of the offense here alleged seldom possess the hardihood to speak out boldly and plainly, but deal in mysterious and ambiguous phrases,— mysterious and ambiguous to the world at large, but read in the light of surrounding circumstances by the party for whom intended, they have no uncertain meaning."[36] Moreover, indirect or ambiguous language might "serve to protect [the perpetrator] in the event of failure to accomplish his extortion."[37]

Political Hyperbole

We have seen that what seems to be a relatively innocuous statement, or a gesture, or even a question may in fact be intended to operate as a threat. The opposite can also be true: sometimes what literally seem to be threats may instead be strong or even vicious statements of political opinion.

An African American minister once declared during a sermon, "We will kill Richard Nixon."[38] Did he mean physically or metaphorically? Prosecutors took it literally, indicting him for threatening the president (he was later released on a technicality). His curiosity aroused by this incident, sociolinguist John Gumperz conducted a study on how people use the word "kill" in the African American community. Gumperz found that the term was routinely used in a metaphorical sense: "He killed that bottle" (he finished it); "That killed him around here" (it destroyed his influence), or "Kill it" (stop doing that). When people referred to physically killing someone, they tended to use euphemisms: "They wiped him out"; "They offed him"; "They wasted him."[39] What Gumperz found among African Americans speakers is true as well in standard English, though perhaps to a lesser degree. Using the word "kill" so lightly is hardly a positive reflection on our society, nor are other joking or hyperbolic threats, but they are a reality that we must recognize.

Indeed, the U.S. Supreme Court has emphasized that political hyperbole should not be confused with a true threat. In *Watts v. United States,* the defendant was a young man who stated that if he was drafted and forced to carry a rifle in the Vietnam war, "the first man I want to get in my sights is [President Johnson]." The Court held that he had not made a "true threat" on the life of the president.[40] What the Court meant by "true threat" in *Watts* is not entirely clear.[41] At the least, it seems to mean that when First Amendment rights are at issue, utterances must be analyzed carefully to ensure that they are more than political metaphor.

Distinguishing political invective from actual threats is not always easy. One relevant consideration is whether the statement is uttered in the context of an ongoing political controversy. If so, it is more likely to constitute a political statement. Another factor is whether the speaker seems to be sincere: Is she likely to carry out the threatened action, and capable of doing so? The minister's statement that *we* will kill the president left many questions regarding whom exactly he meant by "we." If he were a

member of an organized group known to be devoted to violence, it would
be more likely to constitute a threat than if he were merely a man of the
cloth preaching to an ordinary congregation, which typically has neither
the desire nor the means to engage in assassination. The audience and
venue matter. Statements made publicly at political gatherings are likely
to be purely political in nature. Most verbal crimes, as we have seen, occur
surreptitiously with as few potential witnesses as possible.

Now consider *United States v. Kelner*. A member of the Jewish Defense
League held a press conference shortly before Palestinian leader Yassir
Arafat was slated to visit the United States. Dressed in military fatigues
and seated behind a desk that had a revolver on it, he declared "We have
people who have been trained and who are out now and who intend to
make sure that Arafat and his lieutenants do not leave this country alive."
He continued: "We are planning to assassinate Mr. Arafat. . . . It's going to
come off."[42]

The defendant later argued that these statements were not threats of
violence, but rather were extreme statements of political opposition to
Arafat. In the sense that the utterances were made during a political controversy (Arafat's visit), the case seems very similar to that of the minister
who said "we will kill" Richard Nixon, or the young man who wanted to
get his gun sights on President Johnson. On the other hand, it does seem
that the defendant in *Kelner* went out of his way to suggest that his words
should be taken seriously by those who heard them. As the appellate court
pointed out, he seemed dead serious, was wearing a uniform, and had a
.38-caliber pistol in his possession.[43] The jury found him guilty and his
conviction was affirmed by the Second Circuit Court of Appeals.

What can render these cases problematic is that sometimes the prosecutor seems to have his own political motivation. A few years ago, a California
state senator, Tim Leslie, initiated efforts to allow more hunting of mountain lions, which at the time were protected by law. During the public
debate on this proposal, someone posted an anonymous message on the
Internet stating "Let's hunt Sen. Tim Leslie for sport. . . . I think it would
be great if he were hunted down and skinned and mounted for our viewing
pleasure." Not long thereafter, a nineteen-year-old freshman at the University of Texas in El Paso, Jose Eduardo Saavedra, was arrested and accused of
making a death threat. He spent sixteen days in jail fighting extradition to
California, where prosecutors charged him with making a terrorist threat.
Saavedra was apparently the first person to be accused of making an online
threat against a public official.[44] But was this really a threat? Or was it a
dramatic political statement?

The statement was made not in a private email to Leslie, but as a posting to the public at large. This was more like making a statement at a political rally or at an open debate. It was clearly about a contested political issue. And as far as we have been able to determine, there was no evidence that Saavedra had any intention of carrying out his proposal, or had made any preparations to do so. Finally, the email was similar to the "How would you like it if we did this to you?" scenario. This permutation of the Golden Rule is typically aimed at persuading people not to engage in some action, rather than threatening them in a serious way. Someone against capital punishment might ask a proponent, "How would you like it if I strapped you to a chair and fried all your organs with a zillion volts of electricity?" Saavedra's electronic posting seems unlikely to be a genuine threat to kill Mr. Leslie, skin him, and mount his head on the wall as a hunting trophy.

The Internet was also a factor in a recent case, *Planned Parenthood v. ACLA,* which involved pro-life protesters who created posters on Web sites picturing "wanted" or "guilty" doctors who performed abortions. Were they threatening the doctors with violence, which is a federal crime? The posters themselves contained no threatening language. They did not advocate killing the doctors or offer a reward for doing so. The posters did offer a modest reward for "information leading to arrest, conviction and revocation of license to practice medicine" and urged people to "write, leaflet or picket his neighborhood to expose his blood guilt."[45] Although it is possible to "threaten" someone with arrest or revocation of her license to practice medicine, the statute in question refers specifically to "threats of violence,"[46] and there seems to be no such threat, express or implied, in the posters. Rather, the posters seem to be mostly political rhetoric and encouragement to engage in peaceful protest.

Yet it is possible that something that is not initially threatening may become so through the intervention of subsequent events. A new context may arise that makes a formerly innocuous statement more sinister. In this case, three doctors who provided abortions and whose pictures and addresses appeared on similar posters were killed soon thereafter. Thus, when the anti-abortion protesters added the names of the plaintiff doctors to their Web sites, they must have been aware that similar previous postings had led to the murder of some of the doctors depicted in them. In addition, one of the Web sites would strike through the name of a doctor who had been killed and would gray-out names of those who had been wounded.[47]

Is this additional context enough to turn permissible free speech into prohibited threats of violence? The Ninth Circuit decided that it was. There is little doubt that the posters intimidated the doctors, who asked for and received FBI protection. By keeping the posters on their Web sites, the protesters quite likely intended to intimidate them.

More problematic is whether the defendants expressed an intention to personally commit an act of violence against the doctors, or to be responsible for having such an act occur. You can only threaten someone with violence if you express or suggest to them that you will carry out the threatened act, or can incite someone else to do it. The protesters who maintained the Web sites did not seem to be suggesting that they themselves would carry out acts of violence against the doctors. But it is possible that they were suggesting through their posting that, in light of the history of violent attacks against abortion clinics, putting a doctor's face on a wanted poster on their Web site would be likely to induce one of their more radical members or sympathizers to take violent action against the doctor. It would be analogous to a mob boss telling someone, "You know I'm a nice guy, Benny, and I would never lay a finger on you, but my boys aren't as nice as I am. I'm going to have to tell them that you keep selling drugs in my territory, and I can't guarantee your safety when that happens." To us, this is a threat. On the other hand, whether it is sufficiently analogous to the *Planned Parenthood* case is a difficult question that was properly left to a jury, which found that the postings did threaten the doctors.

Conclusion

We have seen that the crimes of language discussed in this and the previous chapter are commonly committed indirectly. If someone were to ask a known hit man, "Do you mind killing my wife?" or were to say, "Maybe you could kill my wife tomorrow," adding that he will pay $10,000 for the job, he would probably be convicted of soliciting murder. Or consider someone stopped for speeding who pulls out his wallet and asks the officer, "Would twenty dollars take care of it?" Surely this is an offer of a bribe, even if phrased in terms of a question or request for information. Similarly, threats are often made indirectly or ambiguously. "Maybe your daughter will have an unfortunate accident the next time she goes skating," and "How would you like it if I punch you in the face?" would surely be taken as threats in the proper circumstances, even though literally they might be considered predictions or questions. As we saw in this chapter, courts have little trouble recognizing indirect or ambiguous threats for what they are.

Yet when the indirect threats are made by law enforcement officers in the context of interrogation of suspects, which we discussed in chapter 5, many courts suddenly begin to interpret such utterances more literally. A common method of persuading suspects to confess is to tell them that they face severe punishment, or even the death penalty, if they do not cooperate. This often takes the form of what seems to be merely a prediction, as in "You're going to get the death penalty if you keep lying."[48] Such a prediction—when made by people who seem to have the power to make it happen—may well be intended, and understood, as a threat.

Although the cases do not speak with one voice, there seems to be a "selective literalism" at work here. When the issue is whether a defendant committed a language crime like solicitation or threatening, courts are seldom overly literal. They readily consider the pragmatic circumstances and are well aware that people who know they are doing something illegal may not express their intentions directly. Yet with issues relating to criminal procedure, as we discussed in part 2, courts often ignore or minimize pragmatic information. For example, they may require that suspects being interrogated invoke their right to counsel by making a direct or literal request for a lawyer. And they tend to view police attempts to gain consent for a search as "requests" even though, under the circumstances, the utterances are likely to be interpreted as commands. They ignore the fact that, because of the asymmetrical power relationship between police and citizens, suspects tend to voice their requests to police indirectly, and to interpret police requests as orders.

Whether courts consciously intend it or not, this selective literalism most often benefits law enforcement. Unfortunately, these benefits to law enforcement come at the cost of an unknown number of false confessions and a loss of confidence in the fairness of the criminal justice system, especially by members of minority communities. We believe that these problems can be minimized if courts recognize across the board that people do not always make their intentions known as directly as possible, and that it is essential to take the pragmatic circumstances into account in understanding what a person means. If the law can recognize the importance of pragmatic information in assessing threats and other language crimes, it should do no less in the area of criminal procedure.

Chapter 11

Perjury

It depends upon what
the meaning of the
word "is" is.

The final language crime that we consider is perjury. Perjury consists of lying under oath: having sworn to tell the truth, a witness speaks falsely. It is a serious crime, since false testimony may cause the innocent to go to prison or allow the guilty to go free.

It is not normally a crime to lie. To commit perjury, a person must first have taken an oath to testify truthfully. Federal law also requires that the person "willfully and contrary to such oath states or subscribes any material matter which he does not believe to be true."[1] This is often called the "false statement" requirement.[2] Perjury involves asserting or declaring that a particular state of affairs exists (or existed in the past), when the speaker knows that not to be the case. If the speaker did not know that the actual and asserted state of affairs were different, she would have made a mere mistake.

Not only must the accused make a false statement, but it must be material. If the false statement relates to a minor matter or something that is unlikely to influence a trial or other official proceeding, it does not constitute perjury, even though we might still call the statement a lie. The law of perjury is aimed at protecting the integrity of official proceedings, not at punishing everyone who speaks untruthfully. Minor or marginally relevant misstatements, even if intentional, are unlikely to undermine the integrity of the governmental process, and thus fall outside the scope of the criminal law.

To decide whether an asserted state of affairs is material and corresponds to reality, we first need to determine the meaning of the assertion or statement. We have seen numerous illustrations so far that people often speak indirectly. When people are engaged in criminal activity, they tend to speak even more obliquely and obscurely, a point that courts have routinely recognized with respect to conspiracies and threats.

What standard of literalness is applied to perjury? Because it is a crime—just like offering bribes, or conspiring, or making certain types of threats—one might expect courts to take a relatively nonliteral approach to determining the meaning of allegedly perjurious statements. That is not true, however, as we will see below.

The *Bronston* Case

The seminal case on the false statement requirement is *Bronston v. United States,* decided by the Supreme Court of the United States. The issue in *Bronston* was "whether a witness may be convicted of perjury for an answer, under oath, that is literally true but not responsive to the question asked and arguably misleading by negative implication."[3] The defendant, Samuel Bronston, was president of Samuel Bronston Productions, Inc., a movie production company. He had personal as well as company bank accounts in various European countries. His company petitioned for bankruptcy. At the bankruptcy hearing, the following exchange occurred between the lawyer for a creditor and Bronston:

Q. Do you have any bank accounts in Swiss banks, Mr. Bronston?
A. No, sir.
Q. Have you ever?
A. The company had an account there for about six months, in Zurich.[4]

The "truth" was that Bronston earlier had a large personal bank account in Switzerland for five years, where he had deposited and drawn checks totaling more than $180,000.

Bronston was tried for perjury. The prosecution's theory at trial was that although his reply to the second question was literally true (his company did have an account there), his answer falsely implied that he had never had a personal Swiss bank account. Bronston was found guilty and the court of appeals upheld his conviction.

The U.S. Supreme Court unanimously reversed. It assumed for purposes of argument that the questions referred to Bronston's personal accounts (that is to say, that "you" referred to Bronston individually). The Court acknowledged that the hearer might reasonably infer from Bronston's answer that he had never had a personal account in Switzerland. Indeed, this inference was implicit in the jury's guilty verdict.

What is so tricky about Bronston's response? The answer lies generally in philosopher H. Paul Grice's Cooperative Principle (see chapter 2). Part of this principle is the *maxim of relation,* which requires that one's contribution to a conversation be relevant to what went on before.[5] While it is true that people sometimes change the topic, it is notable that the above sequence is a question and answer set. Normally, someone who appears to be responding to a question is assumed to be providing information that is relevant to the question. Asked about any personal bank accounts in Switzerland, Bronston responds by mentioning that his company had a business or corporate account there for a time. Company bank accounts are unresponsive to the question, of course. Because the questioner assumes that Bronston has abided by the maxim of relation, he tries to interpret the answer in some way that will make it relevant.

The only way to make sense of the response is to assume that Bronston was communicating that he had no personal bank accounts in Switzerland, but that—in an effort to be as helpful as possible—he volunteered the unrequested information that his company once had such an account. This is how we would interpret Bronston's reply in ordinary conversation, and it is apparently how the examining lawyer understood it. In this light, consider the following example:

Q. Do you have a Chevy?
A. I have a Ford.

Under normal circumstances, if someone asks "Do you have an X?" and you respond merely that you have a Y, you imply that you do not have an X. The hearer assumes that your response is relevant, and understands it as communicating that you do not have a Chevy. Most people would think that your response was misleading at best if, in truth, you have a Chevy in addition to the Ford.[6]

We routinely ascribe meaning by virtue of inferences that we draw from context, and we do so rapidly and unselfconsciously. To take another example, if Bob wants to date Alice but is unsure whether she is married, he might ask a mutual acquaintance about her marital status. The acquaintance could reply, "She has two children." On the surface, the response seems to be entirely irrelevant to the question. But Bob will assume that the acquaintance was trying to cooperate and say something relevant to his question. Because there is at least a loose relationship in our society between marriage and children, Bob will infer that Alice is likely to be married.

In *Bronston,* however, Chief Justice Burger emphasized that the perjury statute refers to what the witness "states," not to what he "implies."[7] It is the responsibility of the examining lawyer to probe a vague or ambiguous answer. If the witness equivocates or evades, it is the lawyer's job to clarify the testimony. Even if Bronston knowingly tried to mislead the examining lawyer with his answer, the "intent to mislead" standard, according to the Court, is too vague and confusing for a jury to apply consistently. If a witness gives a literally true but unresponsive answer, the solution is for the lawyer to follow up with more precise questions, not to instigate a federal perjury prosecution.[8] The perjury laws are not violated simply because a witness's responses are "shrewdly calculated to evade,"[9] as long as the answers are literally true.

The *Bronston* case has come to be seen as establishing a literal truth defense. Interestingly, there is no such "literal" defense for other crimes of language. If someone approaches a person on the street and says, "Give me your wallet—you'd hate to have me blow your brains out," the defendant would almost certainly lose if he argued that under a literal interpretation (that the victim would hate to receive a bullet in the cranium), his utterance was a statement of fact, and therefore not a threat. Why would the Supreme Court insist on literal interpretation with perjury, when courts take a much less literal approach to other language crimes?

One of the main reasons is that perjury typically occurs during the rigidly structured questioning of witnesses in a trial. Lawyers and the judge maintain tight control over the types of questions that are asked and the nature of permissible responses. Witnesses are obligated by law to answer questions, and any unresponsive statement can be ordered stricken from the record. Moreover, lawyers and judges work together with the court reporter (stenographer) to create a written record that is as complete and unambiguous as possible. For example, if a witness points to an exhibit, the judge may state for the record that the witness is pointing to Exhibit F.[10] Unlike more ordinary conversation, where no one systematically clarifies ambiguities, the message of the Supreme Court in *Bronston* is that errors, vagueness, ambiguity, and lack of responsiveness ought to be corrected during the questioning process, not by prosecuting the witness for perjury after the fact.

Moreover, during questioning the lawyers hold all the cards. Lawyers decide what questions to ask, and witnesses have no choice but to answer them. It is not unusual for attorneys to use this power to attempt to create an impression that the facts differ from how the witness recalls them, even if the witness is being truthful. A great deal has been written, especially in the context of rape trials, about how lawyers can exercise this power strategically.[11] It would skew the power relationship between lawyer and witness even more if witnesses could be prosecuted for creating a misleading impression in a dialogue in which the questioner is doing exactly the same thing.[12]

Yet while a literal truth defense may seem appealing, the question of what is "literally" true is, in reality, highly problematic. Consider the following hypothetical situation, which the district court in *Bronston* presented as part of its reason for permitting the perjury statute to reach cases like Bronston's: If it is material to ascertain how many times a person has entered a store on a given day and that person responds to such a question by saying five times when in fact he knows that he entered the store fifty times that day, that person may be guilty of perjury even though it is technically true that he entered the store five times.[13] The Supreme Court responded:

> [T]he answer "five times" is responsive to the hypothetical question and contains nothing to alert the questioner that he may be sidetracked. Moreover, it is very doubtful that an answer which, in response to a specific quantitative inquiry, baldly understates a numerical fact can be described as even "technically true." Whether an answer is true must be determined with reference to the question it purports to answer, not in isolation. An unresponsive answer is unique in this respect because its unresponsiveness by definition prevents its truthfulness from being tested in the context of the question—unless there is to be speculation as to what the unresponsive answer "implies."[14]

The lower court was not entirely off the mark, however. If you are asked how many children you have, and you answer "I have two children," it is certainly true that you have two children, even if you have a total of four. At the same time, there is no doubt that your response is highly misleading, and some people would probably call it a lie. Likewise, the person who says "I was in the store five times" has made an utterance that is, in isolation, a true statement, albeit once again quite misleading.

The reason that most people would consider these responses to be so misleading, or even outright lies, is that we almost automatically consider the verbal context, as well as any pragmatic information, whenever we interpret an utterance. Moreover, communication is inherently a cooperative venture, so we assume that, at least to some extent, other participants in a conversation are cooperating with us. This, of course, is the basis for Grice's Cooperative Principle.

Another aspect of the Cooperative Principle is the *maxim of quantity*, which requires that a person give enough information for purposes of the exchange.[15] If we understand a question as inquiring into the total number of times that a person entered a store, we assume that a person answering "five" is being cooperative and is obeying the maxims of relation and quantity. Thus we infer that when he says "five," he means not merely that he was in the store five times, but that he was there *only* five times. Otherwise, the response would not be sufficiently informative. Because this interpretative process is so natural, even the Supreme Court seems to have been unaware that its example involved inferential reasoning and that the notion of "literal" truth is, therefore, more complex than it might seem.[16]

Obviously, as the *Bronston* Court itself acknowledged, a critical component in evaluating the truthfulness of an answer is the nature of the question. In fact, most answers to questions (e.g., "Yes" or "Five") are elliptical and cannot be processed without considering the question. So perhaps we can make sense of the literal truth defense by suggesting that what the Court meant was that an answer must be literally true not in isolation, but in the context of the question. This approach may help solve the "How many times did you enter the store?" example, because an elliptical answer of "Five" will be expanded to mean "I entered the store (exactly) five times." Interpreting the question as asking about the total number of times that a person entered the store, which seems reasonable, the answer is clearly false. But taking the question into account does not completely solve the problem. Consider the following sequence:

Q. Do you have any children?
A. Two sons, Bob and John.

Suppose the respondent actually has two sons and a daughter. The reply, interpreted in the context of the question, can be expanded to mean "I have two children, Bob and John." This response is literally true, even after the question fills in some of the meaning. But most people, we believe, would consider the above response at least misleading. The reason is that the answer violates the maxim of quantity by not giving enough information.

The problem is that it is not always clear *how much* information the questioner is seeking. If the overall circumstances suggest that the questioner is after the total number of children, the response is false or misleading because the hearer will interpret it (under the maxim of quantity) as providing enough information, and thus infer that the respondent has only two children. But under other circumstances, the answer may be sufficiently informative. For example, if the respondent has two sons attending the local high school and a grown daughter living elsewhere, his answer may be appropriate if the conversation were about the need to hire math teachers at the high school.

This example shows that we need context not just to understand an answer, but also to properly understand the question. Recently an appellate court upheld a perjury conviction for a literally true response, based on an analysis of how the witness most likely understood the question. A general in the Kentucky National Guard was being investigated for inviting officers of the Guard to attend a "Preakness party" at which they were improperly asked to make campaign contributions. During the investigation, one of the officers, Robert DeZarn, was asked:

> Q. Ok. In 1991, and I recognize this is in the period that you were retired, he held the Preakness party at his home. Were you aware of that?
> A. Yes.
> Q. Ok. Sir, was that a political fundraising activity?
> A. Absolutely not.[17]

It turns out that the party at which the contributions were solicited occurred in 1990. In 1991, there was no Preakness party—only a small dinner party, which DeZarn attended. Other questions and answers made it very clear that DeZarn understood the questions as referring to the 1990 party, even though the lawyer misspoke. DeZarn was convicted of perjury, and the appellate court affirmed, rejecting his *Bronston* defense. In light of how DeZarn understood the question, the answer was considered perjured.

Assuming that DeZarn correctly understood what the lawyer meant by the question, the decision seems correct.[18] But it further muddles the literal truth defense. It is apparently no longer good enough if the answer is literally true in light of the question literally interpreted. Rather, we need to determine how the witness understood the question, based not merely on the words of the question, taken in isolation, but in light of the context established by all of the previous testimony and evidence. On the basis of such contextual information, the defendant was found to have understood that when the prosecutor said "1991," he actually meant "1990." Thus, DeZarn was convicted of responding falsely to a question that was not asked, but which he presumably thought was asked. He truthfully answered the question that *was* asked.

DeZarn's conviction is, however, consistent with the plain language of the perjury statute, which requires only that the defendant "willfully and contrary to such oath states or subscribes any material matter which he does not believe to be true."[19] Assuming that DeZarn understood that the prosecutor was asking about 1991, he did just that. But had DeZarn not known that the prosecutor misspoke about the date of the Preakness party, *Bronston* suggests that he could have answered similarly with impunity on the theory that his answer was literally true, he believed it to be true, and it is up to the questioner to ask the right questions. At the core of the problem is the extent to which a witness should be required to cooperate with the questioner by providing relevant information to the questions as the witness understands them.[20]

When the Supreme Court held that Bronston's answer was literally true, because what matters is what a witness "states" and not what he "implies," it might be taken to mean that the maxim of relation does not apply in the courtroom, and that the witness has no obligation, without further prodding, to provide relevant answers to questions. In fact, some linguists have suggested that at least certain of Grice's maxims do not operate in the courtroom, especially when the questioner and respondent are in an adversarial, rather than cooperative, relationship.[21]

But failure to apply the maxim of relation in all cases would mean that we can never be sure that a response is intended to be taken as an answer to a question, as opposed to being an irrelevant comment that is true enough, but does not respond to the question. Consider the following example:

Q. Why weren't you at work yesterday?
A. I was sick.[22]

Suppose that it is true that I was sick, but that I was fine all day until I became sick late at night as a result of spending all day at the beach drinking beer. If we interpret the answer as being responsive, then it must obviously be interpreted in the context of the question and is an outright lie. But what if the speaker, like Bronston in the Supreme Court's analysis, did not intend his reply to respond to the question? Nothing in the answer alerts the questioner to the possibility that the answer may simply be a cute, unresponsive statement. Another illustration:

> Q. I lost a twenty dollar bill—do you know where it is?
> A. I saw it on the floor somewhere.

In reality, I did indeed see the money on the floor, picked it up, and now have it in my pocket. Once again, this reply is highly misleading, because the hearer will assume that it is responsive to the question and sufficiently informative. But it is literally true in isolation.

These observations lead to a disturbing irony. On the one hand, a witness is required to give relevant and relatively complete responses, and we should be able to interpret the answer accordingly. Were it not so, the entire questioning process would collapse. On the other hand, the nature of the adversarial process suggests that it is the questioning lawyer's job to ensure that responses comply with these requirements. But who do we blame when, as seems to have happened in *Bronston,* the witness intentionally gives an unresponsive answer to create a false impression of responsiveness? Do we let Bronston's creditors go uncompensated because their lawyer's trial skills were not sufficiently honed, or do we prosecute the witness for perjury to discourage deceitful conduct?

We believe that the most practical solution is to require the lawyer to clarify unresponsive answers, as the Supreme Court suggested, but only when it is reasonably evident to the lawyer that the answer may not be responsive. If we interpret the question in *Bronston* as asking about personal bank accounts in Switzerland, it should have been evident to the examining lawyer that Bronston's reply about company bank accounts was not responsive to the question. While in ordinary conversation this would lead the hearer to infer that Bronston had no personal accounts in Switzerland, this was a legal setting, and therefore the lawyer should have probed further. Likewise, if you say you have a Ford in response to a question regarding whether you have a Chevy, it is evident that your reply is not responsive and the examiner should probe more deeply.

In contrast, if someone asks why you weren't at work yesterday, and you say that you were sick (when in fact you became sick only that night), there is no way for the questioner to know that this is not responsive, and thus—if this happened during a trial—the lawyer would have no obligation to probe further. Any reasonable person would interpret this answer as responding to the question and communicating that you were not at work because of illness. Even though your response is truthful in isolation, the system would break down if we allow this level of noncooperation. A jury should decide whether such a reply actually communicates something false when considered in light of the question, and whether the defendant knew or believed it to be false.

Similarly, in cases involving the maxim of quantity, especially those involving numbers, it is critical to examine the question closely. Thus, it is not dishonest to say you have $2 in response to a friend's request to borrow that amount, even if you have $10.[23] The answer provides sufficient information in light of the purpose of the question. But a waitress reporting $2 of tips on her tax form when she earned $10 would be subject to prosecution. The question on the form clearly requests her to list all tip income, and there is no reason to think that her reply is not responsive or complete.

The literal truth defense is therefore, in reality, quite limited. As we have seen, we do not normally interpret spoken utterances literally or in isolation of the context. This means that a witness's answers are virtually always understood in the context of the question, which in turn is understood in the context of the entire line of questioning and all kinds of other pragmatic information. Only when the reply is not relevant to the question (that is, not responsive) does it make sense to judge the answer literally, in isolation of the question.

While the maxims of relation and quantity might seem somewhat esoteric, the issue of how relevant and complete an answer must be arose repeatedly in the impeachment proceedings against President Clinton. We now consider those proceedings in greater detail.

Did Clinton Lie?

The impeachment of President William Jefferson Clinton was the perjury trial of the twentieth century. It was based on the U.S. Constitution's provision allowing for impeachment of federal officials who engage in "treason, bribery, or other high crimes and misdemeanors."[24] The impeachment process begins in the House of Representatives. If the House decides to proceed, it sends articles of impeachment to the Senate. The trial itself then occurs in the Senate, where a two-thirds majority is required to remove an official from office.

Briefly stated, President Clinton became sexually involved with a White House intern named Monica Lewinsky. They met several times in or around the Oval Office. There were never allegations that the president coerced or harassed Lewinsky. She seemed infatuated with Clinton and was a willing, even eager, participant. Their sexual shenanigans, according to Lewinsky, consisted of Clinton stroking or fondling her breasts. She also testified that she performed oral sex on him, but not vice versa. They also seem to have played some other sexual games, including "phone sex," but it appears that they never had actual intercourse.[25] Whatever the morality of these activities, there is nothing illegal in having such private affairs.

Enter Paula Corbin Jones. Jones had worked for the State of Arkansas when Clinton was governor. According to Jones, Governor Clinton once had state troopers escort her to a hotel room to meet him. She claims that he tried to induce her to engage in some sort of sexual activity. When it was clear that she was not interested, he let her leave. Eventually, after Clinton became president, Jones—then married and living in California— initiated a civil lawsuit accusing Clinton of sexual harassment and related torts. She was encouraged and assisted in these efforts by Clinton's political opponents, who were eager to embarrass him and undermine his political effectiveness.[26]

Jones was also aided by what is, in retrospect, one of the more short-sighted decisions of the U.S. Supreme Court, *Clinton v. Jones*. Clinton argued that as president, he occupied an office that was unique in power and responsibility, and that he should therefore not be distracted by ordinary lawsuits until after he had left office. The Supreme Court agreed with this proposition to some extent, but concluded that the *Jones* litigation "appears to us highly unlikely to occupy any substantial amount of petitioner's time," and held that therefore the lawsuit could proceed.[27] Except for Justice Scalia, who dissented, the justices were strikingly naive about the political motivations behind Jones's case against Clinton and the amount of time and energy that the president would have to invest in it.

Throughout this time, Kenneth Starr had been operating as independent counsel, under a now-defunct statute, charged with investigating some controversial investments that Clinton and his wife had made while he was governor of Arkansas. This became known as the "Whitewater" investigation. Starr's efforts in ferreting out serious wrongdoing by the Clintons were not meeting with much success, despite enormous effort and the expenditure of many millions of dollars. For that reason he was quite receptive when someone named Linda Tripp contacted his office with allegations against the president that were completely unrelated to the Whitewater investigation. Tripp had pretended to be a friend to Monica Lewinsky and, after gaining her confidence, had surreptitiously (and illegally) taped conversations with Lewinsky in which Lewinsky discussed her relationship with Clinton. All of a sudden, Starr was far more interested in the former intern with her explosive allegations about sex in the White House than he was in the dry and complex business transactions in Arkansas. He successfully applied to the attorney general to have his mandate expanded to include investigating possible obstruction of justice by the president in the Paula Jones lawsuit. At this stage, Starr's investigation into Whitewater, the machinations of Linda Tripp, efforts by wealthy enemies of Clinton to undermine his presidency, and the Jones lawsuit all become inextricably intertwined.

The next step in the *Jones* case was for the plaintiff's lawyers to depose Clinton himself on January 17, 1998. Unbeknownst to Clinton, Tripp had been briefing not only the independent counsel, but also Jones's lawyers about Lewinsky's relationship with the president. Whether Jones's lawyers should even have been allowed to ask Clinton about Lewinsky is debatable, in light of the fact that his relationship with her was entirely consensual and therefore different from the harassment that Jones claimed to have suffered. It would, at most, have confirmed that Clinton was interested in sex, not so unusual a preoccupation. In fact, a judge later decided that evidence regarding Lewinsky would be inadmissible in the Jones lawsuit.[28] Nevertheless, Clinton's deposition explored his relationship with Lewinsky in great detail. The *Jones* case was later dismissed.[29]

Although there is room for debate, the Lewinsky matter was probably not material to the *Jones* case. If that view is correct, Clinton could not have committed perjury in the Jones deposition even if he had been lying. As Judge Wright held, "[T]his case was dismissed on summary judgment as lacking in merit—a decision that would not have changed even had the President been truthful with respect to his relationship with Ms. Lewinsky."[30] In fact, the House of Representatives rejected articles of impeachment that accused Clinton of committing perjury at the deposition, probably for this very reason. The deposition, nonetheless, was the principal topic of Clinton's testimony before a federal grand jury on August 17, 1998. No doubt aware that the perjury case against Clinton was very weak, Starr had convened the grand jury for the purpose of determining whether the president had committed perjury or had obstructed justice in the *Jones* case.[31] Clinton used the literal truth defense as the cornerstone of his grand jury testimony. He stated that it was his job to tell the truth, but it was not his job to help his political enemies accumulate scandalous material:

> Q. Judge Wright had ruled that the attorneys in the *Jones* case were permitted to ask you certain questions.
> A. She certainly did, and they asked them, and I did my best to answer them. I'm just trying to tell you what my state of mind was.
> Q. Was it your responsibility to answer those questions truthfully, Mr. President?
> A. It was. But it was not my responsibility, in the face of their repeated illegal leaking, it was not my responsibility to volunteer a lot of information.[32]

Ultimately, the House of Representatives voted to impeach Clinton for having lied in his testimony before the grand jury. The articles of impeachment did not specify the answers that the House thought were untruthful. Regardless, the focus rested on Clinton's statements about having been alone with Lewinsky, and about whether he had engaged in "sexual relations" with her, given a peculiar legalistic definition of the term. Clinton was ultimately acquitted and finished out his term in office.[33]

How Often Were Clinton and Lewinsky Alone?

A major issue surrounding the Clinton impeachment proceedings was whether he had committed perjury in his testimony regarding how often he and Monica Lewinsky had been alone in the White House. The issue first arose during his deposition in the Paula Jones litigation. It came up again during the grand jury proceedings, where Kenneth Starr's team of lawyers accused him of having lied about the matter in his deposition.

Paula Jones's lawyers spent a fair amount of time during their deposition of Clinton trying to induce him to admit that he and Lewinsky had frequently been alone in or near the Oval Office. Caught with his pants down, Clinton equivocated:

> Q. Now, do you know a woman named Monica Lewinsky?
> A. I do.
> Q. How do you know her?
> A. She worked in the White House for a while, first as an intern, and then in, as the, in the legislative affairs office. . . . [34]

So far, Clinton has told the truth. The questioning continued:

> Q. . . . At any time were you and Monica Lewinsky together alone in the Oval
> Office?
> A. "I don't recall. . . . She—it seems to me she brought things to me once or
> twice on the weekends. In that case, whatever time she would be in there,
> drop it off, exchange a few words and go, she was there."[35]

Certainly the president wished to create the impression that he and
Lewinsky were seldom together alone, and then only serendipitously. The
critical issue for perjury law, however, is whether Clinton made a false
statement. He starts out by testifying that he does not recall. Had he
said nothing else, this would almost certainly have been perjurious. To
say "I don't think so" or "I don't recall" or "I'm not sure" is false if the
speaker does remember something.[36] It stretches credulity to suggest that
Clinton, who admitted that he had a good memory,[37] could have forgotten
his intimate sessions with Lewinsky so easily. Bronston was more careful. He never said, "I don't recall. I think my company had an account in
Switzerland."

But Clinton then continues by qualifying his answer in a way that
would do Bronston proud: he makes a statement that is apparently true
(she brought him things in the weekends),[38] but which does not really
answer the question—it does not address whether they were alone when
she delivered things. The president further states that this might have
happened "once or twice." The evidence, however, is that they were alone
substantially more often than just once or twice.

Is this a successful use of the *Bronston* literal truth defense? Again, it
depends on the question that was asked. If the lawyer had asked how many
times they were alone together, and Clinton answered "Once or twice," his
response would be considered perjurious as a clear violation of the maxim of
quantity. Yet that is not the question. The lawyer simply asks *whether* they
had been alone together, which requires a yes or no answer. Clinton does
not answer that question directly, but his reply suggests that the answer
is yes. At the same time, he apparently tries to throw the questioner off
track by limiting his answer to the time or two that she brought papers to
him, leaving other meetings unmentioned.

The examining lawyer presses on, however, and tries to pin Clinton
down by reformulating his testimony in a way that clarifies the ambiguous
point and simultaneously seeks confirmation from the president that his
proposed clarification is correct:

Q. So I understand, your testimony is that it was possible, then, that you were alone with her, but you have no specific recollection of that ever happening?

A. Yes, that's correct. It's possible that she, in, while she was working there, brought something to me and that at the time she brought it to me, she was the only person there. That's possible.[39]

The House of Representatives, which functioned as prosecutor during the impeachment, called this a "verbose lie."[40] If Clinton's "yes" is taken as a confirmation that he didn't remember what happened exactly, it probably was. But the rest of his answer is once again Bronstonesque. Literally, it is entirely possible that they were alone. Not only is it possible, but that is exactly what seems to have happened. Logically, everything that happens must be possible, or it would never happen.

In ordinary conversation Clinton's answer would be misleading because Grice's maxim of quantity mandates that a cooperative speaker give as much information as is required by the situation. If I have a pen in my pocket and tell you that it is "possible" that I have a pen in my pocket, I have told the truth on a strictly logical level, but I imply that I am not certain (otherwise I would have stated outright that I have a pen in my pocket). Most of us would therefore take Clinton's statement as implying that he is not sure or does not remember whether he and Lewinsky were alone in the Oval Office, and that if they were, it was a spontaneous rather than prearranged meeting.

Normally, we would be inclined to say that the lawyer should not have a duty to press on in such a case. After all, the answer is obviously responsive and there is nothing to suggest to the questioner that the ordinary implications of the word "possible" should not apply. This was not a normal case, however. Unlike the questioner in *Bronston,* Clinton's nemesis already knew the truth, courtesy of Linda Tripp. He easily enough could have clarified the issue.

In fact, the questioning lawyer does try to redeem himself by asking a catch-all question at the end:

Q. At any time have you and Monica Lewinsky ever been alone together in any room in the White House?

A. I think I testified to that earlier. I think that there is a, it is—I have no specific recollection, but it seems to me that she was on duty on a couple of occasions working for the legislative affairs office and brought me some things to sign, something on the weekend. That's—I have a general memory of that.[41]

Notice that, once again, the questioner does not ask about the *total* number of times that Clinton and Lewinsky were alone. He merely asks *whether* they were ever alone. The only relevant answers to this question are "Yes" or "No," or opting out of answering by saying "I don't recall" or "I don't know." At first, it seems that Clinton is opting out by stating that he has no specific recollection, which would clearly be false. But he continues by repeating his story about how Lewinsky came to his office to bring him some papers to sign, which is apparently true and constitutes a roundabout way of saying "Yes." Although Clinton and Lewinsky were alone more than "a couple" of times, the question does not ask about the number of times they were together, so technically the answer does not violate the maxim of quantity.

At the same time, Clinton's answer is misleading in a very interesting way. As mentioned, the question asks only *whether* (not *how often*) Clinton and Lewinsky were together alone. A simple "Yes" could have sufficed. Thus, the answer gives more information than the question calls for by discussing *how often* they were alone. This causes the hearer to reinterpret the question as addressing not merely whether they were alone, but how often. Under this interpretation of the question, Clinton's answer violates the maxim of quantity by creating the false impression that those were the *only* times they were alone together.

Knowing, as Jones's lawyer did, that Clinton and Lewinsky must have been alone on more occasions than Clinton seemed willing to admit, and that he would surely not have forgotten these sexual escapades, this would have been the time for the questioner to close in for the kill. He dropped the ball, however. He failed to pin down *how often* Clinton and Lewinsky were alone in a room in the White House.[42]

Clinton did slip up a few times, however, For one thing, his repeated denials of adequate recollection are incredible. Consider also the following response to a question at his deposition asking the president whether he and Lewinsky were ever alone in the hallway between the Oval Office and the kitchen area:

> I don't believe so, unless we were walking back to the dining room with the
> pizza. I just, I don't remember. I don't believe we were alone in the hallway, no.[43]

In fact, according to the report by Kenneth Starr, that hallway was where much of the activity with Lewinsky took place.[44] If so, Clinton's statement here is clearly false.

When Clinton testified a second time before the grand jury, the topic of whether Clinton had been alone with Ms. Lewinsky arose afresh, complicated by his earlier deposition in the *Jones* case. At the beginning of the grand jury testimony, Clinton read a statement admitting that he had been "alone" with Lewinsky "on certain occasions in early 1996 and once in early 1997."[45] In the questioning that followed, Starr's lawyers did a better job than those who conducted the *Jones* deposition: they finally asked him specifically how many times he and Lewinsky had been alone. Clinton admitted that in addition to the "certain occasions" in 1996, he might have been alone with her as many as nine times in the period from February to December of 1997.[46]

During Clinton's impeachment proceedings in the Senate, his opponents argued emphatically that his admission to the grand jury was inconsistent with what he said in his *Jones* deposition. Yet as Clinton stated to the grand jury, his goal was to be "truthful" during his deposition testimony, but not particularly "helpful."[47] As we have seen, he was anything but cooperative, doing his best to mislead while trying to stay within the bounds of *Bronston*'s literal truth defense.

There is no doubt that at his deposition Clinton evaded, equivocated, or avoided answering certain questions about being alone with Lewinsky, and on a few occasions made false statements on the matter. In the final analysis, however, we believe that Clinton did not lie about these issues nearly as often as his political enemies would have us believe. At the same time, some of his answers in the *Jones* deposition—as Clinton himself later admitted—were surely false.[48]

But Clinton was not impeached for lying at his deposition. He was impeached for lying before the grand jury. There, he admitted to having been alone with Lewinsky on several occasions. Moreover, close analysis of his testimony before the grand jury—at least on this issue—suggests that Clinton really believed he had succeeded at his deposition in misleading without making false statements. The crux of the impeachment trial, then, was whether Clinton lied about whether he had lied. At least with respect to how often they had been together alone, Clinton's testimony before the grand jury—as opposed to his deposition testimony—was relatively truthful.

Did Clinton Have Sexual Relations with "That Woman"?

If nothing else, Clinton's testimony illustrates that it can be very hard to decide whether someone is lying. People differ widely in their judgments on these matters. Some of us take a very literalistic approach, while others—

like Clinton's political opponents in Congress—seem to equate equivocation, evasion, and intentional deception with lying.

A nice illustration of what makes a lie a lie arose during Clinton's deposition in the *Jones* case, when her lawyers presented Clinton with a definition
of the expression "sexual relations." This rather convoluted and legalistic
definition stated that a person engages in sexual relations when the person "knowingly engages in or causes contact" with the erogenous zones of
any person "with an intent to arouse or gratify the sexual desire of any
person."[49] Jones's lawyer never directly asked Clinton if he and Lewinsky
had engaged in oral sex, whether either had touched the other sexually,
or any other direct question that would have required a straightforward
answer. Clinton denied having had sexual relations with Lewinsky under
this definition.

Before the grand jury, Clinton reiterated this position. He argued that
he had parsed the definition very carefully and that he had interpreted it
to only cover contact by the deponent (Clinton) with the erogenous zones
of the other person (Lewinsky), and that it did not include contact by
the other person with the deponent's body parts. He testified that under
this definition his testimony that they did not engage in "sexual relations"
was true. Strictly speaking, Clinton's interpretation of this poorly drafted
definition is probably correct. Yet as Judge Posner and others have pointed
out, for Clinton to have told the truth, he must have allowed Lewinsky
to perform oral sex on him without his having touched her sexually. This
seems a rather remote possibility.[50]

Another of the prosecutor's theories in the grand jury proceedings went
way beyond *Bronston* or any other theory of perjury of which we are aware.
During the deposition, Clinton's lawyer, Robert Bennett, objecting to questions being asked about Lewinsky, had made the following statement:

> I question the good faith of counsel, the innuendo of the question. Counsel is
> fully aware that Ms. Lewinsky has filed—has an affidavit, which they are in
> possession of, saying that there is absolutely no sex of any kind in any manner,
> shape or form with President Clinton.[51]

During the grand jury proceedings, lawyers for special prosecutor Kenneth
Starr accused Clinton of making an "utterly false statement" by not speaking up and correcting his lawyer's comment. Clinton rejoined that Bennett's
statement was not necessarily false: "It depends upon what the meaning
of the word 'is' is."[52]

The response came to symbolize the perception that Clinton exploited the nuances of language to avoid being honest. His lawyer's statement, however, really was literally true. Clinton's physical relationship with Lewinsky had ended some time before Clinton's deposition. Moreover, Clinton was clearly operating in a defensive mode. A federal prosecutor was insinuating that he had committed perjury by not correcting Bennett's true, but possibly misleading, statement.

In fact, the prosecutor may have misquoted Bennett's statement in a way that made it appear to be false. He asked:

> The statement that there *was* no sex of any kind in any manner, shape or form with President Clinton was an utterly false statement. Is that correct?[53]

By switching the lawyer's statement from present to past tense, the prosecutor misquoted the tense of the verb, which was the critical issue in deciding whether the disputed statement by Clinton's lawyer was true or false. Quite possibly the prosecutor's "slip" was unintended. It is natural to change the tense of the verb when paraphrasing what someone said previously.[54] In this case, in any event, it seems highly unlikely that Clinton would have been misled, since he had the transcript of the deposition, with the word "is," right in front of him. But a less perceptive witness might more easily be misled by such a "slip."

What is even more disturbing about this line of questioning is that Starr's attorneys were accusing Clinton of lying by not volunteering to correct his lawyer's statement. There are some rare circumstances under which a person can commit perjury by saying nothing,[55] but only when the person under oath is legally obligated to speak up, which was not the case here. Yet the prosecutors repeatedly insinuated that Clinton committed a crime by saying nothing:

> You are the President of the United States and your attorney tells a United States District Court Judge that there is no sex of any kind, in any way, shape or form, whatsoever. And you feel no obligation to do anything about that at that deposition, Mr. President?[56]

Moreover, the prosecutors characterized the statement by Clinton's lawyer as being "completely false" and "utterly false," even though by all accounts it was true that at the time of the deposition there was no sex of any kind going on between Clinton and Lewinsky.

Unfortunately, it is not all that unusual for lawyers to try to create a misleading impression through their questioning, as happened in this case with Clinton. It is especially disturbing when the lawyers are prosecutors, who have an ethical duty to seek the truth. This phenomenon suggests why the rule in *Bronston* should be upheld. Witnesses should not be sent to prison for perjury when they give a misleading but true answer to a misleading question.

Perjury and Lying

As we noted at the outset of this chapter, lying is not normally a crime. The question in cases like *Bronston* and the Clinton impeachment is not whether they lied, but whether they violated the relevant perjury statutes. To some extent, the strong opinions by many members of the public, as well as politicians, that Clinton lied, or did not lie, often failed to consider the intricacies of perjury law. At the same time, it is impossible to separate the legal concept of perjury from the ordinary concept of lying. If nothing else, exploring the everyday notion of lying may help us understand why people were so divided on the Clinton impeachment.

In a very interesting article, linguists Linda Coleman and Paul Kay suggest that we understand lying not merely by virtue of a definition that focuses on whether a statement is true or false, but rather on which elements of a prototypical lie a statement contains.[57] According to Coleman and Kay, lying contains three elements: a false statement, intent to deceive, and knowledge of falsity. When all three are present, the statement is clearly a lie. When none is present, the statement is clearly not a lie. But what do we make of those statements that contain one or two elements? Coleman and Kay argue that for these, we equivocate about calling the statement a lie. Consider their most Clintonesque example:

> John and Mary have recently started going together. Valentino is Mary's ex-boyfriend. One evening John asks Mary, "Have you seen Valentino this week?" Mary answers, "Valentino's been sick with mononucleosis for the past two weeks." Valentino has in fact been sick with mononucleosis for the past two weeks, but it is also the case that Mary had a date with Valentino the night before. Did Mary lie?[58]

This example contains a literally true statement, with an intent to deceive. Notice that it is very similar to the *Bronston* case. Like Mr. Bronston, Mary made a statement that is true in isolation but that is literally not responsive to the question. At the same time, as in *Bronston*, there is a natural tendency to interpret the answer in a way that would make it responsive: that Mary has not seen Valentino because he's been sick.

Do people think that Mary lied? Coleman and Kay asked sixty-seven people to rank the story on a scale from 1 to 7, where 1 indicates "very sure it is not a lie," 7 indicates "very sure it is a lie," and 4 is the midpoint response, "can't say anything." The result, as the authors might have predicted, was a mean of 3.48, not far from the midpoint, but tending toward Mary's not having lied.

One explanation for this result is that people judge lying not by definitions but rather by how close a statement matches a prototypical lie.[59] But there is another explanation consistent with the facts. Further analysis of the data showed that eighteen respondents (27 percent) thought Mary lied, seven (10 percent) couldn't say, and forty-two (63 percent) thought Mary did not lie.[60] This means that not only were many people uncertain about whether Mary had lied, but that there was significant disagreement over the matter. Perhaps some of the disagreement results from different perceptions of what it means to utter a "false statement." If we look at the perlocutionary effect of the statement (that is, the effect it has on the hearer), there is no difference between Mary's true but deceptive statement and a statement that is actually false. But if we look at the illocutionary force of the statement (the information conveyed), the statement is true.

Coleman and Kay's results suggest that people tend to care about whether a statement conveys false information in judging whether someone lied. But the results further show that it is not all that unusual for people also to concern themselves with whether the statement caused the hearer to believe something false, even if the statement was literally true. Prototypical lies do both. However, because Mary, Bronston, and Clinton all indirectly achieved the same deceptive result as someone who conveys false information directly, we are uncomfortable relieving them from legal responsibility while holding the conventional, and perhaps less skillful, liar guilty of a crime.

In his testimony, Clinton relied on the fact that people often understand words based on how far they stray from the prototype. Lewinsky had denied in her affidavit that the two of them had had a "sexual relationship." Unlike the objection by Clinton's lawyer, which was clearly in the present tense, Lewinsky's affidavit was not so limited. During his deposition in the *Jones* case, Clinton was asked about the statement and testified that Lewinsky's statement was truthful.

Not surprisingly, Kenneth Starr's lawyers came back to this issue during the grand jury proceedings, quizzing him once again about whether her statement was true. Clinton responded:

> I believe at the time that [Lewinsky] filled out this affidavit, if she believed that the definition of sexual relationship was two people having intercourse, then this is accurate. And I believe that is the definition that most ordinary Americans would give it.[61]

Clinton also noted that Lewinsky was not bound by the definition that had been used at his deposition in the *Jones* case, which would clearly have covered her acts of oral sex on him.[62] In other words, Clinton claimed that Lewinsky's statement relied not on the convoluted definition of "sexual relations" that had been given to him, but on the prototypical meaning of the phrase "sexual relationship," which in his view referred to sexual intercourse:

> I believe, I believe that the common understanding of the term, if you say two people are having a sexual relationship, most people believe that includes intercourse. So, if that's what Ms. Lewinsky thought, then this is a truthful affidavit. I don't know what was in her mind. But if that's what she thought, the affidavit is true.[63]

We do not know whether Clinton was correct to assert that the "common understanding" of the phrase "sexual relationship" requires that the parties have engaged in intercourse. But it is true that this phrase, like many others, has a prototypical usage about which practically everyone agrees. Very few people would argue that if two people are having sexual intercourse, they do not have a sexual relationship. There is likely to be much more disagreement about more marginal cases, however.

This explains how people could differ so sincerely in their assessment of whether Clinton lied about his sex life. He clearly intended to mislead people into believing something that was not true. Some felt that was enough to make him a liar. Others did not. Still others thought Clinton lied, but did not believe the lies to be material to his ability to govern, in part because they were largely the result of a perjury trap set by his political opponents. However one comes out on this question, we believe that some of the insights of linguistic theory can help to explain how people could legitimately take different positions on the question.

Conclusion

In light of Clinton's highly misleading testimony, is it time to reexamine the *Bronston* literal truth defense? Should we place so much emphasis on whether the examiner could or should have probed more deeply?

Recall that Bronston falsely implied that he had no personal Swiss bank accounts, but the examining lawyer failed to realize that the reply was unresponsive and thus did not probe more deeply. There are thus two principles that collide in such cases. On the one hand, we should normally be able to assume—even during an adversarial proceeding—that a witness's reply is relevant to the question. On the other hand, lawyers in the courtroom have a unique duty to ensure that the questions they ask and the answers they receive produce a record that is as clear and unambiguous as possible. A common way to do this is by reformulating and seeking confirmation.[64] In the *Bronston* case, the examining lawyer could have clarified the testimony by rephrasing Bronston's answer ("So, are you saying that you have never had a personal bank account in Switzerland?") and persisting until he had a clear confirmation that this was or was not correct.

That is the lesson of *Bronston*, even though it flies in the face of rules regulating ordinary conversation and perhaps also prototypical notions of what it means to lie. The problem with blaming the witness, which is what a perjury prosecution entails, is that he might have given an unresponsive reply without intending to mislead. Or even if he hoped to mislead, it is always possible that if pressed, he would have admitted the truth. It is lawyers and judges, not the witnesses, who control the questioning process.

The Clinton impeachment trial provides another reason to place much of the responsibility on the examining lawyer. When the questioner already knows the truth, which is often the case in a trial, the purpose of questioning is not to acquire information, but to create a clear narrative on the record to support one's case. If a hostile witness fails to cooperate in creating such a narrative, and especially if the witness evades or equivocates and produces no testimony that is useful to the questioner, the lawyer now has a motivation to create a very different record by attacking the witness's credibility. If Jones's lawyers were indeed politically motivated, they might have been more interested in trying to show that Clinton was a liar than in proving that he harassed their client. If this was the case, they would have a reason not to press Clinton too hard on the issue of whether he had ever been alone with Lewinsky. Had they forced the issue, he might have capitulated and admitted that they had met alone on other occasions than those he mentioned. Because of the highly politicized nature of the proceedings, it is impossible to discount this possibility.

Thus, despite our occasional misgivings about the *Bronston* holding, we believe that its placement of primary responsibility on examining lawyers is an important safeguard against advantaging those in the legal system who would rather let a witness look bad based on an incomplete record than to get at the full truth. It warns lawyers that if they believe that a witness is equivocating or may not be telling the truth, they must clarify the witness's testimony, instead of trying to create a record that will allow them to refer the matter to local prosecutors. And it removes an incentive for a lawyer to ask misleading questions to set a perjury trap. We also believe that limitations on the doctrine—applying it only when it is evident that an answer was true, but unresponsive—are appropriate.

This duty of examining lawyers—to create a clear and unambiguous record—also helps explain why other crimes of language have no equivalent to the literal truth defense. If someone asks a hit man to "knock off" or "blow away" her husband, or if a suspect tells a potential witness that he will "get" her if she testifies, the argument that these words taken literally have a largely innocuous meaning would fall on deaf ears. The reason, of course, is that there is no one present on such occasions whose job it is to clarify ambiguities of this sort. Because courtroom questioning is tightly structured and—subject to the judge's supervision—entirely managed by the examining lawyer, whether and how the truth emerges is controlled as much by the lawyers as it is by the witnesses. Moreover, witnesses are generally counseled by lawyers before they testify to listen very carefully to the question, to answer only the question that is asked, and not to volunteer any information. Ordinary rules of conversation apply with significantly less force in such a rigidly structured environment.

There are thus valid institutional reasons for interpreting language relatively literally in a perjury prosecution. In contrast, language used to commit other sorts of language crimes should be viewed more realistically, especially in light of the tendency of perpetrators to speak circuitously.

Chapter 12

Where Do We Go from Here?

There are two sensible ways of organizing a book that draws on learning from both linguistics and law. We chose to organize this book around legal issues, since ultimately our point is that advances in linguistics and the psychology of language can contribute to understanding and improving the legal system. We could instead have organized the book around recurring linguistic issues, but we believe that would have made the book less useful. Apart from chapter 2, in which we introduced some basic linguistic concepts, we decided to subordinate the analytical tools we use to the purpose of our analysis.

Of course, what we refer to as the "legal system" is an abstraction that includes vast numbers of people doing a large variety of jobs in different institutional settings. Among those we discuss in this book are law enforcement officials, prosecutors, defense lawyers, judges, legislators, and academics who testify as experts. Any response to the issues we raise must come from within these settings. With this in mind, we conclude the book by summarizing some of the suggestions we have made, organized in terms of the institutions that will have to implement any changes.

Law Enforcement

As noted in chapters 3 and 4, recent U.S. Supreme Court decisions have been generous to law enforcement agencies when interpreting the language used in encounters between the police and suspects. These decisions have held that some coercive or otherwise questionable police practices do not violate the U.S. Constitution. That does not mean that such practices are right, of course, or even that they are likely to be effective in the effort to reduce crime. The Supreme Court reviews law enforcement practices only for the purpose of deciding whether they do or do not violate the federal Constitution. Thus, state and local governments, as well as law enforcement agencies themselves, are free to initiate a higher level of professionalism that effectively fights crime, improves their relationships with the community, and at the same time protects the rights of citizens.

The professional practice that we recommend most strongly is that all encounters between the police and suspects be videotaped whenever possible. Taping is required in a few states, and it has been the law for many years in the United Kingdom and Australia.

Taping has several benefits. It preserves a record of the exact words that were used, which is a prerequisite for determining whether a request for consent or a waiver of *Miranda* rights occurred within the bounds of the law. In addition, a taped record is the best evidence for the jury. A confession may pass constitutional muster and therefore be admissible, but a jury still needs to decide whether the defendant is guilty. With access to an appropriately made recording of the entire interrogation, the jury can make a reasoned decision about how seriously to take the confession. Without one, the issue may devolve into a swearing contest between the defendant and interrogating officers about what was said over the course of many hours. Even if the officers and the defendant are being as forthright as they can be, the jury will not have available the evidence that it needs to decide what happened, simply because our memory for exact words is quite limited. Finally, recording encounters between the police and suspects is likely to lead to a more routine use of professional police practices, which can serve to protect the rights of citizens, to reduce the risk of error in the criminal justice system, and to increase respect for legal institutions generally.

Taping will, of course, involve some expense and inconvenience, especially when the encounter between the police and a citizen is in the field. These factors largely explain why it was not routinely done in the past.

But today, audiotaping costs almost nothing, and videotaping is almost as cheap. The recording equipment has also become extremely compact. There is absolutely no technical impediment to routine videotaping inside the police station, and doing so in the field is also increasingly feasible.

Our second recommendation is that law enforcement agencies should use special procedures when questioning the young, the mentally handicapped, and non-native speakers of English, or continue to refine existing procedures for those agencies that already have them in place. The Central Park jogger case in New York, in which five youths served substantial prison terms after confessing to a rape they did not commit, should simply never have happened. The most vulnerable suspects should not be able to waive their rights without representation, or at least without the presence of an adult relative.

Third, consensual searches should be used with care. One consequence of the Supreme Court's tolerant attitude toward "requests" for consent to search is that it presents police officers with a greater opportunity to engage in racial profiling in deciding which cars to stop and when to seek "consent" to search on the nation's highways. While the extent to which racial profiling occurs remains somewhat unclear, the practice is extremely divisive and undermines confidence in law enforcement institutions by minority communities. For this reason, whether legislatively or by executive order, police departments in some states have stopped using consensual searches altogether, or have placed limitations on when they can be used in an effort to reduce abuses. Others should follow suit.

It is possible, of course, that conducting searches of cars along established drug corridors is an effective law enforcement technique in the war against drugs. This may explain the Supreme Court's reluctance to assess the issue of consent in this context. Yet if it is truly necessary to search automobiles along the nation's highways, it should be done in a transparent and constitutional manner, not by manipulating the meaning of the acts of requesting and consenting in order to single out minority drivers.

Fourth, we recommend that police departments consistently use appropriate procedures for voice lineups and for identifying speakers on tape recordings. Such procedures are already, to a large extent, in place with eyewitness identifications. Under some circumstances, the courts have required them as a constitutional matter. Even when not required, however, adopting more professional procedures can only serve to enhance the status and prestige of law enforcement agencies in the community, while helping to make the system more fair in individual cases.

Legislatures and the Executive Branch

Another way to improve the criminal justice system on either a state or national basis is through legislation. As mentioned, some states have made racial profiling or consent searches during a traffic stop illegal or subject to special restrictions. Governors can also play a role in improving the criminal law. An outgoing governor of Illinois pardoned some inmates and commuted the sentences of others on death row based on a study showing serious miscarriages of justice in the state's capital punishment scheme. Practically speaking, it seems unlikely that his approach will be adopted on such a grand scale. But the mere possibility that governors might use their clemency powers may encourage other actors in the legal system to bring greater fairness and concern for accuracy into the legal system.

Courts

We have been critical of some Supreme Court rulings involving linguistic encounters in the context of criminal procedure. All too often the Court has interpreted utterances by suspects in a literal manner, with little attention to pragmatic circumstances, as though they were construing a contract or will. Of course, as a practical matter, important precedents like the *Busta-monte* or *Davis* cases are unlikely to be modified or overruled in the near future. But the federal Constitution simply sets a minimum standard. State courts need not always follow suit, especially when a state constitution offers greater protection than federal law. In that event, a state court might well decide that when a suspect requests counsel in words that are easily enough understood as such by fair-minded people, he should not be interrogated further without his lawyer's permission. State court decisions may also offer more protection to the most vulnerable members of society, who frequently do not understand their rights or much else that is happening to them when charged with a crime.

Second, courts should not admit out-of-court confessions or statements by witnesses unless the judge or jury who must evaluate those statements has the best possible evidence of what was said. There is no reason that courts cannot require, under state rules of evidence, that a confession not be admitted unless it was videotaped, or unless perhaps there was a very good reason for not videotaping it. Because our memory for exact words is so frail, the system should encourage participants in the legal system to preserve the best evidence of what was said. Only then can we be sure that the truth will be presented at trial.

Finally, courts should take great care in evaluating the reliability of the identification of voices on tape, as we suggest in chapter 7. Instead of rubber-stamping questionable identifications, they should take steps to ensure that the person identifying the voices on the tape is truly familiar with them, or that circumstances in which the tape was made provides a good indication of reliability.

Attorneys

Although judges and juries are the ones who decide cases in the Anglo-American legal system, it is up to the attorneys in a case to bring the facts of the case, and the arguments based on those facts, to the attention of the judge and jurors. The law governing identification by voice is a half-century behind the scientific research. No one other than defense lawyers has a stake in introducing this material. They should begin to do so, just as they have begun to insist on educational experts who point out some of the shortcomings in eyewitness identification.

Defense lawyers have the same responsibility with respect to identification of authors. As work in stylistic analysis develops, lawyers who repeatedly face issues of identification should closely follow that research and seek expert analysis to the extent that the analysis meets current evidentiary standards.

Prosecutors have even higher ethical duties because they represent the power of the state. Despite the strong lawyerly desire to win cases, they should never stray from the ideal of seeking justice. They have the discretion and even the obligation not to prosecute weak cases. If they decide to prosecute, they should refrain from introducing evidence that they know is unreliable. They should therefore resist the temptation to introduce the work of experts who use methodologies that cannot be shown to have a scientific basis. And they should be very careful in using confessions from vulnerable witnesses. Despite the understandable pressure on prosecutors (who are often elected officials) to obtain convictions in high-profile cases, they have little to gain—and much to lose—if it later turns out that they helped convict an innocent person, while allowing a guilty one to roam free.

Moreover, the law should be less tolerant of lawyers, whether prosecutors or defense attorneys, who engage in efforts to mislead or manipulate witnesses during questioning, and sometimes even judges during argument. In the heat of battle, there are constant accusations of discovery abuses and other bad conduct. In chapter 11, we discussed the law of perjury. We observed that the "literal truth" standard employed by the courts allows clever witnesses to make statements that are intended to mislead the questioner and manipulate the truth-finding process. Perhaps we should insist that witnesses speak more forthrightly in court. Lawyers—as officers of the court—should do no less. If the legal system wishes to demand more of witnesses, it should begin by demanding more of itself.

Linguists, Psychologists, and Other Scholars

It is convenient to think of experts as either coming from a group of people specially trained to participate as experts in the judicial process, or as being practicing members of disciplines with something to contribute. In the first group, conflicts of interest are patent. People who make a living from investigating and testifying have an inherent stake in convincing the system to permit them to continue investigating and testifying. That has triggered controversies about such areas as handwriting analysis, microscopic hair analysis, and ballistic comparisons.

When scholars without such motivations or special training get involved in judicial proceedings, the situation becomes more complicated. Such scholars do not make a living from testifying in court, so money is less of a driving force, but they may nonetheless find the process exciting or intellectually stimulating. As difficult as it may sometimes be, it is of the utmost importance that academics acknowledge the weaknesses, as well as the strengths, of the methodologies they employ. In an era in which scientific validity is essential for expert opinion testimony to be admissible, this candor will serve two important functions. First, it will permit courts to make informed decisions about whether to permit the testimony in the first place. There is absolutely no reason for an academic linguist to be embarrassed if a judge decides that his or her subfield is not appropriate for trial testimony. Even when it is not admitted into evidence, linguistic evidence may be helpful to law enforcement in investigating a crime or to lawyers preparing for trial. Second, greater candor about the weaknesses of a methodological approach will promote the research that is necessary to address those concerns.

In addition, when linguists testify as experts they should not state conclusions that are stronger than the evidence and underlying theory warrant. Even the most reliable research can be called into question if its proponent makes exaggerated claims about it. It is the job of lawyers, not expert witnesses, to make arguments based upon the evidence. Consider cases in which linguists analyze a suspect's written confession to determine whether it really is a verbatim record of what the suspect said during interrogation, an issue that we discussed in chapter 8. A linguist in such a case could not testify that, based on her analysis, the defendant was innocent, even if she was convinced that this was true. Nor could she testify that in her opinion the police coerced the defendant into signing his confession, or even that the confession was not an accurate record of what the defendant said. What she could properly conclude, if the evidence is strong enough and properly analyzed, is that in a number of respects the language of the confession was more like the language of police officers than the defendant, and that therefore it was unlikely to be a verbatim record of what the defendant actually said. Linguists who carefully circumscribe their conclusions in this way are far more likely to be allowed to testify than those who make more aggressive claims.

Finally, linguists interested in the legal ramifications of their field should continue to explore human language as a matter of basic research (see chapter 2). Sometimes this learning may be useful in the trial context. Sometimes it may not. On other occasions, it is potentially useful but its reliability has not yet been proven. Yet even when it is not particularly relevant to factual issues in a specific case, linguistics can help us better understand the workings of the legal system in general, as we hope to have shown throughout this book.

Linguistic expertise has been favorably compared to fingerprint or DNA evidence. Especially the latter has come to be regarded as a highly useful tool of the criminal justice system, helping exonerate the innocent while at the same time solving crimes that police had long ago given up hope of resolving. As we have seen, the current state of the art is that when it comes to identifying people by their voices or writing style, linguistic expertise has not yet reached that level of reliability. At present, such linguistic expertise is most useful in eliminating a suspect as the perpetrator. As the fields develop, however, there is reason to expect that the evidentiary problems that we have highlighted in the areas of speaker and author identification can be solved by continuing advances in the language sciences. It may well be that in the foreseeable future forensic identification techniques will advance sufficiently to be used to identify with reasonable certainty the voice on a tape or the author of a threatening letter.

Some of the other problems we have discussed do not lend themselves as easily to such solutions. Thus, when it comes to resolving some of the inconsistencies in the system, such as the law's unwillingness to recognize a suspect's indirect request for counsel, while being quite willing to recognize an indirect threat, we are less optimistic. Fixing these problems requires political will. That is something we cannot provide.

Our central purpose in this book has been to illustrate some of the ways in which linguistics, cognitive psychology, philosophy of language, and related fields can help us better understand the workings of our legal system. Often enough the system gets it right. Judges and jurors have pretty good intuitions about language, for the most part. They can usually tell when an utterance is a threat or a lie. But there are also many aspects of language that are not intuitively obvious, such as how long we remember a voice that we heard once or twice, or how well we recall exact words. Although we engage in countless conversations during our lives, people tend not to realize how much information we communicate indirectly, and why. And even though we all use prototypical reasoning in understanding what a word means, most people think that meaning is something found in a dictionary, rather than our brains. Thus, apart from its increasing promise in helping to solve specific crimes where language is an issue, linguistics may be even more useful in helping us understand important aspects of the legal system.

Of course, a better appreciation of how the legal system works not only helps us recognize the problems it has in dealing with language, but also points out ways to solve them. We hope that the issues that we have discussed in this book, and the solutions that we recommend, will give the players in the criminal justice system a framework for making the changes that are needed to assure that the guilty receive their just deserts, and the innocent remain free.

Notes

Chapter One

1. See Schneckloth v. Bustamonte, 412 U.S. 218 (1973).
2. People v. Krueger, 412 N.E.2d 537, 538–39 (Ill. 1980).
3. See Segerstrom v. State, 783 S.W.2d 847 (Ark. 1990), involving a fifteen-year-old defendant with attention deficit disorder and a mental age of six years.
4. United States v. Hamilton, 107 F.3d 499, 510 (7th Cir. 1997).
5. See United States v. Knox, No. 97-5492, 1998 U.S. App. LEXIS 27655 (6th Cir. 1998).
6. This scenario is discussed by Robert Eagleson, *Forensic Analysis of Personal Written Texts: A Case Study,* in *Language and the Law* 362–73 (John Gibbons ed., 1994).
7. People v. Hood, 878 P.2d 89, 94–95 (Colo. Ct. App. 1994).
8. People v. Warren, 113 Ill. App. 3d 1 (1983).
9. United States v. DeZarn, 157 F.3d 1042, 1045 (6th Cir. 1998).
10. See, e.g., Lawrence M. Solan, *Law, Language, and Lenity,* 40 William and Mary Law Review 57 (1998); Peter M. Tiersma, *A Message in a Bottle: Text, Autonomy, and Statutory Interpretation,* 76 Tulane Law Review 431 (2001).
11. See, e.g., Peter Tiersma, *The Rocky Road to Legal Reform: Improving the Language of Jury Instructions,* 66 Brooklyn Law Review 1081 (2001); Lawrence M. Solan, *Refocusing the Burden of Proof In Criminal Cases: Some Doubt about Reasonable Doubt,* 78 Texas Law Review 105 (1999).

Chapter Two

1. See Fed. R. Evid. 901(b)(5), discussed in chapter 7.
2. See Fed. R. Evid. 801(d)(2), discussed in chapter 6.

3. See Noam Chomsky, *Language and Mind* (2d ed. 1972); Noam Chomsky, *Aspects of the Theory of Syntax* (1965), for seminal work. For an excellent book that sets forth some of Chomsky's ideas accessibly, see Neil Smith, *Chomsky: Ideas and Ideals* (1999).

4. See, e.g., Leonard Bloomfield, *Language* (1933); Edward Sapir, *Language* (1921). For a discussion of the development of the generative perspective, see Frederick Newmeyer, *Generative Linguistics: A Historical Perspective* (1996) (especially chap. 4, "Has There Been a 'Chomskyian Revolution' in Syntax?" at 23); Federick J. Newmeyer, *Linguistic Theory in America: The First Quarter-Century of Transformational Generative Grammar* 35–38 (1986).

5. See Garland Cannon, *Oriental Jones: A Biography of Sir William Jones, 1746–1794* (1964).

6. The parallel between Jones and Chomsky was drawn by scholars commenting on Chomsky's early work. Charles Hockett, whose structuralist perspective on linguistics was largely supplanted by Chomsky's new approach, nonetheless likened Chomsky's paradigm shift to the contributions Jones had made to the field in the late eighteenth century. Charles Hockett, *Sound Change*, 41 Language 185 (1965).

7. The seminal book is Elizabeth F. Loftus, *Eyewitness Testimony* (1979). For an account of the trials in which Loftus participated as a witness, see Elizabeth Loftus and Katherine Ketcham, *Witness for the Defense: The Accused, the Eyewitness, and the Expert Who Puts Memory on Trial* (1991).

8. Both have articles in *Eyewitness Testimony: Psychological Perspectives* (Gary L. Wells and Elizabeth F. Loftus eds., 1984), along with many other interesting articles.

9. Barry Scheck, Peter Neufeld, and Jim Dwyer, *Actual Innocence: Five Days to Execution, and Other Dispatches from the Wrongly Accused* 263–64 (2000).

10. We do not mean to imply that our brains contain separate areas each of which is exclusively dedicated to a specific module. While studies of people with brain injuries suggest that this is true to some extent, see Steven Pinker, *Words and Rules* (1999), other evidence suggests that the brain is quite plastic and that these various subsystems are present in various areas of the brain. See, e.g., Jeffrey L. Elman, Elizabeth A. Bates, Mark H. Johnson, Annette Karmiloff-Smith, Domenico Parisi, and Kim Plunkett, *Rethinking Innateness* (1996). These are open issues that go well beyond the scope of this book. Nonetheless, it is useful, and to a large extent empirically justified, to regard these various linguistic capacities as separate subsystems.

11. For an introduction to phonology, see Michael Kenstowicz, *Phonology in Generative Grammar* (1994).

12. For an introduction to the study of syntax, see Robert Freidin, *Foundations of Generative Syntax* (1992). There is controversy in the field over the extent to which syntax is dependent on the meaning of the ideas being conveyed. Discussion of that issue goes well beyond the scope of this book.

13. Actually, aspiration occurs at the beginning of a syllable—not a word. Compare *despot* (unaspirated *p*) with *repair* (aspirated).

14. As we will see, we identify speakers not only by their voices, but also by the way they pronounce the sounds of their languages.

15. The title of this subsection derives from Gary F. Marcus, *The Algebraic Mind* (2001), which discusses numerous psychological phenomena, including syntax, which operate in a rule-like fashion.

16. For an interesting and accessible introduction to these developments, see Mark C. Baker, *The Atoms of Language: The Mind's Hidden Rules of Grammar* (2001).

17. Interestingly, when the subject is questioned, the word "that" is not permissible. Compare "Who do you think that Bill saw?" with "Who do you think that saw Bill?" The first is dramatically better than the second to most native speakers of English. See Baker, *The Atoms of Language,* at 39–44 for details of how contemporary linguistics explains this fact.

18. This is not to say that linguists all agree that "direct object" is the appropriate unit of explanation. Many use various structural relations within a sentence as defined by certain diagrams that set forth syntactic relationships.

19. Noam Chomsky, *Aspects of the Theory of Syntax* 21 (1965).

20. This example is adapted from Freidin, *Foundations of Generative Syntax,* at 97.

21. We have each written about this elsewhere. See Peter M. Tiersma, *Legal Language* (1999); Lawrence M. Solan, *The Language of Judges* (1993).

22. 18 U.S.C. § 2252.

23. 513 U.S. 64 (1994).

24. N.J. Stat. Ann. § 2C:15-1(a).

25. See United States v. Scheetz, 293 F.3d 175, 187 (4th Cir. 2002).

26. Vicki L. Smith, *Prototypes in the Courtroom: Lay Representations of Legal Concepts,* 61 Journal of Personality and Social Psychology 857 (1991).

27. See Lawrence M. Solan, *Learning Our Limits: The Decline of Textualism in Statutory Cases,* 1997 Wisconsin Law Review 235.

28. Eleanor Rosch, *Cognitive Representations of Semantic Categories,* 104 Journal of Experimental Psychology: General 192 (1975).

29. See, e.g., Edward E. Smith and Steven A. Sloman, *Similarity—Versus Rule-Based Categorization,* 22 Memory and Cognition 377 (1994); Geoffrey Murphy and Daniel L. Medin, *The Role of Theories in Conceptual Coherence,* 92 Psychological Review 289 (1985).

30. For an attempt to answer this question in detail, see Ray S. Jackendoff, *The Architecture of the Language Faculty* (1996).

31. Smith v. United States, 508 U.S. 223, 229 (1993).

32. See George A. Miller, *Contextuality,* in *Mental Models in Cognitive Science: Essays in Honor of Phil Johnson-Laird* 1 (J. Oakhill and A. Garnham eds., 1996).

33. Paul Grice, *Logic and Conversation,* in *Syntax and Semantics 3: Speech Acts* 41, 45 (P. Cole and J. Morgan eds., 1975).

34. Some have argued that Grice's entire system can be reduced to a principle of relevance, broadly defined. See Dan Sperber and Deirdre Wilson, *Relevance: Communication and Cognition* (1986).

35. Georgia Green makes this point in her excellent introduction to pragmatics. Georgia M. Green, *Pragmatics and Natural Language Understanding* (2d ed. 1996).

36. J. L. Austin, *How to Do Things with Words* (1962).

37. John Searle, *Speech Acts* (1969).

38. See Peter M. Tiersma, *Reassessing Unilateral Contracts: The Role of Offer, Acceptance and Promise,* 26 U.C. Davis Law Review 1 (1992).

39. See John R. Searle, *Indirect Speech Acts,* in *Pragmatics: A Reader* 265 (Steven Davis ed., 1991).

40. See, e.g., *John Searle and His Critics* (Ernest Lepore and Robert Van Gulick eds., 1991). For an expansive discussion of speech act analysis of legal events, including its limitations, see Jonathan Yovel, *Rights and Rites: Initiation, Language and Performance in Law and Legal Education,* 2 Stanford Agora, wysiwyg://2/http://lawschool.stanford.edu/agora/volume2/yovel.shml (2002).

41. We discuss some of these cases in Peter Tiersma and Lawrence M. Solan, *The Linguist on the Witness Stand: Forensic Linguistics in American Courts*, 78 Language 221 (2002).

42. Although this book is limited to criminal law, it may be worth mentioning that morphology can be a helpful tool in trademark disputes. For instance, is the *Mc-* in McDonald's a general morpheme of the language that can be used to indicate that a business offers low-cost goods or services of reasonable quality (as in *McSleep Inns*)? Or is it part of the name (trademark) McDonald's? Such issues are obviously linguistic questions, and courts deciding trademark cases usually allow linguistic expertise to be taken into consideration. See Quality Inns International, Inc. v. McDonald's Corp., 695 F. Supp. 198 (D. Md. 1988). See also Roger Shuy, *Linguistic Battles in Trademark Disputes* (2002).

43. See *Language in the Legal Process* (Janet Cotterill ed., 2002); *Language in the Judicial Process* (Judith N. Levi and Anne G. Walker eds., 1990); *Language and the Law* (John Gibbons ed., 1994). Gibbons's book deals largely with cases in Australia.

44. Shuy, *Linguistic Battles*; Roger Shuy, *Language Crimes: The Use and Abuse of Language Evidence in the Courtroom* (1993); Roger Shuy, *The Language of Confession, Interrogation and Deception* (1998).

45. Much of the literature reporting on linguists' experience in the American legal system is discussed in Judith N. Levi, *Language as Evidence: The Linguist as Expert Witness in North American Courts*, 1 Forensic Linguistics 1 (1994).

46. Perhaps just as important, linguists and psychologists sit on jury reform committees in some states. Tiersma is a member of the California committee on jury instruction reform; Solan is a member of the advisory committee to the New York Jury Trial Project.

47. The discussion in this section is an expansion of our discussion in Tiersma and Solan, *The Linguist on the Witness Stand.*

48. Jennifer L. Mnookin, *Fingerprint Evidence in an Age of DNA Profiling*, 67 Brooklyn Law Review 13 (2001).

49. This discussion has made its way into the scientific community. The fall 2003 issue of *Issues in Science and Technology* published several articles on questions of the scientific validity of the forensic sciences. See D. Michael Risinger and Michael J. Saks, *A House with No Foundation*; David Faigman et al., *The Limits of the Polygraph*; Jennifer L. Mnookin, *Fingerprints: Not a Gold Standard*; Paul Giannelli, *Crime Labs Need Improvement.*

50. 293 F. 1013 (D.C. Cir. 1923).

51. Id. at 1014 (emphasis added).

52. Peter W. Huber, *Galileo's Revenge: Junk Science in the Courtroom* (1991).

53. 509 U.S. 579 (1993).

54. For a clear discussion of the three cases and some of their ramifications, see Margaret A. Berger, *The Supreme Court's Trilogy on the Admissibility of Expert Testimony*, in Federal Judicial Center, *Reference Manual on Scientific Evidence* 9 (2d ed. 2000).

55. 727 F. Supp. 570, 572 (S.D. Cal. 1989).

56. 951 F.2d 1128 (9th Cir. 1991).

57. 509 U.S. at 592–93.

58. Id. at 590.

59. Id. at 593.

60. 522 U.S. 136 (1997).

61. 526 U.S. 137 (1999).

62. Id. at 149.

63. Id. at 152.

64. Fed. R. Evid. 702 (as amended December 1, 2000).

65. Joseph Sanders, *Complex Litigation at the Millennium:* Kumho *and How We Know,* 64 Law and Contemporary Problems 373 (2001). Sanders relies on somewhat different psychological research, but the point he makes is the same.

Part Two

1. 384 U.S. 757 (1966).

2. Id. at 761 n.5.

3. United States v. Wade, 388 U.S. 218 (1967) (voice sample); Gilbert v. California, 388 U.S. 263 (1967) (handwriting sample).

Chapter Three

1. 536 U.S. 194, 199 (2002).

2. 412 U.S. 218 (1973).

3. Carroll v. United States, 267 U.S. 132, 151 (1925); California v. Acevedo, 500 U.S. 565 (1991).

4. 412 U.S. 218 (1973).

5. Bumper v. North Carolina, 391 U.S. 543, 548 (1968).

6. *Bustamonte,* 412 U.S. at 224.

7. 367 U.S. 568, 602 (1961).

8. 412 U.S. at 226.

9. Id. at 221.

10. Research shows this to be a significant motivating force in people's behavior. See Tom Tyler, *Why People Obey the Law* (1990).

11. John R. Searle, *Speech Acts: An Essay in the Philosophy of Language* 58–59 (1969).

12. 412 U.S. at 220–22.

13. See John R. Searle, *Indirect Speech Acts,* in *Pragmatics: A Reader* 265 (Steven Davis ed., 1991).

14. *The MacMillan Dictionary of Quotations* 34 at *Assassination* 5 (1967).

15. Consider some other types of indirect commands (at least, in the right context). None of these are literally imperatives, although all could be phrased as such: "You are standing on my foot" ("Get off my foot!"); "I would like you to go now" ("Go now!"); "Officers will henceforth wear ties at dinner" ("Officers, wear ties at dinner!"); "Would you mind not making so much noise?" ("Be quiet!"); "How many times have I told you not to eat with your fingers?" ("Don't eat with your fingers!"). The examples are from Searle, *Indirect Speech Acts,* at 268–69.

16. Robin T. Lakoff, *Talking Power: The Politics of Language* 30 (1990).

17. See Bumper v. North Carolina, 391 U.S. at 548–49 (when four officers appeared at the defendant's residence and falsely claimed to have a warrant, consent to search the house was not voluntary).

18. John R. Searle, *A Classification of Illocutionary Acts,* 5 Language in Society 1, 5 (1976).

19. Bustamonte v. Schneckloth, 448 F.2d 699, 701 (9th Cir. 1971).

20. The situation in *Bustamonte* is actually a bit more complicated since the driver and owner of the car really had not committed any crime, and Bustamonte, who had committed a crime, was not the individual in control of the automobile. In the typical case, the person who can consent and the person who stands to lose are the same individual. Because of

its prominence in legal history, we continue to illustrate our points about requests and commands with *Bustamonte,* asking to reader to put such nuances to one side.

21. The example is from United States v. Zapata, 997 F.2d 751, 754 n.1 (10th Cir. 1993).

22. United States v. Gomez, 1991 WL 266552 (9th Cir.).

23. United States v. Chaidez, 906 F.2d 377, 382 (8th Cir. 1990).

24. United States v. Randolph, 789 F. Supp. 407, 408 (D.D.C. 1992).

25. State v. Johnson, 346 A.2d 66, 68 (N.J. 1975).

26. United States v. $24,339.00 in United States Currency, 1995 WL 507517 at *2 (E.D. Tex.).

27. United States v. Brugal, 209 F.3d 353, 369 (4th Cir. 2000).

28. United States v. Johnson, 71 F. Supp. 2d 1379, 1382 (M.D. Ga. 1999).

29. United States v. Garcia, 897 F.2d 1413, 1416 (7th Cir. 1990).

30. United States v. Valdiosera-Godinez, 932 F.2d 1093, 1095 (5th Cir. 1991).

31. United States v. Yusuff, 96 F.3d 982, 984 (7th Cir. 1996).

32. United States v. Mondragon Farias, 43 F. Supp. 2d 1276, 1279 (D. Utah 1999) (consent held not voluntary because videotape revealed no audible response).

33. United States v. Baker, 2000 WL 146878 (W.D.N.Y.).

34. United States v. Erwin, 155 F.3d 818, 821–22 (6th Cir. 1998).

35. United States v. Price, 54 F.3d 342, 346–47 (7th Cir. 1995).

36. United States v. Zapata, 180 F.3d 1237, 1240 (11th Cir. 1999).

37. United States v. Badru, 97 F.3d 1471, 1475 (D.C. Cir. 1996).

38. United States v. Rich, 992 F.2d 502, 504 (5th Cir. 1993) (emphasis added).

39. United States v. Aloi, 9 F.3d 438, 440 (6th Cir. 1993) (emphasis added).

40. United States v. McGill, 125 F.3d 642, 643 (8th Cir. 1997) (emphasis added).

41. For discussion of how we understand a particular use of an expression to be the "literal" meaning, see Sam Glucksberg and Matthew S. McGlone, *Understanding Figurative Language: From Metaphors to Idioms* (2001).

42. See Randolph Quirk et al., *A Comprehensive Grammar of the English Language* § 4.49, at 219–21 (1985).

43. For a good, accessible introduction to linguistic pragmatics, see Georgia M. Green, *Pragmatics and Natural Language Understanding* 90 (2d ed. 1996).

44. United States v. Price, 54 F.3d 342, 346–47 (7th Cir. 1995) (emphasis added).

45. 529 U.S. 334 (2000).

46. United States v. Pulido-Baquerizo, 800 F.2d 899 (9th Cir. 1986).

47. See, e.g., United States v. Herzbrun, 723 F.2d 773, 776 (11th Cir. 1984); United States v. Skipwith, 482 F.2d 1272 (5th Cir. 1973).

48. United States v. Griffin, 530 F.2d 739 (7th Cir. 1976). Alternatively, the court held that he consented only to the officers' entry, but that once inside, they could search what was in plain view.

49. United States v. Benitez, 899 F.2d 995, 997–99 (10th Cir. 1990).

50. United States v. Wilson, 895 F.2d 168, 171–72 (4th Cir. 1990).

51. See United States v. Gallego-Zapata, 630 F. Supp. 665, 675 (D. Mass. 1986) (nodding or shrugging shoulders by defendant with limited English in response to agent's request to search jacket were gestures of passivity and not consent to search); United States v. Benitez-Arreguin, 973 F.2d 823 (10th Cir. 1992) (holding that pantomimic gestures by defendant with limited English, including shrugging shoulders and holding up

hands as if to signify that he did not know anything, did not constitute consent to search his bags).

52. See Thomas Y. Davies, *Recovering the Original Fourth Amendment,* 98 Michigan Law Review 547 (1999).

53. Samuel Walker, *Taming the System: The Control of Discretion in Criminal Justice 1950–1990* 48 (1993).

54. One commentator has suggested that minority drivers may be disproportionately inclined to consent to searches, perhaps because of a belief in their communities that it is dangerous to refuse compliance with police requests. Marcy Strauss, *Reconstructing Consent,* 92 Journal of Criminal Law and Criminology 211, 242–44 (2002).

55. David A. Harris, *"Driving While Black" and All Other Traffic Offenses: The Supreme Court and Pretextual Traffic Stops,* 87 Journal of Criminal Law and Criminology 544, 561 (1997).

56. See David Cole, *Race, Policing, and the Future of the Criminal Law,* Human Rights, Summer 1999, at 5.

57. One study found that 95 percent of people who were asked to consent to a search did so. State v. Carty, 790 A.2d 903, 911 (N.J. 2002).

58. Solomon Moore, *Race Profiling Suit Challenges CHP's Tactics,* Los Angeles Times, May 28, 2001, B1.

59. State v. Carty, 790 A.2d 903, 905 (N.J. 2002). In addition, as a result of a federal lawsuit against the New Jersey State Police for alleged racial profiling, the State Police agreed to request detained motorists for consent to searches only when they have reasonable suspicion to believe that the search will reveal evidence of a crime. Suspects must be notified that they have the right to refuse. See Wesley MacNeil Oliver, *With an Evil Eye and an Unequal Hand: Pretextual Stops and Doctrinal Remedies to Racial Profiling,* 74 Tulane Law Review 1409, 1415, 1477–78 (2000).

60. According to a study in Ohio, which for a period of time required a warning of this sort, the consent rate did not change substantially. Illya Lichtenberg, *Miranda in Ohio: The Effects of Robinette on the "Voluntary" Waiver of Fourth Amendment Rights,* 44 Howard Law Journal 349 (2001).

61. We are not the first to make this recommendation. Among others, see Oliver, *With an Evil Eye,* who—as we do—links consent searches to the issue of racial profiling.

62. 412 U.S. at 233.

63. Id. at 231.

64. 536 U.S. at 203. See also Ohio v. Robinette, 519 U.S. 33 (1996).

65. United States v. Gray, 883 F.2d 320, 321 (4th Cir. 1989).

66. State v. Johnson, 346 A.2d 66 (N.J. 1975) ("where the State seeks to justify a search on the basis of consent it has the burden of showing that the consent was voluntary, an essential element of which is knowledge of the right to refuse consent"); State v. Ferrier, 960 P.2d 927, 933–34 (Wash. 1998) (requiring a warning to residents in a home search that they need not consent). These warnings are probably not sufficient, however, because they do not tell motorists that they are free to be on their way. Without adding this additional information, motorists may believe that if they refuse consent, officers will simply detain them for who knows how long.

67. See Janice Nadler, *No Need To Shout: Bus Sweeps and the Psychology of Coercion,* 2002 Supreme Court Review 153.

68. 412 U.S. at 231–32.

69. Id. at 227.

70. Note, incidentally, that while liberal judges have often been accused of engaging in "result-oriented" jurisprudence, this analysis reveals that moderate and conservative judges are just as capable of doing so.

71. This point has been a theme of some very interesting empirical research in the relationship between social psychology and criminal justice. See Tyler, *Why People Obey the Law.*

Chapter Four

1. Brown v. Mississippi, 297 U.S. 278, 286 (1936).

2. Ashcraft v. Tennessee, 322 U.S. 143, 154 (1944).

3. The relay technique was still used in 1971, when a court held that a confession obtained after seven and one-half hours of questioning while depriving the suspect of food and water was coercive. United States ex rel. Burgos v. Follette 448 F.2d 130 (2d Cir. 1971). See also Xiao v. Reno, 837 F. Supp. 1506 (N.D. Cal. 1993) (interrogation methods in China described, including deprivation of sleep, food, and water, and use of cattle prod).

4. See David N. Nissman and Ed Hagen, *Law of Confessions* (2d ed. 1994). The voluntariness of confessions has also been required for at least two centuries in England. See Rex v. Warickshall, 168 Eng. Rep. 234 (1783).

5. Fikes v. Alabama, 352 U.S. 191 (1957).

6. Withrow v. Williams, 507 U.S. 680, 693 (1993).

7. Reck v. Pate, 367 U.S. 433, 440 (1961).

8. 378 U.S. 478 (1964).

9. 451 U.S. 477 (1981).

10. Bane v. State, 587 N.E.2d 97, 103 (Ind. 1992).

11. Bunch v. Commonwealth, 304 S.E.2d 271, 275 (Va.), *cert. denied,* 464 U.S. 977 (1983).

12. Clark v. Murphy, 331 F.3d 1062 (9th Cir. 2003).

13. 412 N.E.2d 537, 538–39 (Ill. 1980).

14. 459 N.E.2d 1137, 1139 (Ill. App. Ct. 1984).

15. State v. Moore, 744 S.W.2d 479, 480 (Mo. Ct. App. 1988) ("Maybe [I] should have an attorney."); People v. Bestelmeyer, 212 Cal. Rptr. 605, 607, 609 (Ct. App. 1985) ("I just thinkin', maybe I shouldn't say anything without a lawyer and then I thinkin' ahh."). In both cases the invocation was held ineffective and the police were allowed to continue interrogation.

16. State v. Campbell, 367 N.W.2d 454, 456 (Minn. 1985).

17. Poyner v. Commonwealth, 329 S.E.2d 815, 823 (Va.), *cert. denied,* 474 U.S. 888 (1985).

18. Even the statement "I have a right to an attorney" is not a literal request for counsel, so that a court might have held even this statement not to invoke the right.

19. See, e.g., Maglio v. Jago, 580 F.2d 202, 203, 205 (6th Cir. 1978) ("Maybe I should have an attorney" held to invoke right to counsel); People v. Traubert, 608 P.2d 342, 344 (Colo. 1980) ("I think I need to see an attorney" held valid invocation); Singleton v. State, 344 So. 2d 911, 912–13 (Fla. Dist. Ct. App. 1977) ("Maybe I had better ask my mother if I should get [an attorney]" held valid invocation); Sleek v. State, 499 N.E.2d 751, 753–54 (Ind. 1986) ("Well, I feel like I ought to have an attorney around" held valid invocation);

United States v. Prestigiacomo, 504 F. Supp. 681, 683 (E.D.N.Y. 1981) ("maybe it would be good to have a lawyer" held valid invocation).

20. Janet E. Ainsworth, *In a Different Register: The Pragmatics of Powerlessness in Police Interrogation,* 103 Yale Law Journal 259, 301–16 (1993).

21. Id. at 312.

22. Robin Lakoff, *Language and Women's Place* 18 (1975).

23. Id. at 14–17.

24. William M. O'Barr, *Linguistic Evidence: Language, Power, and Strategy in the Courtroom* 64–71 (1982). For updated discussion, see John M. Conley and William M. O'Barr, *Just Words: Law, Language, and Power* 65–66 (1998).

25. Davis v. United States, 512 U.S. 452, 459 (1994).

26. Id. at 455–56.

27. It would make sense to have this be part of the *Miranda* warning, which we discuss in chapter 5. This suggestion is from Greg Webb, *Exploration in the Practical Use of Formalism* (2002) (unpublished undergraduate paper, Princeton University).

28. 446 U.S. 291, 293–95 (1980).

29. Id. at 300–301.

30. See United States v. Gomez, 927 F.2d 1530, 1533 (11th Cir. 1991) (officer told suspect that cooperation was a good idea because he was facing a sentence of ten years to life; held to constitute interrogation).

31. Brewer v. Williams, 430 U.S. 387, 392–93 (1977).

32. The Court itself suggested that the difference lay in the fact that *Innis* involved *Miranda* and the right against compelled self-incrimination, while *Brewer* depended on the Sixth Amendment right to counsel. See *Innis,* 446 U.S. 291, 300 n.4. The relevance of this distinction escapes us, however, since a question should be a question under either constitutional right.

33. People v. Ferro, 460 N.Y.S.2d 585 (1983).

34. 63 N.Y.2d 316 (1984), *cert. denied,* 472 U.S. 1007 (1985).

35. For an important work that relates the degree of suggestibility to the likelihood of making a false confession, see Gisli H. Gudjonnson, *The Psychology of Interrogations, Confessions and Testimony* (1992). The "Gudjonnson Suggestibility Scales" are widely cited in the literature.

36. Estimates range from 35 to 840 annually throughout the United States. Barry Scheck, Peter Neufeld, and Jim Dwyer, *Actual Innocence: Five Days to Execution and Other Dispatches from the Wrongly Convicted* 92 (2000). See also Richard A. Leo, Miranda *and the Problem of False Confessions,* in *The* Miranda *Debate: Law, Justice, and Policing* 271 (Richard A. Leo and George C. Thomas eds., 1998); Richard A. Leo and Richard J. Ofshe, *The Consequences of False Confessions: Deprivations of Liberty and Miscarriages of Justice in the Age of Psychological Interrogation,* 88 Journal of Criminal Law and Criminology 429 (1998) (examining sixty cases of police-induced false or probably false confessions). The Leo and Ofshe article also lists a large number of published reports of false confessions. See id. at 430 n.4.

For an argument that the number of false confessions is actually quite a few less than these statistics would suggest, see Paul G. Cassell, *Protecting the Innocent from False Confessions and Lost Confessions—and from* Miranda, 88 Journal of Criminal Law and Criminology 497, 520 (estimating that the number of wrongful convictions resulting from false confessions each year in the United States is probably around ten, and is at most around 394). On the difficulties of making such calculations, see Richard A. Leo and Richard J. Ofshe, *Missing the Forest for the Trees: A Response to Paul Cassell's "Balanced Approach" to the False Confessions Problem,* 74 Denver University Law Review 1135 (1997).

37. The project is described in Scheck, Neufeld, and Dwyer, *Actual Innocence.*

38. See generally www.innocenceproject.org (last visited March 11, 2004). The Innocence Project reports that of the first seventy of these exonerations, fifteen resulted at least in part from false confessions. For some actual examples involving false confessions, see *DNA Results Exonerate Man Jailed for 17 Years,* Los Angeles Times, Aug. 27, 2002, A7; Brooke A. Masters, *Death Row to Freedom: A Journey Ends,* Washington Post, February 13, 2001, A1; Henry Weinstein, *DNA Testing Clears Texas Murderer and "Accomplice,"* Los Angeles Times, Oct. 14, 2000, A10.

39. On the linguistic features of leading questions, see Peter M. Tiersma, *Legal Language* 164–65 (1999).

40. Roger W. Shuy, *The Language of Confession, Interrogation, and Deception* 98, 176–79 (1998).

41. Richard J. Ofshe and Richard A. Leo, *The Decision to Confess Falsely: Rational Choice and Irrational Action,* 74 Denver University Law Review 979, 1020–21 (1997).

42. Id. at 995.

43. Id. at 1118.

44. Bram v. United States, 168 U.S. 532, 557–58 (1897).

45. Ofshe and Leo, *Decision to Confess Falsely,* at 1115.

46. Id. at 1066.

47. Id. at 1067.

48. Id. at 1078–79.

49. Shuy, *The Language of Confession,* at 94–106.

50. For a discussion of problems with police reports of confessions in England, see Malcolm Coulthard, *Powerful Evidence for the Defence: An Exercise in Forensic Discourse Analysis,* in *Language and the Law* 414 (John Gibbons ed., 1994).

51. See also Richard A. Leo, *The Impact of* Miranda *Revisited,* 86 Journal of Criminal Law and Criminology 621, 681 (1996).

52. For discussion of the Australian experience, including some cases in which the recorder may be strategically turned off and on, see John Gibbons, *Forensic Linguistics* (2003).

53. Steve Mills, *Law Mandates Taping of Police Interrogations,* Chicago Tribune, July 18, 2003, C1. Currently, two other states—Alaska and Minnesota—require taping of police interrogation sessions. Leonard Post, *Illinois to Tape Police Questioning,* National Law Journal, Aug. 4, 2003, 1.

54. Leo, *The Problem of False Confessions,* at 278–79.

Chapter Five

1. 384 U.S. 436 (1966).

2. Escobedo v. Illinois, 378 U.S. 478 (1964).

3. See, e.g., Brown v. Mississippi, 297 U.S. 278, 286 (1936); Ashcraft v. Tennessee, 322 U.S. 143, 154 (1944).

4. 384 U.S. at 479.

5. See, e.g., Paul G. Cassell, *The Costs of the* Miranda *Mandate: A Lesson in the Dangers*

of Inflexible, "Prophylactic" Supreme Court Inventions, 28 Arizona State Law Journal 299 (1996).

6. 530 U.S. 428 (2000).

7. Roger W. Shuy, *Ten Unanswered Language Questions about Miranda,* 4 Forensic Linguistics 175, 176 (1997).

8. See McCay Vernon et al., *The* Miranda *Warnings and the Deaf Suspect,* 14 Behavioral Science and Law 121, 122–23 (1996).

9. Thomas Grisso, *Juveniles' Capacities to Waive* Miranda *Rights: An Empirical Analysis,* 68 California Law Review 1134, 1152–53 (1980).

10. 475 U.S. 412, 421 (1986).

11. Fare v. Michael C., 442 U.S. 707, 725 (1979).

12. See Shuy, *Ten Unanswered Language Questions,* at 176. In addition, police sometimes ask the suspect to read the warning or ask him to explain or paraphrase it. See Lois B. Oberlander and Naomi E. Goldstein, *A Review and Update on the Practice of Evaluating* Miranda *Comprehension,* 19 Behavioral Science and Law 453, 459 (2001).

13. Shuy, *Ten Unanswered Language Questions,* at 187–88.

14. Faulkner v. State, 727 S.W.2d 793, 798 (Tex. Ct. App. 1987).

15. See Smith v. Zant, 855 F.2d 712 (11th Cir. 1988); United States v. Robles-Ramirez, 93 F. Supp. 2d 762 (W.D. Tex. 2000); Alabama v. Caldwell, 611 So. 2d 1149 (Ala. Crim. App. 1992).

16. For an overview of cases going both directions, see Charles C. Marvel, *Annotation, Mental Subnormality of Accused as Affecting Voluntariness or Admissibility of Confession,* 8 A.L.R.4th 16 (1981).

17. Mental retardation is defined as having an IQ score of "about 70 or below." "Mild retardation" describes those whose IQs range from about 50 or 55 up to 70; "moderate retardation" describes those whose IQs range from 35 or 40 to 50 or 55. American Psychological Association, *Diagnostic and Statistical Manual of Mental Disorders (DSM-IV)* 40 (4th ed. 1994).

18. Taylor v. Rogers, 1996 U.S. App. LEXIS 25350, at *9 (6th Cir. 1996). See also Rice v. Cooper, 148 F.3d 747 (7th Cir. 1998), *cert. denied,* 526 U.S. 1160 (1999).

19. For a summary, see Lois B. Oberlander, Naomi E. Goldstein, and Alan M. Goldstein, *Competence to Confess: Evaluating the Validity of* Miranda *Rights Waivers and Trustworthiness of Confessions,* in *Handbook of Psychology,* vol. 11, *Forensic Psychology* (Alan M. Goldstein ed., 2002).

20. Morgan Cloud, George B. Shepherd, Alison Nodvin Barkoff, and Justin V. Shur, *Words without Meaning: The Constitution, Confessions, and Mentally Retarded Suspects,* 69 University of Chicago Law Review 495, 499 (2002).

21. Gilliam v. State, 579 A.2d 744 (Md. Ct. App. 1990).

22. People v. Reid, 554 N.E.2d 174, 189 (Ill. 1990). For an Illinois opinion holding that a seventeen-year-old defendant with an IQ of less than 67 did not understand and waive his rights, see People v. Higgins, 607 N.E.2d 337 (Ill. Ct. App. 1993).

23. People v. Williams, 476 N.Y.S.2d 788, 790 (Ct. App. 1984). The court noted that the detective gave the warning in simple terms, which may help explain the decision.

24. See Oberlander and Goldstein, *Review and Update,* at 464.

25. Colorado v. Connelly, 479 U.S. 157, 168 (1986) ("Whenever the State bears the burden of proof in a motion to suppress a statement that the defendant claims was obtained in violation of our *Miranda* doctrine, the State need prove waiver only by a preponderance

of the evidence."). *Connelly* reaffirmed Lego v. Twomey, 404 U.S. 477 (1972), on this issue.

26. People v. W.C., 657 N.E.2d 908 (Ill. 1995).

27. Segerstrom v. State, 783 S.W.2d 847 (Ark. 1990).

28. Grisso, *Instruments for Assessing and Understanding,* at 87.

29. Grisso, *Juveniles' Capacities to Waive* Miranda *Rights,* at 1160–61.

30. Naomi Goldstein, Risk Factors for False Confessions in Adolescent Offenders, paper presented at the European Association of Psychology and Law Conference, Lisbon, Portugal, June 2001 (on file with authors).

31. In re Gault, 387 U.S. 1 (1967).

32. 442 U.S. 707, 725 (1979). The Court did not specifically decide whether *Miranda* fully applies to juvenile proceedings, however.

33. See Robert E. McGuire, *Note, A Proposal to Strengthen Juvenile* Miranda *Rights: Requiring Parental Presence in Custodial Interrogations,* 53 Vanderbilt Law Review 1355 (2000). For a discussion on the efficacy of this approach, see Oberlander and Goldstein, *Review and Update,* at 461–63.

34. In the matter of B.M.B., 955 P.2d 1302 (Kan. 1998).

35. States have taken different approaches to this issue. For summary and critical discussion, see Barry C. Feld, *Juveniles' Waiver of Legal Rights: Confessions,* Miranda *and the Right to Counsel,* in *Youth on Trial* 105 (Thomas Grisso and Robert G. Schwartz eds., 2000).

36. United States v. Higareda-Santa Cruz, 826 F. Supp. 355 (D. Or. 1993).

37. People v. Jiminez, 863 P.2d 981 (Colo. 1993).

38. United States v. Short, 790 F.2d 464, 468–69 (6th Cir. 1986).

39. United States v. Ghafoor, 897 F. Supp. 2d 90 (S.D.N.Y. 1995) (suspect answered questions in understandable English and never asked investigators to repeat a question).

40. Commonwealth v. Maldonado, 451 N.E.2d 1146 (Mass. 1983).

41. United States v. Doe, 819 F.2d 206 (9th Cir. 1985). In another case involving an Apache, United States v. Bernard S., 795 F.2d 749 (9th Cir. 1986), a seventeen-year-old Apache-speaking defendant claimed to understand his rights, as explained with the help of his mother, and then answered questions in English; the court held the waiver valid even though the defendant had to ask his mother and an Apache-speaking officer for occasional translation during the English-language interview.

42. People v. Cook, 558 N.E.2d 1268, 1273–74 (Ill. App. Ct. 1990).

43. See, e.g., Commonwealth v. Gil, 471 N.E.2d 30 (Mass. 1984) (testimony of witnesses and Polish-born defendant's ability to speak English at other court proceedings disproved claim that he did not understand *Miranda* warning); Hernandez v. State, 978 S.W.2d 137, 141 (Tex. Ct. App. 1998) (suspect whose primary language was Spanish was held to have validly waived his rights when there was no evidence presented that he did not understand); State v. Nguyen, 833 P.2d 937, 944 (Kan. 1992) (Vietnamese suspect whose answers during interrogation showed he spoke English "reasonably well" was held to have made a valid waiver); United States v. Bing-Gong, 594 F. Supp. 248, 256 (N.D.N.Y. 1984), *cert. denied,* 479 U.S. 818 (1986) (Chinese-speaking defendant held to have understood rights in light of ability to answer questions in English, failure to ask for an interpreter, and close relationship to English speakers); United States v. Abou-Saada, 785 F.2d 1, 10 (1st Cir. 1986) (the defendant answered the officer's questions in English, and therefore must have understood *Miranda* warning).

44. Paul Feldman, *Turkish to Tagalog—L.A. Courts Hear It All,* Los Angeles Times, May 5, 1985, pt. 1.

45. Perri v. Director, Department of Corrections, 817 F.2d 448, 452 (7th Cir. 1987).

46. United States v. Fung, 780 F. Supp. 115 (E.D.N.Y. 1992).

47. State v. Teran, 862 P.2d 137 (Wash. Ct. App. 1993).

48. United States v. Hernandez, 913 F. 2d 1506, 1510 (10th Cir. 1990), *cert. denied,* 499 U.S. 908 (1991). See also United States v. Hernandez, 93 F.3d 1493, 1503 (10th Cir. 1996) (*Miranda* warning held adequate even though translation was imperfect and did not translate the word "waive").

49. United States v. Villegas, 928 F.2d 512, 518–19 (2d Cir. 1991).

50. People v. Merrero, 459 N.E.2d 1158 (Ill. App. Ct. 1984).

51. 826 F. Supp. 355, 359–60 (D. Or. 1993). The court decided, however, that the defendant was not shown the Spanish language card, and did not understand the English warning.

52. United States v. Soria-Garcia, 947 F.2d 900, 901–3 (10th Cir. 1991).

53. United States v. Yunis, 859 F.2d 953, 964–65 (D.C. Cir. 1988); see also Colorado v. Spring, 479 U.S. 564, 574 (1987) (holding that the Constitution "does not require that a criminal suspect know and understand every possible consequence of the Fifth Amendment privilege"; the suspect must simply comprehend the basic meaning of the warnings).

54. Le v. State, 947 P.2d 535, 543 (Okla. Crim. App. 1997).

55. See People v. Merrero, 459 N.E.2d 1158 (Ill. App. Ct. 1984); Liu v. State, 628 A.2d 1376, 1380 (Del. 1993). See also United States v. Zapata, 997 F.2d 751 (10th Cir. 1993) (in determining whether a suspect's consent to a search was voluntary, his upbringing in a country—Mexico—where people must acquiesce to police demands to avoid dire consequences was irrelevant).

56. To be prelingually deaf means to have lost one's hearing before the age at which one normally acquires a spoken language. Thus, it refers to people deaf from birth, or who become deaf at an age of one or two years.

57. McCay Vernon et al., *The Miranda Warnings and the Deaf Suspect,* 14 Behavioral Science and Law 121, 123 (1996).

58. To be more specific, around 75 percent of prelingually deaf Americans use ASL. Jamie McAlister, *Deaf and Hard-of-Hearing Criminal Defendants: How You Gonna Get Justice If You Can't Talk to the Judge?* 26 Arizona State Law Journal 163, 175 (1994).

59. See Victoria Fromkin and Robert Rodman, *An Introduction to Language* 416–21 (5th ed. 1993); Edward S. Klima and Ursula Bellugi, *The Signs of Language* (1979).

60. People v. Gaylord, 210 A.D.2d 980 (N.Y. 1994); People v. Brannon, 486 N.W.2d 83 (Mich. Ct. App. 1992).

61. State v. Mason, 633 P.2d 820, 826 (Or. Ct. App. 1981).

62. People v. Smith, 37 Cal. Rptr. 2d 524 (Ct. App. 1995); State v. Hindsley, 614 N.W.2d 48 (Wis. Ct. App. 2000).

63. Rosen v. Montgomery County, 121 F.3d 154 (4th Cir. 1997).

64. See McAlister, *Deaf and Hard-of-Hearing Criminal Defendants,* at 180 n.113; Jo Anne Simon, *The Use of Interpreters for the Deaf and the Legal Community's Obligation to Comply with the ADA,* 8 Journal of Law and Health 155, 177 (1993–1994); Vernon et al., *The Miranda Warnings and the Deaf Suspect,* at 123.

65. See, e.g., Mich. Comp. Laws Ann. § 93.505(1) (West 1997).

66. See McAlister, *Deaf and Hard-of-Hearing Criminal Defendants*, at 181; Vernon et al., *The Miranda Warnings and the Deaf Suspect*, at 123.

67. See Vernon et al., *The Miranda Warnings and the Deaf Suspect*, at 130; McAlister, *Deaf and Hard-of-Hearing Criminal Defendants*, at 190.

68. Lawrence S. Leiken, *Police Interrogation in Colorado: The Implementation of Miranda*, 47 Denver Law Journal 1, 15 (1970). See also Connecticut v. Barrett, 479 U.S. 523 (1987) (after being read his rights, the defendant stated that he would not make a written statement without the presence of his attorney, but that he would talk to police about the crime that he was suspected of having committed; his oral statements were admitted into evidence); North Carolina v. Butler, 441 U.S. 369 (1979) (suspect said he would talk to police but refused to sign written waiver form; oral statement was used to convict him).

69. See Leiken, *Police Interrogation*, at 15 (27 percent of suspects believed that the right to counsel attached only at the trial stage).

70. Some of the versions of the *Miranda* warning in actual use already address certain of these issues. Oberlander and Goldstein present a version that, in addition to having some minor linguistic changes, contains a fifth element: "If you decide to answer questions now without a lawyer present, you will still have the right to stop answering at any time until you talk to a lawyer." Oberlander and Goldstein, *Review and Update*, at 458.

71. 492 U.S. 195, 203 (1989).

72. State v. Medina, 685 A.2d 1242 (N.J. 1996), *cert. denied*, 520 U.S. 1190 (1997).

73. An actual form of the warning that incorporates several of these points is given in the District of Columbia. Charles J. Ogletree, *Are Confessions Really Good for the Soul? A Proposal to Mirandize* Miranda, 100 Harvard Law Review 1826, 1827 (1987). Another form of the *Miranda* warnings that provides more explicit information in plain language is sometimes administered to juveniles. Nissman, *Law of Confessions* § 6:21, at 6-39.

74. Richard A. Leo, *The Impact of* Miranda *Revisited*, 86 Journal of Criminal Law and Criminology 621, 681 (1996).

75. Thomas Grisso, *Instruments for Assessing Understanding and Appreciation of Miranda Rights* (1998).

76. See Saul M. Kassin and Katherine Neumann, *On the Power of Confession Evidence: An Experimental Test of the Fundamental Difference Hypothesis*, 21 Law and Human Behavior 469 (1997); Saul M. Kassin and Holly Sukel, *Coerced Confessions and the Jury: An Experimental Test of the "Harmless Error" Rule*, 21 Law and Human Behavior 27 (1997). A study by Leo and Ofshe found that 73 percent of false confessors whose cases went to trial were convicted. Richard A. Leo and Richard J. Ofshe, *The Consequences of False Confessions: Deprivations of Liberty and Miscarriages of Justice in the Age of Psychological Interrogation*, 88 Journal of Criminal Law and Criminology 429, 484 (1998) (examining sixty cases of police-induced false or probably false confessions).

77. See Leo, *The Impact of* Miranda *Revisited*, at 645. The point is controversial, however. See Paul G. Cassell, *Protecting the Innocent from False Confessions and Lost Confessions—And from* Miranda, 88 Journal of Criminal Law and Criminology 497, 549 (1998). For discussion of the status of empirical evidence, see George C. Thomas III, *Plain Talk about the* Miranda *Empirical Debate: A "Steady-State" Theory of Confessions*, 43 UCLA Law Review 933 (1996).

78. Jeffrey Toobin, *Viva Miranda*, New Republic, Feb. 16, 1987, at 11 (survey in 1984 showed that 93 percent of those surveyed knew they had a right to a lawyer if arrested).

79. Id. at 12.

80. We are not the first to make this point. See, e.g., Richard A. Leo, Miranda *and the Problem of False Confessions,* in *The* Miranda *Debate: Law, Justice, and Policing* 271 (Richard A. Leo and George C. Thomas eds., 1998).

81. Rogers v. Richmond, 365 U.S. 534, 540–44 (1961) (holding that reliability of a confession was not a factor in determining voluntariness, focusing instead on police conduct).

82. State v. Jones, 6 P.3d 323 (Ariz. Ct. App. 2000). See also State v. Miller, 765 A.2d 693 (N.H. 2001).

Part Three

1. See Robin T. Lakoff, *Talking Power: The Politics of Language* 85–12 (1990).

2. See, e.g., William M. O'Barr, *Linguistic Evidence: Language, Power and Strategy in the Courtroom* (1982); John Conley and William O'Barr, *Rules versus Relationships* (1990); John Conley and William O'Barr, *Just Words: Law, Language, and Power* (1998).

3. See Gregory M. Matoesian, *Law and the Language of Identity: Discourse in the William Kennedy Smith Rape Trial* (2001). For an excellent linguistic analysis of a rape case, see Susan Ehrlich, *Representing Rape: Language and Sexual Consent* (2001).

4. Quoted from the transcript in Matoesian, *Law and the Language of Identity,* at 61.

5. Andrew Taslitz, *Rape and the Culture of the Courtroom* (1999).

6. See, e.g., Anthony G. Amsterdam and Jerome Bruner, *Minding the Law* (2000); Bernard S. Jackson, *Making Sense in Law* (1995).

Chapter Six

1. 18 U.S.C. § 3500(e).

2. In New York, for example, the governing statute states: "In an action for libel or slander, the particular words complained of shall be set forth in the complaint, but their application to the plaintiff may be stated generally." N.Y. Civ. Prac. L. & R. § 3016(a).

3. A shorter version of this section appeared in Lawrence M. Solan, *The Written Contract as Safe Harbor for Dishonest Conduct,* 77 Chicago-Kent Law Review 87 (2001).

4. Jacqueline Strunk Sachs, *Recognition Memory for Syntactic and Semantic Aspects of Connected Discourse,* 2 Perception and Psychophysics 437 (1967).

5. Alan Baddeley, *Human Memory: Theory and Practice* 74–79 (1990).

6. N. C. Ellis and R. A. Hennelly, *A Bi-Lingual Word-Length Effect: Implications for Intelligence Testing and the Relative Ease of Mental Calculation in Welsh and English,* 1 British Journal of Psychology 43 (1980).

7. Moshe Naveh-Benjamin and Thomas J. Ayres, *Digit Span, Reading Rate, and Linguistic Relativity,* 38 Quarterly Journal of Experimental Psychology 739 (1986).

8. Baddeley, *Human Memory,* at 172.

9. Robert J. Jarvella, *Syntactic Processing of Connected Speech,* 10 Journal of Verbal Learning and Verbal Behavior 409 (1971). This line of research is important. If our ability to recall exact words gets worse after we've processed a clause, and worse yet after we've processed an entire sentence, then units such as "clause" and "sentence" indeed have some psychological status in the way we use and process language, as linguistic theory predicts.

10. Amina Memon and A. Daniel Yarmey, *Earwitness Recall and Identification: Comparison of the Cognitive Interview and the Structured Interview,* 88 Perception and Motor Skills 797, 802 (1999).

11. Marcia K. Johnson, John D. Bransford, and Susan K. Solomon, *Memory for Tacit Implications of Sentences,* 98 Journal of Experimental Psychology 203–5 (1973). To eliminate the inference, the experimenters changed "broke" to "just missed."

12. Elizabeth F. Loftus and John C. Palmer, *Reconstruction of Automobile Destruction: An Example of the Interaction between Language and Memory,* 13 Journal of Verbal Learning and Verbal Behavior 585 (1974).

13. Of course, important questions are still unanswered: How long does it take for memory of the substance of what was said to decay? What factors influence how we recall what we have heard? Do certain aspects of speech tend to be forgotten first?

14. P. N. Johnson-Laird and C. E. Bethell-Fox, *Memory for Questions and Amount of Processing,* 6 Memory and Cognition 496 (1978).

15. Id. at 500.

16. Thorn v. Sundstrand Aerospace Corp., 207 F.3d 383, 388–89 (7th Cir. 2000).

17. Examples abound. See, e.g., International Brotherhood of Teamsters, AFL-CIO v. Executive Jet Aviation Inc., 53 F.3d 331 (6th Cir. 1995) (court found that although plaintiff did not spell out the exact words of a conversation a witness had with the plaintiff, it did convey the essence of the conversation, namely that plaintiff had made disparaging remarks about the company); Lovell v. Ponway Unified School District, 90 F.3d 367, 374 (9th Cir. 1996) (court held that exact words of what the student said are not necessary when determining whether he violated a law by threatening to kill a teacher because of a scheduling change).

18. 38 F.3d 936, 938 (7th Cir. 1994).

19. 973 F.2d 746, 750 (9th Cir. 1992).

20. Id. at 751.

21. Id.

22. Fed. R. Evid. 801(c).

23. Fed. R. Evid. 802.

24. Fed. R. Evid. 801(d)(2)(A).

25. Fed. R. Evid. 801(d)(2)(B).

26. 5 Jack B. Weinstein and Margaret A. Berger, *Weinstein's Federal Evidence* § 802.02[3] (Joseph M. McLaughlin ed., 1997).

27. Fed. R. Evid. 801(d)(2) (Advisory Committee Note).

28. For a good set of readings on this issue, see *Eyewitness Testimony: Psychological Perspectives* (Gary L. Wells and Elizabeth F. Loftus eds., 1984).

29. See Neil v. Biggers, 409 U.S. 188 (1972).

30. 18 U.S.C. § 3500(e).

31. United States v. Leshuk, 65 F.3d 1105, 1111 (4th Cir. 1995).

32. United States v. Clemons, 676 F.2d 122, 123 (5th Cir. 1982).

33. Howard v. Moore, 131 F.3d 399, 405 (4th Cir. 1997).

34. Roger Shuy, *The Language of Confession, Interrogation, and Deception* 58–68 (1998).

35. Malcolm Coulthard, *On the Use of Corpora in the Analysis of Forensic Texts,* 1 Forensic Linguistics 27 (1994). The *Bentley* case provided the plot for the film *Let Him Have It.*

36. Richard J. Ofshe and Richard A. Leo, *The Decision to Confess Falsely: Rational Choice and Irrational Action,* 74 Denver University Law Review 979, 1018 (1997).

37. Id. at 1121–22.

38. The Innocence Project Web page, www.innocenceproject.org (last visited March 15, 2004).

39. The "science" of hair comparison has led to the conviction of many other innocent people, according to the Innocence Project. See www:innocenceproject.org/causes/index. php. We discuss this issue briefly in chapter 7.

40. Raymond Bonner, *Death Row Inmate Freed after DNA Test Clears Him,* New York Times, August 24, 2001, A11.

41. Not all do. According to Scheck and his co-authors, prosecutorial and police misconduct rank high among the factors that lead to false convictions. See Barry Scheck, Peter Neufeld, and Jim Dwyer, *Actual Innocence: Five Days to Execution and Other Dispatches from the Wrongly Convicted* 263 (2000).

42. For discussion of this issue in the context of a recent case, see Tim Bryant, *Tests of Convicts Have Only Just Begun,* St. Louis Post-Dispatch, August 4, 2002, B 4 (reporting on release of Larry Johnson, who served eighteen years in prison for a rape he did not commit; much of the article reports on differences between the prosecutor and Barry Scheck with respect to making DNA samples available for testing). For general discussion of psychological and political factors that make it difficult for prosecutors to accept the prospect of post-conviction analysis, see Daniel S. Medwed, *The Zeal Deal: Prosecutorial Resistance to Post-Conviction Claims of Innocence,* 84 Boston University Law Review 125 (2004).

43. Based on a LEXIS search ("cellmate w/8 confess!") conducted on the combined database of federal and state cases on July 12, 2002. Obviously, this search will not reveal cases in which the court discusses a confession to someone in prison, but doesn't call that person a cellmate. Our point is not that this search is complete—it is merely that testimony by other prisoners about confessions is not an uncommon occurrence.

44. 107 F.3d 499, 510 (7th Cir. 1997).

45. 132 F.3d 463 (9th Cir. 1997).

46. This is only a partial solution because we believe that additional measures should also be imposed. For instance, inmates reporting the confession should routinely be required to explain to the jury what they are receiving in exchange for their testimony. In addition, an instruction that tells the jury to treat such testimony with caution is a good idea. See California Jury Instructions, Criminal, 3.20 (6th ed. 1996).

47. United States v. De Leon, 474 F.2d 790 (5th Cir.), *cert. denied,* 414 U.S. 853 (1973).

48. United States v. Marchisio, 344 F.2d 653, 665 (2d Cir. 1965).

49. 171 F.2d 800, 812 (D.C. Cir. 1948).

50. Id. at 814 (Prettyman, J. dissenting).

51. A related question is whether, in a perjury indictment, the government must allege the exact words that make up the crime. Generally, courts have held that they do not, since the defendant can ask for a bill of particulars. But there are limits. When an indictment alleges neither exact words nor enough of the substance to put the defendant on notice of what the government claims was false about the testimony, the indictment may be dismissed. See United States v. Slawik, 548 F.2d 75 (3d Cir. 1977).

52. 18 U.S.C. § 1001(a).

53. See, e.g., United States v. Massey, 550 F.2d 300 (5th Cir. 1977) (false statements made to FBI agent; conviction based on agent's testimony about conversation); United States v. Ratner, 464 F.2d 101, 102 (9th Cir. 1974) ("When Special Agent Greene asked him about his tax returns for the years 1964 and 1965, he represented 'that he had no bank account, business or personal, in either San Jose or Red Wood [*sic*] City for either of the retail outlets'; and that he had only four bank accounts, all in Los Angeles County during 1964 and 1965, two business and two personal, which he specified (Ex. 56)").

54. United States v. Poindexter, 951 F.2d 369 (D.C. Cir. 1991).

55. Id. at 387–88.

Chapter Seven

1. Ludovic Kennedy, *The Airman and the Carpenter* 267 (1985).

2. John F. Condon, *Jafsie Tells All! Revealing the Inside Story of the Lindbergh-Hauptmann Case* 149 (1936).

3. Jim Fisher, *The Lindbergh Case* 248 (1987).

4. Id.

5. In his testimony, Lindbergh left out the words "over here." Transcript at 109, State v. Hauptmann, 180 A. 809 (N.J. 1935). In fact, there is dispute over what the kidnapper actually said. Lindbergh had apparently told the grand jury that the words were "Hey, doc." Kennedy, *The Airman and the Carpenter,* at 209. Others quoted the kidnapper as having said: "Hey, Doctor! Hey, Doctor, over here." George Waller, *Kidnap: The Story of the Lindbergh Case* 75 (1961). We thank Ronelle Delmont for providing us with a compact disk containing the transcript.

6. Transcript, State v. Hauptmann, at 113–14.

7. A. Scott Berg, *Lindbergh* 315 (1998).

8. See Regina v. Morin, 37 C.R. (4th) 395 (Ontario Ct. App. 1995). The voice identification aspect of the case is discussed in A. Daniel Yarmey, A. Linda Yarmey, Meagan J. Yarmey, and Lisa Parliament, *Common Sense Beliefs and the Identification of Familiar Voices,* 15 Applied Cognitive Psychology 283 (2001).

9. There is an extensive literature on problems with eyewitness testimony. For a collection of articles that provide a good introduction to some of the research in this area, see *Eyewitness Testimony: Psychological Perspectives* (Gary L. Wells and Elizabeth F. Loftus eds., 1984). See also Brian L. Cutler and Steven D. Penrod, *Mistaken Identification: The Eyewitness, Mistaken Identity and the Law* (1995).

10. 409 U.S. 188 (1972).

11. Id. at 195.

12. Id. at 198.

13. Id. at 199–200.

14. 432 U.S. 98 (1977).

15. Id. at 114.

16. Commonwealth v. Miles, 648 N.E.2d 719, 728–29 (Mass. 1995).

17. 845 F. Supp. 625 (N.D. Ill. 1994).

18. Id. at 628.

19. Id.

20. 351 A.2d 787 (N.J. Super. Ct. App. Div. 1976).

21. Id. at 788.

22. See, e.g., Macias v. State, 673 So. 2d 176 (Fla. Ct. App. 1996) (playing a short tape-recording of only the defendant to the victim for identification); State v. Pendergrass, 586 P.2d 691, 696 (Mont. 1978) (allowing victim to overhear defendant's voice in police station).

23. State v. Blevine, 536 A.2d 1002 (Conn. App. Ct. 1988).

24. State v. Pickney, 714 So. 2d 854 (La. Ct. App. 1998).

25. 378 N.E.2d 51 (Mass. 1978).

26. 4 F.3d 800 (9th Cir. 1993).

27. 913 F.2d 372 (7th Cir. 1990).

28. See Government of the Virgin Islands v. Sanes, 57 F.3d 338 (3d Cir. 1995) (finding identification sufficiently reliable when fifteen days elapsed between last attack and positive voice identification, and victim making identification testified that she had engaged assailant in conversation during two separate attacks with hope that she would be able to identify his voice); Tate v. Morris, No. 89-3570, 1990 WL 117367 (6th Cir. 1990) (*Biggers* criteria met when victim heard rapist's voice on many occasions, including phone calls made subsequent to the assault).

29. Fed. R. Evid. 901(b)(5).

30. Fed. R. Evid. 901, Advisory Committee's Notes. In light of these remarks, the word "opinion" in the rule is best understood as referring to lay opinion.

31. United States v. Plunk, 153 F.3d 1011, 1023 (9th Cir. 1998) (citations omitted).

32. United States v. Carrasco, 887 F.2d 794 (7th Cir. 1989) (person who identified voices was an eyewitness and active participant in the recorded conversations); People v. Griffin, 592 N.E.2d 930 (Ill. 1992) (participant in conversation testified that the tape recording was accurate and identified the voice of the defendant).

33. See Mutz v. State, 862 S.W.2d 24 (Tex. Ct. App. 1993) (permitting identification of ex-father-in-law's voice, when witness and defendant lived near each other and marriage had lasted seven years; United States v. Puentes, 50 F.3d 1567 (11th Cir. 1995) (permitting agent to testify that he knew voice on a particular tape belonged to defendant based on agent's hearing defendant's voice frequently during a two-month wiretap).

34. See United States v. Ladd, 527 F.2d 1341, 1342 (5th Cir. 1976).

35. D. Michael Risinger, Mark P. Denbeaux, and Michael J. Saks, *Exorcism of Ignorance as a Proxy for Rational Knowledge: The Lessons of Handwriting Identification "Expertise,"* 137 University of Pennsylvania Law Review 731, 752 (1989).

36. 913 F.2d 372 (7th Cir. 1990).

37. No. 97-5492, 1998 U.S. App. LEXIS 27655 (6th Cir. 1998).

38. See United States v. Pheaster, 544 F.2d 353, 369 (9th Cir. 1976).

39. 841 F.2d 1320 (7th Cir. 1988).

40. The problem in *Zembrana* was compounded by providing the jury with transcripts during the trial, once again with the defendant's name in the margin. The court of appeals stressed that the judge did not admit the transcripts into evidence, warned the jury that it could not consider the names in the transcripts to constitute substantive evidence, and did not let the jury take the transcripts with them during their deliberation. Still, this procedure was quite suggestive, and in this age of word processing capabilities it is quite unnecessary. It would be easy enough to use pseudonyms, or letters like *A* and *B*.

41. 841 F.2d at 1339.

42. United States v. Townsend, 1999 U.S. App. LEXIS 13872 (5th Cir. 1999).

43. Trial of William Hulet, 5 Howell's State Trials 1185 (1660).

44. Id. at 1186.

45. Id. at 1187.

46. Id. at 1195.

47. Id. at 1185 n.1.

48. One of the most prolific writers on this subject is A. Daniel Yarmey, a Canadian psychologist. For a good summary of the research in this area, see A. Daniel Yarmey, *Earwitness Speaker Identification,* 1 Psychology, Public Policy and Law 792 (1995).

49. Yarmey et al., *Common Sense Beliefs,* at 283.

50. See Harry Hollien, Wojciech Majewski, and E. Thomas Doherty, *Perceptual Identification of Voices under Normal, Stress and Disguised Speaking Conditions,* 10 Journal of Phonetics 139 (1982).

51. A. Daniel Yarmey, *Voice Identification over the Telephone,* 21 Journal of Applied Social Psychology 1868–76 (1991).

52. Kenneth A. Deffenbacher, John F. Cross, Robert E. Handkins, June E. Chance, Alvin G. Goldstein, Richard Hammersley, and J. Don Read, *Relevance of Voice Identification Research to Criteria for Evaluating Reliability of an Identification,* 123 Journal of Psychology 109 (1989). The reported study was conducted by two co-authors of the article, Goldstein and Chance.

53. Id. at 117.

54. United States v. Infelice, 506 F.2d 1358, 1365 (7th Cir. 1974).

55. Frances McGehee, *The Reliability of the Identification of the Human Voice,* 17 Journal of General Psychology 249 (1937). The results are reported in a useful survey article, Ray Bull and Brian R. Clifford, *Earwitness Voice Recognition Accuracy,* in *Eyewitness Testimony: Psychological Perspectives* 92, 116 (Gary L. Wells and Elizabeth F. Loftus eds., 1984).

56. Frances McGehee, *An Experimental Study of Voice Recognition,* 31 Journal of General Psychology 53 (1944).

57. Deffenbacher et al., *Relevance of Voice Identification Research,* at 116.

58. People v. Rendon, 709 N.Y.S.2d 698, 701 (App. Div. 2000).

59. No. 97-5492, 1998 U.S. App. LEXIS 27655 at *9–10 (6th Cir. 1998).

60. Elizabeth F. Loftus, *Eyewitness Testimony* 33–36 (1979); Hadyn D. Ellis, *Practical Aspects of Face Memory,* in *Eyewitness Testimony* (Wells and Loftus eds.).

61. Howard Saslove and A. Daniel Yarmey, *Long-Term Auditory Memory: Speaker Identification,* 65 Journal of Applied Psychology 111 (1980).

62. Harry Hollien, *The Acoustics of Crime,* at 258–63 (1990); Marianne Jessen, *Phonetic Manifestations of Cognitive and Physical Stress in Trained and Untrained Police Officers,* 4 Forensic Linguistics 124–47 (1997).

63. Gudrun Klasmeyer and Walter F. Sendlmeir, *The Classification of Different Phonation Types in Emotional and Neutral Speech,* 4 Forensic Linguistics 104 (1997).

64. Saslove and Yarmey, *Long-Term Auditory Memory,* at 115.

65. 351 A.2d 787 (N.J. Super. Ct. App. Div. 1976).

66. Yarmey et al., *Common Sense Beliefs.*

67. Hollien et al., *Perceptual Interpretation of Voices,* at 142.

68. Ricardo Molina de Figueiredo and Helena de Souza Britto, *A Report on the Acoustic Effects of One Type of Disguise,* 3 Forensic Linguistics 168 (1996).

69. Frank Schichting and Kirk P. H. Sullivan, *The Imitated Voice—A Problem for Voice Lineups?* 4 Forensic Linguistics 148 (1997).

70. The International Association for Forensic Phonetics (IAFP) has regular conferences to discuss advances in the field; it also has a code of conduct governing expert testimony by its members. See www.iafp.net. The *International Journal of Speech, Language and the Law* (formerly *Forensic Linguistics*) publishes a great deal of the relevant literature.

71. See, e.g., Geoff Lindsey and Allen Hirson, *Variable Robustness of Nonstandard /r/ in English: Evidence from Accent Disguise,* 6 Forensic Linguistics 278–88 (1999); Herbert Masthoff, *A Report on a Voice Disguise Experiment,* 3 Forensic Linguistics 160–67 (1996).

72. See Hollien, *Acoustics of Crime*, at 197, for many citations to the literature.

73. See Ellis, *Practical Aspects of Face Memory*, at 36.

74. See Daniel A. Yarmey, *The Psychology of Eyewitness Testimony* 130–31 (1979).

75. Olaf Köster and Niels O. Schiller, *Different Influences of the Native Language of a Listener on Speaker Recognition*, 4 Forensic Linguistics 18, 25 (1997).

76. For a variation on this study by Goggin and his colleagues, see C. P. Thompson, *A Language Effect in Voice Identification*, 1 Applied Cognitive Psychology 121 (1987). See also J. Goggin, C. P. Thompson, G. Strube, and L. R. Simental, *The Role of Language Familiarity in Voice Identification*, 19 Memory and Cognition 448 (1991).

77. Hollien, *Acoustics of Crime*, at 198.

78. For a study on how foreign accent can help identify a speaker—or eliminate a suspect—see Henry Rogers, *Foreign Accent in Voice Discrimination: A Case Study*, 5 Forensic Linguistics 203 (1998). On the difficulty that many speakers have in successfully imitating regional accents (in Swedish), see Duncan Markham, *Listeners and Disguised Voices: The Imitation and Perception of Dialectal Accent*, 6 Forensic Linguistics 289 (1999).

79. People v. King, 584 N.Y.S.2d 153 (App. Div. 1992) (not permitting lay witness to testify about whether defendant speaks with a Jamaican accent). But see People v. Sanchez, 492 N.Y.S.2d 683 (Sup. Ct. 1985) (permitting lay witness to testify about perpetrator's accent, but acknowledging that expert linguistic testimony might sometimes be necessary).

80. United States v. Vega, 860 F.2d 779 (7th Cir. 1988).

81. *Biggers*, 409 U.S. at 199.

82. Deffenbacher et al., *Relevance of Voice Identification Research*, at 115.

83. Yarmey, *Earwitness Speaker Identification*, at 803.

84. Amy J. Bradfield and Gary L. Wells, *The Perceived Validity of Eyewitness Identification Testimony: A Test of the Five Biggers Criteria*, 24 Law and Human Behavior 581 (2000).

85. Yarmey et al., *Common Sense Beliefs*.

86. For a summary of this work, see Lawrence M. Solan, *Refocusing the Burden of Proof in Criminal Cases: Some Doubt about Reasonable Doubt*, 78 Texas Law Review 105, 125–29 (1999).

87. If so, it calls into question a statement in the Advisory Committee's notes to Rule 901 that "aural voice identification is not a subject of expert testimony." Rule 901, Advisory Committee Note, subd. (b), example (5).

88. Niels O. Schiller and Olaf Köster, *The Ability of Expert Witnesses to Identify Voices: A Comparison between Trained and Untrained Listeners*, 5 Forensic Linguistics 1 (1998).

89. See Ricci v. Urso, 974 F.2d 5, 6 (1st Cir. 1992) (holding that detective did not have expert training in voice identification).

90. See, e.g., Michael J. Saks, *Merlin and Solomon: Lessons from the Law's Formative Encounters with Forensic Identification Science*, 49 Hastings Law Journal 1069 (1998).

91. See, e.g., United States v. Alvarez, 860 F.2d 801 (7th Cir. 1988).

92. 218 F.3d 496 (5th Cir. 2000).

93. Id. at 499.

94. See, e.g., United States v. Everett, 825 F.2d 658 (2d Cir. 1987); United States v. Barrett, 703 F.2d 1076, 1084 n.14 (9th Cir. 1983). See 4 Jack B. Weinstein and Margaret A. Berger, *Weinstein's Federal Evidence* § 702 [02] (Joseph M. McLaughlin ed., 1997).

95. United States v. Alexander, 816 F.2d 164, 168–69 (5th Cir. 1987).

96. See Hollien, *Acoustics of Crime*; Francis Nolan, Speaker Identification Evidence: Its Forms, Limitations, and Roles (2001) (unpublished manuscript, University of Cambridge).

97. See id. at 90–91.

98. See Oscar Tosi, Herbert Oyer, William Lashbrook, Charles Pedrey, Julie Nicol, and Ernest Nash, *Experiment on Voice Identification,* 51 Journal of the Acoustical Society of America 2030 (1972).

99. Lawrence G. Kersta, *Voiceprint Identification,* 196 Nature 1253 (1962). Kersta wrote: "It is my opinion . . . that identifiable uniqueness does exist in each voice, and that masking, disguising, or distorting the voice will not defeat identification if the speech is intelligible." Id. at 1257. For a discussion of Kersta's role, see Paul C. Giannelli and Edward J. Imwinkelreid, *Scientific Evidence* § 10-2, at 299 (2d ed. 1993).

100. Committee on Speech Communication of the Acoustical Society of America, *Speaker Identification by Speech Spectrograms: A Scientist's View of Its Reliability for Legal Purposes,* 47 Journal of the Acoustical Society of America 597, 603 (1970).

101. See Peter Ladefoged and Ralph Vanderslice, *The Voiceprint Mystique,* Working Papers in Phonetics, Department of Linguistics, UCLA, November, 1969.

102. See, e.g., State v. Cary, 239 A.2d 680 (N.J. Super. Ct. Law Div. 1968).

103. Frye v. United States, 293 F. 1013, 1014 (D.C. Cir. 1923). See chapter 2 for discussion of this statement.

104. See, e.g., State ex rel. Constance L. Trimble v. Hedman, 192 N.W.2d 432, 458 (Minn. 1971). For a catalogue of these early cases, see David L. Faigman, David H. Kay, Michael J. Saks, and Joseph Sanders, 2 *Modern Scientific Evidence* § 25-1.0, at 190 (1997). See also Lisa Rafferty, *Note, Anything You Say Can and Will Be Used against You: Spectrographic Evidence in Criminal Cases,* 36 American Criminal Law Review 291 (1999).

105. See Tosi et al., *Experiment on Voice Identification.* This was not Tosi's first study, but it was the seminal one.

106. Id. at 2041.

107. The letter was published as Peter Ladefoged, *An Opinion on Voiceprints,* 19 UCLA Working Papers in Phonetics 84 (1971). Our thanks to Peter Ladefoged for providing us with a copy of the letter.

108. Peter Ladefoged, *A Course in Phonetics* 194 (2d ed. 1985).

109. See, e.g., Commonwealth v. Lykus, 327 N.E.2d 671 (Mass. 1975). See Faigman et al., *Modern Scientific Evidence,* and Rafferty, *Anything You Say,* for lists of cases.

110. Fed. R. Evid. 702. See chapter 2 for a more detailed history of changes in the law governing the admissibility of expert evidence.

111. Committee on the Evaluation of Sound Spectrograms, Assembly of Behavioral and Social Sciences, National Research Council, On the Theory and Practice of Voice Identification (1979). The chair of this committee was Richard H. Bolt, thus giving the report its name.

112. Id. at 2.

113. Id. at 60.

114. United States v. Maivia, 728 F. Supp. 1471, 1477 (D. Haw. 1990) (citations omitted).

115. Hollien, *Acoustics of Crime,* at 210; see also Francis Nolan, *The Phonetic Bases of Speaker Recognition* 25 (1983).

116. See Faigman et al., *Modern Scientific Evidence;* Rafferty, *Anything You Say.*

117. 509 U.S. 579 (1993). See chapter 2 for discussion.

118. 974 P.2d 386 (Alaska 1999).

119. Id. at 402.

120. 218 F.3d 496 (5th Cir. 2000).

121. 974 P.2d at 388.

122. 218 F.3d at 498–99.

123. Based on aural analysis of the voices, however, Koenig agreed with Cain that the voice on the tape was probably not the defendant's. Id. at 499.

124. Id. at 503–4.

125. Bruce E. Koenig, *Spectrographic Voice Identification,* 13 FBI Crime Lab Digest 105, 115 (1986).

126. Id.

127. Id. at 117.

128. For discussion of avenues of research that have yielded impressive results, see Joseph P. Campbell Jr., *Speaker Recognition: A Tutorial,* 85 Proceedings of the IEEE 1437 (1995); Wojciech Majewski and Czeslaw Basztura, *Integrated Approach to Speaker Recognition in Forensic Applications,* 3 Forensic Linguistics 50 (1996); J. C. L. Ingram et al., *Formant Trajectories as Indices of Phonetic Variation for Speaker Identification,* 3 Forensic Linguistics 129 (1996).

129. R. Rodman, D. McAllister, D. Bitzer, L. Cepeda, and P. Abbitt, *Forensic Speaker Identification Based on Spectral Moments,* 9 Forensic Linguistics 22 (2002).

130. A. P. A. Broeders, *Forensic Speech and Audio Analysis: Forensic Linguistics 1998– 2001: A Review,* paper presented at 13th INTERPOL Forensic Science Symposium, Lyon, France, October 16–19, 2001 (copy on file with authors).

131. See www.nist.gov/speech/tests/spk/.

132. For discussion, see Jean-François Bonastre et al., Person Authentication by Voice: A Need for Caution (on file with Solan).

133. Lawrence M. Solan and Peter M. Tiersma, *Hearing Voices: Speaker Identification in Court,* 54 Hastings Law Journal 373 (2003).

134. See, e.g., Roy S. Malpass and Patricia G. Devine, *Research on Suggestion in Lineups and Photospreads in Eyewitness Testimony: Psychological Perspectives* 64 (Gary L. Wells and Elizabeth F. Loftus eds., 1984).

135. For some suggestions, see Frances Nolan and Esther Grabe, *Preparing a Voice Lineup,* 3 Forensic Linguistics 74 (1996); A. P. A. Broeders, *Earwitness Identification: Common Ground, Disputed Territory and Uncharted Areas,* 3 Forensic Linguistics 3 (1996). See also U.S. Department of Justice, Office of Justice Programs, National Institute of Justice, *Eyewitness Evidence: A Guide for Law Enforcement* (1999).

136. See, e.g., California Jury Instructions: Criminal, No. 2.91 (6th ed. 1996).

137. United States v. Magana, 118 F.3d 1173, 1208 (7th Cir. 1997).

138. Id.

139. We propose such an instruction in an appendix to Solan and Tiersma, *Hearing Voices.*

140. See United States v. Downing, 753 F.2d 1224 (3d Cir. 1985). For a recent holding, see People v. Lee, 726 N.Y.S.2d 361 (N.Y. 2001). For discussion of the admissibility of such expert testimony under various circumstances, see Faigman et al., *Modern Scientific Evidence* §§ 11-1.0 et seq.

141. For discussion, see D. Michael Risinger, *Navigating Expert Reliability: Are Criminal Standards of Certainty Being Left on the Dock?* 64 Albany Law Review 99, 142 n.171 (2000).

142. See Government of the Virgin Islands v. Sanes, 57 F.3d 338, 341 (3d Cir. 1995).

143. Commonwealth v. Pagano, 710 N.E.2d 1034, 1040 (Mass. App. Ct. 1999) (rejecting testimony of Professor Yarmey as not responsive to particular issues in the case).

144. See, e.g., United States v. Leon, No. 90-6571, 1992 U.S. App. LEXIS 14323 (6th Cir. 1992).

Chapter Eight

1. Don Foster, *Author Unknown: On the Trail of Anonymous* 46 (2000).

2. Jonathan Bate, *A Literary Detective Gets the Wrong Man,* Sunday Telegraph (London), April 29, 2001, 13. Bate is King Alfred Professor of English at Liverpool University.

3. James Bone, *Poem Not Shakespeare's After All, Scholar Admits,* The Times (London), June 22, 2002, 20; William Neiderkorn, *A Scholar Recants on His "Shakespeare" Discovery,* New York Times, June 20, 2002, sec. E, 1. Later in this chapter we will find Foster, also well known for correctly identifying the author of the novel *Primary Colors* in 1996, to be an important figure in some high-profile legal cases, including the Unabomber and JonBenét Ramsey investigations.

4. When part of this profile contains information about race, serious societal concerns are raised. See chapter 3 for some discussion. But criminal profiling generally has been part of law enforcement procedure for many years. For recent discussion, see Frederick F. Schauer, *Profiles, Probabilities, and Stereotypes* (2003).

5. The anecdotal linguistic literature contains accounts of expert linguists testifying as to authorship. Chief among them is Gerald McMenamin, to whom we return below. See, e.g., Gerald McMenamin, *Forensic Stylistics* (1993), discussing the author's experiences in such cases.

6. Daubert v. Merrell Dow Pharmaceuticals, Inc., 509 U.S. 579 (1993).

7. See McMenamin, *Forensic Stylists.*

8. American Board of Forensic Document Examiners, "What Do the Terms 'Forensic Science' and 'Forensic Document Examination' Mean?" www.abfde.org/fd_faq.htm#terms.

9. See D. Michael Risinger, Mark P. Denbeaux, and Michael J. Saks, *Exorcism of Ignorance as a Proxy for Rational Knowledge: The Lessons of Handwriting Identification "Expertise,"* 137 University of Pennsylvania Law Review 731 (1988).

10. See United States v. Hines, 55 F. Supp. 2d 62, 69 (D. Mass. 1999) (allowing handwriting expert to point out similarities, but not to render an opinion of co-authorship).

11. For a recent example, see United States v. Paul, 175 F.3d 906 (11th Cir. 1999). The trial court did not seem to recognize the difference between handwriting and spelling error analysis. For critical discussion, see D. Michael Risinger, *Defining the "Task at Hand": Non-Science Forensic Science after* Kumho Tire Co. v. Carmichael, 57 Washington and Lee Law Review 767, 789–92 (2000).

12. Some examples are given in McMenamin, *Forensic Stylistics,* at 82, 86.

13. Transcript of State v. Hauptmann, at 1074. We are grateful to Ronelle Delmont for providing us with a compact disc containing the transcript.

14. Id. at 1077–87.

15. Id. at 1242.

16. Testimony of Clark Sellers, id. at 1392 ("I am convinced that the differences between the request and conceded writings and the ransom notes are due to natural variation characteristics of the writer and attempted disguise.").

17. Id. at 1287, discussed in Jim Fisher, *The Lindbergh Case* 303–4 (1987).

18. Transcript of State v. Hauptmann, at 1290.

Notes to Pages 153–158

19. McMenamin, *Forensic Stylists,* at 32–83.

20. Below is the text of one of the notes (quoted in McMenamin, *Forensic Stylistics,* at 82):

> Dear Sir!
>
> Have 50 000 $ redy 2500 $ in 20 $ bills 1 5000 $ in 10 $ bills and 10 000 $ in 5 $ bills. After 2–4 days we will inform you were to deliver the Mony.
>
> We warn you for making anyding public or for the polise the child is in gut care.
>
> Indication for all letters are signature and 3 holes.

21. State v. Hauptmann, 180 A. 809, 826 (N.J. 1935).

22. Evidence scholars have raised this question in connection with the *Hauptmann* case, especially as it applies to handwriting analysis. See, e.g., Risinger, Denbeaux, and Saks, *Exorcism of Ignorance.*

23. Other misspellings, like "gut" for *good,* suggest the writer was German rather than Dutch, however.

24. 704 F.2d 86 (3d Cir. 1983).

25. Id. at 87.

26. Id. at 88.

27. Id.

28. The lower court had relied in part on the celebrated case United States v. Hearst, 412 F. Supp. 893 (N.D. Cal. 1976), *aff'd,* 563 F.2d 1331 (9th Cir. 1977), *cert. denied,* 435 U.S. 1000 (1978). That case involved a prosecution against Patricia Hearst, a kidnapped newspaper heiress, who was accused and later convicted of having joined her captors in various politically motivated crimes. The authorship issue arose over whether Hearst had herself authored various written and oral statements that she made during this period. The court held her offer of expert testimony that she was not the author inadmissible under the *Frye* standard. For discussion, see Jeffrey D. Menicucci, *Stylistics Evidence in the Trial of Patricia Hearst,* 1977 Arizona State Law Journal 387.

29. 704 F.2d at 90.

30. Id. at 91.

31. Amos Tversky and Daniel Kahneman, *Evidential Impact of Base Rates,* in *Judgment under Uncertainty: Heuristics and Biases* 156–57 (Daniel Kahneman et al. eds., 1982).

32. Foster, *Author Unknown,* at 67.

33. See Terry Pristin, *From Sonnets to Ransom Notes; Shakespeare Sleuth Helps Police in Literary Detection,* New York Times, November 19, 1997, B1.

34. The material for this section are taken from Foster, *Primary Colors;* Steve Thomas with Don Davis, *JonBenét: Inside the Ramsey Murder Investigation* (2000); John Ramsey and Patsy Ramsey, *The Death of Innocence: JonBenét's Parents Tell Their Story* (2001); Lawrence Schiller, *Perfect Murder Perfect Town* (1999), and a review of many newspaper articles and Internet sites. Interestingly, there seems to be no significant debate about the facts concerning Foster's positions. Different sources discuss different facts, but no significant controversies are raised.

35. The letter is available at www.acandyrose.com/donaldfoster.htm, and elsewhere on the Web. The text of that letter corresponds closely to press reports describing it. See Lisa Levitt Ryckman, *Book Details Linguistic Scholar's Role in Ramsey Case,* Denver Rocky Mountain News, April 11, 2000, 4A. For Foster's account, see Foster, *Author Unknown,* at 16–17.

36. See Ryckman, *Book Details Linguistic Scholar's Role in Ramsey Case.*

37. See Ramsey and Ramsey, *The Death of Innocence,* at 322–23. Shiller tells the story similarly, *Perfect Murder Perfect Town* at 738.

38. Thomas, *JonBenét,* at 315.

39. Ramsey and Ramsey, *The Death of Innocence,* at 431.

40. Thomas, *JonBenét,* at 317.

41. Gerald R. McMenamin, *Forensic Linguistics: Advances in Forensic Stylistics* 205 (2002).

42. Donald Foster, *The Message in the Anthrax,* Vanity Fair 180 (October 2003).

43. The first bombings were focused on universities and airlines, hence the prefix *una.* James Fitzgerald, *The Unabom Investigation,* paper presented at the meeting of the International Association of Forensic Linguistics, Malta, July 2001.

44. The information about the bombs comes from the affidavit of Terry D. Turchie, an FBI agent whose affidavit formed part of the basis for the FBI's obtaining a search warrant for Theodore Kaczynski's Montana cabin. The affidavit is available online at www.unabombertrial.com/documents/turchie_affidavit.html and through Westlaw at 1996 WL 330432 (D. Mont. Doc.).

45. The manifesto was published on September 17, 1995, and is widely available on the Internet. See www.unabombertrial.com/manifesto/index.html.

46. This brief sketch comes from a statement by David's lawyer, Anthony P. Bisceglie, transcribed by Reuters and published in part in the New York Times, April 9, 1996, A18, and from the Turchie Affidavit.

47. Turchie Affidavit ¶ 99.

48. The report, entitled "A Text Comparison of the 'T' (Ted) Documents and the 'U' (Unabom) Documents" [hereafter Fitzgerald Report], can be found as attachment 4 of the Turchie Affidavit.

49. Turchie Affidavit ¶ 112.

50. Turchie Affidavit ¶¶ 108–30. Donald Foster, who consulted in the case, provides a fascinating account of some of the common allusions running through the Unabomber's documents. See Foster, *Author Unknown,* at 95–142.

51. Fitzgerald Report, at 15.

52. Turchie Affidavit ¶ 113.

53. Turchie Affidavit ¶ 199.

54. See Memorandum of Points and Authorities in Support of Defendant's Motion to Suppress, March 3, 1997, 1997 WL 101898 (E.D. Cal. Doc.) at *28–31.

55. Abigail van Buren, *Dear Abby,* February 20, 1996.

56. This discussion comes from Declaration of Robin T. Lakoff, Ph.D., dated March 2, 1997. Our thanks to John Balazs for providing us with this documentation.

57. We are also aware from personal communication that the FBI had consulted with linguist Roger Shuy, although we do not know at what stage of the investigation that occurred.

58. Declaration of Donald W. Foster, dated April 11, 1997, ¶ 5. The declaration can be found at www.unabombertrial.com/documents/donfoster041197.html.

59. Id. ¶ 7.

60. Declaration of Robin T. Lakoff, Ph.D., dated May 4, 1997, ¶ 9.b. Foster apparently wrote a second declaration, in response to Lakoff's, but it was not filed and is therefore not publically available. See Foster, *Author Unknown,* at 109.

61. Turchie Affidavit ¶ 108.

62. David Kaczynski Affidavit, dated February 8, 1997. The affidavit can be found at www.unabombertrial.com/documents/david_depo.html.

63. The Critique was submitted as an appendix to Kaczynski's motion to suppress evidence, and can be found at 1997 WL 101890 (E.D. Cal. Doc.) at *32.

64. Id. at *36.

65. Id. at *37.

66. 83 F. Supp. 2d 515 (D.N.J. 2000), aff'd, 262 F.3d 405 (3d Cir.), cert. denied, 534 U.S. 826 (2001).

67. The opinion does not contain this detail, but the FBI report, which we obtained, does.

68. In both sets of documents, some were typed, others handwritten.

69. FBI Report, dated January 5, 2000, 9.

70. Thus, it is not our position that Roy Van Wyk was wrongly convicted. We have no opinion about that, and certainly recognize that there was evidence in support of the prosecution.

71. 83 F. Supp. 2d at 522.

72. Id. at 521 n.10, quoting Gerald McMenamin, Forensic Stylistics, 58 Forensic Science International 1, 170 (1993).

73. Id. at 523.

74. Id. at 522.

75. For discussion of this history, see Risinger, Denbeaux, and Saks, Exorcism of Ignorance.

76. See, e.g., United States v. Rutherford, 104 F. Supp. 2d 1190 (D. Neb. 2000); United States v. Hines, 55 F. Supp. 2d 62 (D. Mass. 1999). See also the discussion earlier in this chapter concerning questioned document examiners.

77. 524 U.S. 936 (1998).

78. See United States v. Starzekpyzel, 880 F. Supp. 1027 (S.D.N.Y. 1995).

79. This sort of expertise has sometimes been permitted to rebut handwriting experts. For discussion, see D. Michael Risinger, Navigating Expert Reliability: Are Criminal Standards of Certainty Being Left on the Dock? 64 Albany Law Review 99, 142 n.171 (2000). Risinger notes that as a general matter, educational experts are much more often permitted to testify when offered by the government than when offered by a defendant in a criminal case. Id. at 131–32.

80. www.innocenceproject.org (visited March 15, 2004).

81. For research suggesting that this is the case for expert testimony on the issue of insanity, see Richard Rogers, R. Michael Bagby, Marnie Crouch, and Brian Cutler, Effects of Ultimate Opinions on Juror Perceptions of Insanity, 13 International Journal of Law and Psychiatry 225 (1990).

82. For discussion, see David L. Faigman, David H. Kay, Michael J. Saks, and Joseph Sanders, 2 Modern Scientific Evidence § 25-1.0, at 193 (1997); Risinger, Defining the "Task at Hand."

83. Paul Gianelli and Emmie West, Hair Comparison Evidence, 37 Criminal Law Bulletin 514 (2001).

84. See Carole E. Chaski, Who Wrote It? Steps toward a Science of Authorship Identification, 233 National Institute of Justice Journal 15 (1997), available at www.ncjrs.org/pdffiles/jr000233.pdf. Disclosure: Solan is on the board of the Institute for Linguistic Evidence, of which Chaski is the executive director.

85. Carole E. Chaski, *Empirical Evaluations of Language-Based Author Identification Techniques*, 8 Forensic Linguistics 1 (2001).

86. See D. I. Holmes, *Authorship Attribution*, 28 Computers and the Humanities 87 (1994).

87. Chaski, *Language-Based Author Identification*, at 30.

88. Id. at 36–40.

89. Id. at 22–23.

90. Id. at 20–21.

91. Id. at 24–26.

92. Chaski, *Who Wrote It*, at 20.

93. Chaski, *Language-Based Author Identification*, at 11 ("While this is a very promising and even exciting result, it is by no mans enough evidence to proclaim that the technique actually has a 'zero' error rate. . . . A better way to interpret this result is to state that, in the context of this experiment, the syntactic feature technique shows a 100 per cent correct matching rate. Since the context of this experiment includes controlling for dialect and document size, this is a rigorous result.").

94. Id. at 10.

95. Tim Grant and Kevin Baker, *Identifying Reliable, Valid Markers of Authorship: A Response to Chaski*, 8 Forensic Linguistics 66, 75–76 (2001). For discussion of the types of opinions that are appropriate in testimony based on linguistic analysis, see A. P. A. Broeders, *Some Observations on the Use of Probability Scales in Forensic Identification*, 6 Forensic Linguistics 228 (1999). The same point is made more generally by Wilfrid Smith, *Computers, Statistics and Disputed Authorship*, in *Language and the Law* 374, 380 (John Gibbons ed., 1994).

96. Chaski, *Language-Based Author Identification*, at 35.

97. McMenamin, *Forensic Linguistics*, at 137–61.

98. Krzysztof Kredens, Forensic Linguistics and the Status of Linguistic Evidence in the Legal Setting (2000), Ph.D. diss., University of Lodz.

99. The findings are summarized in a table. See id. at 143.

100. Moshe Koppel and Jonathan Schler, *Exploiting Stylistic Idiosyncrasies for Authorship Attribution*, available at www.cs.biu.ac.il/aaahtmlfiles/indexpeopefiles/fmembers.html.

101. McMenamin, *Forensic Linguistics*, at 157–59.

102. Robert Eagleson, *Forensic Analysis of Personal Written Texts: A Case Study*, in *Language and the Law* 362 (John Gibbons ed., 1994).

103. For example, the farewell letter contained the following sentence: "Since his accident at work he's slowed down before that he wanted it everynight always woke up with a horn everymorning ready to go for it again." Eagleson, *Forensic Analysis*, at 368.

104. Roger W. Shuy, *The Language of Confession, Interrogation, and Deception* 153–73 (1998).

105. Malcolm Coulthard, *On the Use of Corpora in the Analysis of Forensic Texts*, 1 Forensic Linguistics 27 (1994). The press on both sides of the Atlantic reported on the 1998 court decision. See, e.g., Duncan Campbell, *The Bentley Case: Justice at Last, 45 Years Too Late for Meek and Sheeplike Derek Bentley*, The Guardian, July 31, 1998, 4. For a similar analysis of a different case by Coulthard, see Malcolm Coulthard, *Powerful Evidence for the Defence: An Exercise in Forensic Discourse Analysis*, in *Language and the Law* 414 (John Gibbons ed., 1994).

106. Coulthard reports that Bentley's IQ was at the bottom 1 percent of the population. According to one of the two standardized intelligence tests used most routinely in the United States, about 1.9 percent of the population has an IQ of 69 or lower. David Wechsler, *Wais-III: Administration and Scoring Manual* 25 (1997). Apparently, Bentley's IQ was lower than that.

107. The written statement is reproduced by Coulthard, *On the Use of Corpora,* at 41–42.

108. Regina v. Bentley, [2001] 1 Cr. App. R. 21 (Crim. Div. 1998).

Part Four

1. Thus, it is not our goal to replace judges with linguists. See Dennis Patterson, *Against a Theory of Meaning,* 73 Washington University Law Quarterly 1153 (1995); Dennis Patterson, *Fashionable Nonsense,* 81 Texas Law Review 841 (2003); Brian Bix, *Can Theories of Meaning and Reference Solve the Problem of Legal Determinacy?* 16 Ratio Juris 281 (2003). Rather, our goal is to bring to light generalizations that will enable the legal system to be more reflective in its handling of language-based issues.

Chapter Nine

1. 18 U.S.C. § 373 (2000).

2. See, e.g., People v. Morocco, 237 Cal. Rptr. 113, 115 (Ct. App. 1987) (the "gist of a solicitation is the request"); People v. Gordon, 120 Cal. Rptr. 840, 844 (Ct. App. 1975).

3. People v. Rubin, 158 Cal. Rptr. 488 (Ct. App. 1979), *cert. denied,* 449 U.S. 821 (1980).

4. John Searle, *Speech Acts: An Essay in the Philosophy of Language* 62 (1969).

5. United States v. Rahman, 189 F.3d 88 (2d Cir. 1999).

6. Id. at 117.

7. United States v. American Airlines, 743 F.2d 1114, 1116 (5th Cir. 1984).

8. Anna Wierzbicka, *English Speech Act Verbs: A Semantic Dictionary* 187 (1987).

9. See id. at 51.

10. 18 U.S.C. § 373 (2000) (emphasis added).

11. United States v. Rahman, 34 F.3d 1331, 1333 (7th Cir. 1994).

12. Id. at 1334. These conversations have been reconstructed as well as possible from the Seventh Circuit's opinion.

13. Id. at 1334–45.

14. See Roger W. Shuy, *Language Crimes* 3–7 (1993). On the tendency to interpret written language very literally, see Peter M. Tiersma, *A Message in a Bottle: Text, Autonomy, and Statutory Interpretation,* 76 Tulane Law Review 431 (2001).

15. 34 F.3d at 1338–39.

16. Id. at 1339.

17. People v. Hood, 878 P.2d 89, 94–95 (Colo. Ct. App. 1994).

18. United States v. Talley, 164 F.3d 989, 994 (6th Cir. 1999).

19. See State v. Ysea, 956 P.2d 499, 503 (Ariz. 1998).

20. United States v. Hartsfield, 976 F.2d 1349, 1354 (10th Cir. 1992), *cert. denied,* 507 U.S. 943 (1993); United States v. Brown, 943 F.2d 1246, 1250 (10th Cir. 1991); United States v. Green, 175 F.3d 822, 832 (10th Cir. 1999).

21. See United States v. Gore, 154 F.3d 34, 40–41 (2d Cir. 1998).

22. Matsushita Elec. Indus. Co. v. Zenith Radio Corp., 475 U.S. 574, 586 (1986) ("conduct as consistent with permissible competition as with illegal conspiracy does not, standing alone, support an inference of antitrust conspiracy").

23. Georgia Green, *Linguistic Analysis of Conversation as Evidence regarding the Interpretation of Speech Events,* in *Language in the Judicial Process* 247, 259 (J. N. Levi and A. G. Walker eds., 1990).

24. United States v. Romer, 148 F.3d 359, 364 (4th Cir. 1998), *cert. denied,* 525 U.S. 1141 (1999). For those unfamiliar with the American bureaucracy, the IRS refers to the Internal Revenue Service, which collects federal taxes in the United States. See also Dewberry v. State, 4 S.W.3d 735 (Tex. Crim. App. 1999) (use of "we" by co-defendant in murder case was evidence that the defendant and co-defendant acted together).

25. People v. Gerenstein, 580 N.Y.S.2d 489, 491 (App. Div. 1992).

26. United States v. Gibbs, 190 F.3d 188, 200 (3d Cir. 1999).

27. See D. Michael Risinger, Michael J. Saks, William C. Thompson, and Robert Rosenthall, *The* Daubert/Kumho *Implications of Observer Effects in Forensic Science: Hidden Problems of Expectation and Suggestion,* 20 California Law Review 1 (2002).

28. *Gibbs,* 190 F.3d at 209–10.

29. Id. at 210.

30. The word is associated with hip-hop culture in Philadelphia and apparently derives from the word "joint," hence its primary meaning. It can, as the agent testified, be used to refer to almost any noun. Thanks to Jenny Ball, Stephanie Burdine, Bethany Dumas, and Christine Kessler, all of whom responded to a query on this word that was posted on the *Forensic Linguistics* listserver.

31. *Gibbs,* 190 F.3d at 195. On the issues raised by police testifying as experts on drug jargon, see Joelle Moreno, What Happens When Dirty Harry Becomes an (Expert) Witness for the Prosecution? (unpublished manuscript on file with authors).

32. Childress v. State, 807 S.W.2d 424, 433 (Tex. Ct. App. 1991).

33. *Gibbs,* 190 F.3d at 202.

34. See Daniel Hays Lowenstein, *Political Bribery and the Intermediate Theory of Politics,* 32 UCLA Law Review 784, 798 (1985).

35. See, e.g., Cal. Pen. Code §§ 67–68; 92–95.

36. 32 Cal. Rptr. 479, 481 (Ct. App. 1963).

37. People v. Vollman, 167 P.2d 545 (Cal. Ct. App. 1946).

38. Stephen Braun, *Alderman Depicts Chicago's Venal Side,* Los Angeles Times, May 14, 1996, pt. A.

39. The Supreme Court requires a nexus between the gift and some particular contemplated act by the public official. United States v. Sun-Diamond Growers of Calif., 526 U.S. 398 (1999).

40. United States v. Myers, 692 F.2d 823, 831 (2d Cir. 1982). Myers retained only $15,000; the rest went to other participants in the scheme. He later complained about this and was promised an additional $35,000.

41. Id. at 831.

42. Id. at 842.

43. As an illustration, consider a public official who accepts money after making a promise to engage in an official action that favors the giver. The promise seems to be sincere and is intended by the official to create in the hearer the belief that the official

sincerely intends to carry it out. In reality, however, the official does not intend to fulfill the promise. From a speech act perspective, this counts as a promise. Of course, the legal system could require that to commit a specified language crime, a person must not only engage in a particular speech act, but must also sincerely intend to carry it out. For the most part, however, subjective sincerity does not seem to be a requirement for bribery. If it were, corrupt public officials could accept numerous bribes without fearing prosecution, simply by making promises that seem sincere to the hearer but that they secretly do not intend to perform.

Chapter Ten

1. 18 U.S.C. § 115 (threats to assault, kidnap, or murder, a U.S. official); 18 U.S.C. § 871 (threats against president and successors to the presidency).

2. The crimes of robbery, extortion, and blackmail are obviously closely related. All seek to get money or other items of value from the victim. A robber usually threatens immediate harm; an extortionist threatens harm in the future; and the blackmailer threatens a particular type of future harm: exposing embarrassing secrets. See Steven Shavell, *An Economic Analysis of Threats and Their Illegality: Blackmail, Extortion, and Robbery,* 141 University of Pennsylvania Law Review 1877 (1993).

3. Bruce Fraser, *Threatening Revisited,* 5 Forensic Linguistics 159, 171 (1998).

4. Crown Cork & Seal Co. v. NLRB, 36 F.3d 1130 (D.C. Cir. 1994).

5. United States v. Hoffman, 806 F.2d 703 (7th Cir. 1986).

6. Id. at 720–21

7. United States v. Taylor, 972 F.2d 1247, 1249 (11th Cir. 1992). The court's *"sic's"* have been omitted.

8. Id. at 1250–52.

9. See Peter M. Tiersma, *The Language and Law of Product Warnings,* in *Language in the Legal Process* 54 (Janet Cotterill ed., 2002).

10. Dawn Hobbs and Mark van de Kamp, *Vintners Alert after Sabotage Warning,* Santa Barbara News-Press, Feb. 25, 1999, A1.

11. Frederick Schauer, *Categories and the First Amendment: A Play in Three Acts,* 34 Vanderbilt Law Review 265, 270 (1981) (the First Amendment does not protect the right to "fix prices, breach contracts, make false warranties, place bets with bookies, threaten, [or] extort").

12. See United States v. Lee, 6 F.3d 1297 (8th Cir. 1993) (en banc), *cert. denied,* 511 U.S. 1035 (1994). What complicates the situation is that some threats are protected by the First Amendment. Hence, in this case the court of appeals reversed Lee's original conviction because the jury instructions did not make it clear that only certain types of threats could form the basis of a conviction (e.g., a threat "intended to cause residents of the Tamarack Apartments to reasonably fear the use of imminent force or violence"). The court remanded for a new trial with corrected jury instructions. Id. at 1304. The U.S. Supreme Court has recently held that burning a cross with intent to intimidate is not protected by the First Amendment. Virginia v. Black, 538 U.S. 343 (2003).

13. See Brandenburg v. Ohio, 395 U.S. 444 (1969).

14. United States v. Baker, 890 F. Supp. 1375 (E.D. Mich. 1995), *aff'd sub nom.* United States v. Alkhabaz, 104 F.3d 1492 (6th Cir. 1997).

15. 890 F. Supp. at 1387.

16. 104 F.3d at 1501.

17. Id. at 1496.

18. This does not mean that what he did is not or should not be criminal. If the men actually intended to carry out the acts, they would arguably be guilty of conspiracy, and there may well be other crimes that might have been committed.

19. Cignetti v. Healy, 89 F. Supp. 2d 106, 125 (D. Mass. 2000).

20. Because this is a very subjective inquiry, many courts do not look at the defendant's actual (subjective) intent, but instead focus on whether "a reasonable person would foresee that the listener will believe he will be subjected to physical violence upon his person." United States v. Orozco-Santillan, 903 F.2d 1262, 1265-66 (9th Cir. 1990).

21. People v. Benavides, 255 Cal. App. 2d 563 (1967).

22. Vietnamese Fishermen's Ass'n v. Knights of the Ku Klux Klan, 543 F. Supp. 198 (S.D. Tex. 1982).

23. Mickens v. United States, 926 F.2d 1323 (2d Cir. 1991).

24. For a more detailed discussion regarding the meaning of gestures of this sort, see Peter Tiersma, *Nonverbal Communication and the Freedom of "Speech,"* 1993 Wisconsin Law Review 1525.

25. People v. Hines, 780 P.2d 556, 558 (Colo. 1989).

26. Holt v. United States, 565 A.2d 970, 972 (D.C. Ct. App. 1989). See also People v. Czemerynski, 786 P.2d 1100, 1103 (Colo. 1990) (defendant told young woman that if she did not "talk dirty" to him, he would "get" her).

27. *The American Heritage Dictionary of the English Language* (3d ed. 1992) (definition 13f).

28. True threats often seem to involve profanity. Hannes Kniffka, *Eine Zwischenbilanz aus der Werkstatt eines "forensischen" Linguisten: Zur Analyse anonymer Autorschaft,* 185 Linguistische Berichte 75 (2000).

29. State v. Myers, 603 N.W.2d 300, 388 (Neb. 1999) (holding that this statement was a threat in furtherance of a conspiracy and thus not subject to the hearsay rule).

30. People v. Warren, 113 Ill. App. 3d 1 (1983).

31. 139 Cal. Rptr. 675 (Ct. App. 1977).

32. People v. Cassandras, 188 P.2d 546 (Cal. Ct. App. 1948).

33. State v. Methe, 422 N.W.2d 803, 805-6 (Neb. 1988).

34. For more on indirect threats, with some Japanese examples, see Nobuhiko Yamanaka, *On Indirect threats,* 8 International Journal of Semiotics and Law 37 (1995).

35. People v. Oppenheimer, 26 Cal. Rptr. 18, 24-25 (Ct. App. 1962).

36. People v. Choynski, 30 P. 791 (Cal. 1892).

37. People v. Sanders, 188 Cal. 744 (1922).

38. John J. Gumperz, *Discourse Strategies* 187 (1982).

39. Id. at 197.

40. Watts v. United States, 394 U.S. 705, 706 (1969).

41. It is clear that a "true threat" must count as a threat, linguistically speaking. What is less clear is whether, in addition to requiring an actual threat, the Supreme Court would also require that when the First Amendment is involved, the government must prove that the speaker actually was sincere, particularly because the statute in *Watts* contained a willfulness requirement. The court in *Watts* did not decide the issue. See id. at 707-8.

Several courts have since considered the matter. While the point is controversial, most seem to have come to the conclusion that a "true threat" requires only that it fulfill the linguistic requirements that we have set forth in this chapter—namely, that the speaker intend the hearer to believe that he intends to carry out the threatened action, and not that he actually intend to do so. See, e.g., *Hoffman,* 806 F.2d at 707 ("Contrary to the dissent's interpretation of case law, the government is not required to establish that the defendant actually intended to carry out the threat."); United States v. Kelner, 534 F.2d 1020, 1025 (2d Cir. 1976) ("it is the utterance which the statute makes criminal, not the specific intent to carry out the threat"); United States v. Roberts, 915 F.2d 889, 890 (4th Cir. 1990) ("Roberts correctly does not contend that the government must prove his intention or present ability actually to carry out the threat.").

See also Jeremy Martin, *Deconstructing "Constructive Threats": Classification and Analysis of Threatening Speech after* Watts *and* Planned Parenthood, 31 St. Mary's Law Journal 751 (2000).

42. 534 F.2d 1020, 1021 (2d Cir. 1976).

43. Id. at 1028.

44. Amy Harmon, *Student Charged with Online Terrorist Threat,* Los Angeles Times, May 25, 1996, A1; Carl Ingram, *Internet Debate Rages around GOP Legislator Controversy,* Los Angeles Times, June 24, 1996, A3.

45. Planned Parenthood of the Columbia/Willamette, Inc. v. American Coalition of Life Activists, 290 F.3d 1058, 1065 (9th Cir. 2002).

46. Freedom of Access to Clinic Entrances Act, 18 U.S.C. § 248 (1994).

47. 290 F.3d at 1063–65.

48. Richard J. Ofshe and Richard A. Leo, *The Decision to Confess Falsely: Rational Choice and Irrational Action,* 74 Denver University Law Review 97, 1082–83 (1997).

Chapter Eleven

1. 8 U.S.C. § 1621(1).

2. See Peter Tiersma, *The Language of Perjury,* 63 Southern California Law Review 373 (1990).

3. 409 U.S. 352, 353 (1973).

4. Id. at 354.

5. Paul Grice, *Studies in the Way of Words* 27 (1989).

6. See Tiersma, *Language of Perjury,* at 389–90.

7. 409 U.S. at 358.

8. Id.

9. Id. at 362.

10. See Peter M. Tiersma, *Legal Language,* at 175–79 (1999).

11. For a recent example, see Gregory M. Matoesian, *Law and the Language of Identity: Discourse in the William Kennedy Smith Rape Trial* (2001).

12. See Lawrence M. Solan, *Perjury and Impeachment: The Rule of Law or the Rule of Lawyers,* in *Aftermath: The Clinton Impeachment and the Presidency in the Age of Political Spectacle* 199 (Leonard V. Kaplan and Beverly I. Moran eds., 2001).

We realize that the questioning lawyers, unlike the witnesses, are not under oath, so they are technically not subject to the perjury laws. Our point is not that lawyers are committing perjury, but that it would be hypocritical for the legal system to allow lawyers to insinuate untruths with impunity in their questions, while prosecuting a witness for doing the same in her answer.

13. *Bronston,* 409 U.S. at 355 n.3.

14. Id. at 355–56.

15. Grice, *Studies,* at 26.

16. For a discussion of some of the complexities of the notion of literal meaning, see John Searle, *Literal Meaning,* in *Expression and Meaning* 117 (1979); Mira Ariel, *The Demise of a Unique Concept of Literal Meaning,* 34 Journal of Pragmatics 361 (2003), as well as other articles in that volume of the journal.

17. United States v. DeZarn, 157 F.3d 1042, 1045 (6th Cir. 1998).

18. See United States v. Alberti, 568 F.2d 617 (2d Cir. 1977) (holding that defendant understood that question about whether gambling took place at an establishment "almost twenty-four hours a day" was a figure of speech that actually meant merely that the game was played regularly); Tiersma, *Language of Perjury,* at 414–19.

19. 18 U.S.C. § 1621(1).

20. Some who do work in linguistic pragmatics propose that Grice's maxims should be reduced to a broader principle of relevance. Dan Sperber and Deirdre Wilson, *Relevance: Communication and Cognition* (1986).

21. See, e.g., M. B. W. Sinclair, *Law and Language: The Role of Pragmatics in Statutory Interpretation,* 46 University of Pittsburgh Law Review 373, 383–84 (1985) (rules of syntax and semantics remain the same over variant kinds of language use, while maxims of pragmatics do not; maxim of quantity does not apply in courtroom cross-examination, citing *Bronston v. United States* as support); Steven Levinson, *Pragmatics* 121–22 (1983) (the maxim of quantity is in abeyance during cross-examination, but the maxim of quality should still apply).

22. See Tiersma, *Language of Perjury,* at 392; see also Linda Coleman and Paul Kay, *Prototype Semantics: The English Word* Lie, 57 Language 26, 31–32 (1981).

23. For other relevant examples, see Lawrence M. Solan, *The Clinton Scandal: Some Legal Lessons from Linguistics,* in *Language in the Judicial Process* (Janet Cotterill ed., 2002).

24. U.S. Const. art. II, § 4.

25. See *The Starr Report: The Evidence* 127 (Phil Kuntz ed., 1998) (noting Lewinsky grand jury testimony that she performed oral sex on the president approximately nine times). For a general description of the background facts, see Richard A. Posner, *An Affair of State: The Investigation, Impeachment, and Trial of President Clinton* 16–58 (1999).

26. See, e.g., Deborah L. Rhode, *Conflicts of Commitment: Legal Ethics in the Impeachment Context,* 52 Stanford Law Review 269 (2000).

27. 520 U.S. 681, 702 (1997).

28. See Jones v. Clinton, 993 F. Supp. 1217, 1218–19 (E.D. Ark. 1998).

29. Jones v. Clinton, 990 F. Supp. 657 (E.D. Ark. 1998). Jones appealed the dismissal, and Clinton finally settled the matter by paying her $850,000. See Jones v. Clinton, 36 F. Supp. 2d 1113, 1123 (E.D. Ark. 1999).

30. Id. at 1131. Earlier in the same opinion, Judge Wright presents somewhat inconsistent positions on the status of the Lewinsky evidence in the *Jones* litigation. She explains that her decision not to admit the evidence was not, contrary to popular belief, because it was irrelevant to that case, but because allowing it to be considered would have inordinately delayed the proceedings. Id. at 1122 n.7.

31. The Supreme Court has held that a person may be prosecuted for responding falsely to questions about wrongful acts that are not themselves subject to prosecution. Brogan v. United States, 522 U.S. 398 (1998). For discussion, see Solan, *Perjury and Impeachment,* at 205–6.

32. Kuntz, *Starr Report Evidence*, at 361.

33. The Senate also rejected the remaining article relating to obstruction of justice in the *Jones* case. See Jones v. Clinton, 36 F. Supp. at 1123.

34. The text of the deposition was intended to be kept under seal and had never officially been made available to the public. The text used here is from www.cnn.com/ALLPOLITICS/1998/03/13/jones.v.clinton.docs/clinton (hereinafter "Clinton Deposition"), at 48. Excerpts of the deposition in other sources confirm that the version relied on here is authentic. See Steven D. Strauss and Spencer Strauss, *The Complete Idiot's Guide to Impeachment of the President* 206-7 (1998).

35. Clinton Deposition, at 52-53. This excerpt is also available in Jones v. Clinton, 36 F. Supp. 2d at 1127-28.

36. Clinton himself admitted as much in his grand jury testimony. Kuntz, *Starr Report Evidence*, at 382. Somewhat ironically, Kenneth Starr seemed to experience similar lapses of memory when he testified—perhaps dishonestly—before the House Judiciary Committee in the impeachment proceedings. For examples, see Solan, *Perjury and Impeachment*, at 211 n.26.

37. Kuntz, *Starr Report Evidence*, at 378.

38. Her bringing papers to him was apparently a ruse, however. See Lewinsky's testimony before the grand jury in Kuntz, *Starr Report Evidence*, at 141.

39. Clinton Deposition, at 53. See also Jones v. Clinton, 36 F. Supp. 2d at 1128.

40. Trial Memorandum of the U.S. House of Representatives, at 72 (Jan. 11, 1999) (available at 1999 WL 9933).

41. Clinton Deposition, at 59.

42. As Judge Posner notes, "Jones's lawyers did not conduct a skillful examination of Clinton; in particular, they failed to ask him about specific sex acts and to follow up his often meandering and evasive answers with questions designed to pin him down. As a result, many of his answers, though probably lies, would not expose him to a prosecution for perjury." Posner, *An Affair of State*, at 44-45. We concur. Posner does argue that Clinton clearly committed perjury regarding other matters, however. Id. at 30. Indeed, he considers Clinton's equivocation regarding whether he and Lewinsky were alone to be an example of a "clearly perjurious" statement. Id. at 45. As to that conclusion, we concur in part and dissent in part.

43. Clinton Deposition, at 58-59.

44. *The Starr Report: The Findings of Independent Counsel Kenneth W. Starr on President Clinton and the Lewinsky Affair, with Analysis of the Staff of the Washington Post* 183 (1998) (hereinafter *Starr Report*).

45. Jones v. Clinton, 36 F. Supp. 2d at 1128.

46. Kuntz, *Starr Report Evidence*, at 362-63.

47. Id. at 361.

48. Neil A. Lewis, *Exiting Job, Clinton Accepts Immunity Deal*, New York Times, Jan. 20, 2001, A1.

49. Kuntz, *Starr Report Evidence*, at 420.

50. Posner, *An Affair of State*, at 47-48.

51. Clinton Deposition, at 54, quoted in Kuntz, *Starr Report Evidence*, at 373.

52. Id.

53. Kuntz, *Starr Report Evidence*, at 373 (emphasis added). Note that in the Kuntz book, which contains the entire grand jury transcript, there are quotation marks after the

word "was" and before "no sex," and also after the word "Clinton." We have omitted them because they were most likely added by the court reporter.

54. The prosecutor might argue that he was not quoting the verb, and that—as the quotation marks in the transcript suggest—his verbatim quotation began with the word "no." Yet because the tense of the verb is the critical issue, he should have quoted it correctly.

55. See Tiersma, *Language of Perjury,* at 409–14.

56. Kuntz, *Starr Report Evidence,* at 373.

57. Coleman and Kay, *Prototype Semantics.*

58. Id. at 31.

59. Steven Winter relies heavily on this position in his discussion of perjury. See Steven L. Winter, *A Clearing in the Forest: Law, Life, and Mind* (2001).

60. Coleman and Kay, *Prototype Semantics,* at 39.

61. Kuntz, *Starr Report Evidence,* at 359.

62. Id.

63. Id.

64. On the role of reformulation during courtroom questioning, see Bilyana Martinovski, *The Role of Repetitions and Reformulations in Court Proceedings: A Comparison of Sweden and Bulgaria* (2001) (Gothenburg Monographs in Linguistics 18).

Subject Index